# DATE DUE

| | | | |
|---|---|---|---|
| | | | |
| | | | |
| | | | |
| | | | |
| | | | |
| | | | |
| | | | |
| | | | |
| | | | |
| | | | |
| | | | |
| | | | |
| | | | |
| | | | |
| | | | |
| | | | |

DEMCO 38-296

# ELECTRICITY
# RETAIL WHEELING
# HANDBOOK

# ELECTRICITY RETAIL WHEELING HANDBOOK

by

## John M. Studebaker

Published by
**THE FAIRMONT PRESS, INC.**
700 Indian Trail
Lilburn, GA 30247

HD 9685 .U5 S794 1995

Studebaker, John M.

Electricity retail wheeling **ion Data**
 handbook

Electricity retail wheeling handbook / by John M. Studebaker.
 p. cm.
 Includes index.
 ISBN 0-88173-204-4
 1. Electric utilities--United States. 2. Interconnectneed electric utility
systems--United States. 3. Electric utilities--Law and legislation--United
States. I. Title.
 HD9685.U5S794        1995        333.79'32--dc20            95-19036
                                                                         CIP

Published by The Fairmont Press, Inc.
700 Indian Trail
Lilburn, GA  30247

Printed in the United States of America

10 9 8 7 6 5 4 3 2 1

ISBN 0-88173-204-4   FP

ISBN 0-13-389370-7   PH

While every effort is made to provide dependable information, the publisher, authors, and
editors cannot be held responsible for any errors or omissions.

Distributed by Prentice Hall PTR
Prentice-Hall, Inc.
A Simon & Schuster Company
Upper Saddle River, NJ  07458

Prentice-Hall International (UK) Limited, London
Prentice-Hall of Australia Pty. Limited, Sydney
Prentice-Hall Canada Inc., Toronto
Prentice-Hall Hispanoamericana, S.A., Mexico
Prentice-Hall of India Private Limited, New Delhi
Prentice-Hall of Japan, Inc., Tokyo
Simon & Schuster Asia Pte. Ltd., Singapore
Editora Prentice-Hall do Brasil, Ltda., Rio de Janeiro

# DEDICATION

*This book is dedicated to Virginia for her continued support;
to my daughter, Jacqueline Allcorn and her husband, Terry;
and their children, Nathan and Laurah, for the love and joy
they provide to me.*

# Table of Contents

# List of Figures

# Foreword

This publication is divided into four basic sections as follows:

**I.  UNDERSTANDING ELECTRIC
UTILITY BASICS.**
Chapters 1 through 3.

**II.  ELECTRICITY RETAIL WHEELING –
THE PROCESSES INVOLVED.**
Chapter 4 through 6.

**III.  ELECTRICITY RETAIL WHEELING ALTERNATIVES.**
Chapter 7.

**IV.  APPENDIX A THROUGH G.**
Important background data to assist in
reducing electric utility costs.

# Retail Wheeling of Electricity
# An Overview

As with any undertaking, a logical procedure must be established. In this publication, the discussion of retail wheeling of electricity is the predominate theme. However, before we discuss and analyze the retail wheeling process, we must understand the basics of electricity as it relates to generation, transmission and delivery to the retail customer. To accomplish this end, a basic overview of regulation processes and electricity tariff schedule provisions is included in the following section. Please read this section with great care as it provides the foundation upon which will be built the understanding of retail wheeling of electricity. Remember, a successful retail wheeling strategy will require an understanding of how the process functions.

## ACKNOWLEDGEMENTS

The author wishes to express his thanks to the many electric utilities, regulatory agencies, students and clients whose information, insight and comments have assisted in making this publication possible.

Every effort has been made to provide dependable and accurate information. However, changes occur almost on a daily basis due to the very active environment that encompasses the electricity retail wheeling industry. The things that cause these revisions such as regulatory changes, competition, customer requirements, etc. are very important for the retail electricity purchaser to be aware of on a continuing basis. This publication will address these issues as they currently exist as well as provide strategies for the future so that the electricity purchaser can be assured that their electricity costs are as low as is possible.

# Introduction

In the 1970's, most electric utilities had insufficient generating capacities to meet their customer's growing demands. As a result of this lack of capacity, the electric utility industry began massive capital construction programs to build what they and their customers considered "reasonable generating capacity" to meet their expected future needs.

In general, the electric utility industry felt that growth would continue to be at the then current rate for an indefinite period of time. Lending credibility to this viewpoint was the natural gas shortages at the time which appeared to greatly broaden the potential for the use of electricity. Also, the electric utility industries projected an ever increasing demand for energy together with an ever increasing cost of oil. On top of this, federal and state regulatory agencies, in agreement with the "ever increasing demand" philosophy, encouraged the electric utilities to spend and commit to future spending enormous sums of money on generating facilities.

As is so often the case, the scenario that was envisioned never materialized. Customers' demands did not continue increasing at an unabated rate; and, most importantly, oil prices did not continue to escalate. Since these things did not happen as anticipated, the obvious results occurred – overcapacity in electricity base load became more and more widespread. In addition, the commitments requiring long-term capital investments became less attractive and in some cases unaffordable. Change had to take place!

As a result of the overexpectations in the 1970's concerning electrical requirements, today's electrical prices on a cost per million Btu basis are often more expensive than other forms of energy. Many electric utilities are now finding themselves in the position of having large base load excess capacity availability. The decline in oil and gas prices, the deregulation of natural gas and imbalances on their system will be worsened by continuing deregulation in the electricity industry in the form of retail wheeling. Electricity generation and distribution pricing in the United States is changing in a way that has never before taken place in this industry. True competition for customers is taking place at a pace that would not have even been imagined five years ago. The electricity environment is changing so rapidly that by the time you read this publication, there will be new things occurring that were not available at the time of its writing.

The purpose of this publication, from an electricity purchaser's viewpoint, is to sort out all of the potential pitfalls and opportunities that both currently as well as in the future of retail wheeling may reduce or increase electricity costs. To accurately assess electricity costs, a purchaser must have at least a minimal understanding of how electricity flows from where it is to where the purchaser is, and how costs are accumulated in the process. There are other publications that currently address specific areas of retail wheeling of electricity in one manner or another. There are also many seminars held annually in the United States that address various aspects of retail wheeling of electricity. Why add one more publication to what appears to be an already cluttered field? Most publications as well as seminars address specific areas of the retail wheeling process but do not tie all of the loose ends together. Also, it seems that an assumption exists that everyone knows all of the basics so the publications and seminars can concentrate on one or two specific areas of information. This publication is not written from a theoretical perspective, but is intended to be of value to an electricity purchaser that needs to know the best and least costly method of obtaining electricity at their facility, both currently as well as in the future, based upon their usage characteristics.

The philosophy I use is quite simple – "how can I get electricity as inexpensively as possible when I need it, and not lay awake at nights worrying about whether what I did will work." If this appeals to you, then this publication can help you realize your goals of least cost and best reliability in the purchase of electricity both currently as well as in the future.

# SECTION I

## *Understanding Electric Utility Basics*

### Chapters 1 – 3

# Chapter 1

# Electricity – An Overview

Today the electric utility industry is at the same place the natural gas industry was several years ago. They generally discourage cogeneration and retail wheeling (transportation of power purchased by customers from third party electric suppliers). The time it will take before the same forces which successfully convinced regulators to allow the transportation of third party supplied natural gas, can not be estimated accurately. However, if the natural gas scenario is any indicator, it probably will not be long in coming.

The electric utility industry must recognize that change is inevitable and that to resist is counter productive and detrimental to its own well being. Ultimately, electric consumers will have the right to choose the least expensive, best suited source of power. In many instances, unfortunately, electric utilities do not accept or suggest the innovative measures required to assist the consumer in their quest for reduced costs. When this occurs, the regulators will devise the means for the utilities to reduce the consumer's cost for electrical power. But for the utilities, many traditional cost recovery and operational procedures currently enjoyed will be forfeited.

Electric utilities must become market responsive if they want to remain viable in their industries. Failure to do so will subject them to a process of fierce competition from third party suppliers and regulatory imposition of mandatory retail wheeling of power. The long-term outlook for electrical power alternatives is good and for many companies the savings realized through these various alternatives will be even more cost reducing than has been possible in the natural gas area. The electric utility industry is at the threshold of change and the prospects of cost reduction are great. However, as changes occur, an awareness on a continuing basis must be maintained. To be able to understand how changes occur in electric utilities, a knowledge of what they are and how they are regulated must be available.

Probably one of the most discussed, least understood areas in electricity today is retail wheeling. This is the process whereby the customer purchases electricity (kVA/kW and kWh) from a utility other than their own serving utility. This procedure, from the customer's viewpoint, is very similar to customer transportation of natural gas where the customer purchases the actual natural gas themselves and utilizes the serving utility only to transport the natural gas to their point of use. While this process works well in natural gas and causes most natural gas utilities no real supply or cost problems, the same is not true for electric utilities where retail wheeling of electricity takes place. The reason for this is that most natural gas utilities do not actually have the natural gas they sell, but purchase their system supplies on the open market. In electricity, the serving utility normally generates all or at least a portion of the electricity they sell the customer. When a customer elects to not use the serving utility's electricity, the utility's generation utilization is reduced, causing increased costs to occur for the utility. Many electric utilities are now finding themselves in the position of having large base load excess capacity availability. The decline in oil and gas prices, the deregulation of natural gas utility transportation, and imbalances on their system will be worsened by customer wheeling of electricity. The utilities also maintain that electric generating facility costs that have been incurred must be recovered from their customers, and that any reduction in the customer base through the use of wheeled power would, of necessity, increase costs to the remaining retail sales customers.

In electricity utility service, the commodity being sold is produced by the utility that serves the customer. In this case, if the customer obtains their electricity from a source other than the local electric company (retail wheeling), the electric utility suffers a real loss – not having a sale for the electricity they produce. Retail wheeling can have a very real impact on the very existence of an electric utility. How the origination points of the commodity (electricity/natural gas) vary are shown on Figure 1.1 following.

**Figure 1.1** Commodity Origination Points – Electricity versus Natural Gas

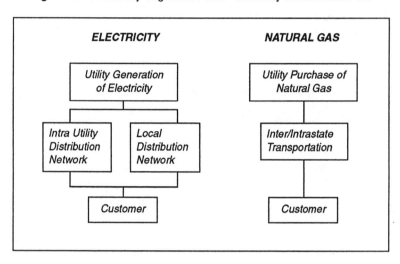

Figure 1.1 shows that an electric utility generates its commodity (electricity) where a natural gas utility generally purchases its commodity (natural gas). While this difference may seem to be of no particular concern to the customer, it is of great importance to an electric utility. Since the electric utility generates its commodity, it relies upon its customers to purchase the electricity it generates. If customers have the choice to not purchase the generated electricity, the utility has to find other customers or reduce its generation output which affects its overall system efficiency. Another electric utility worry is customer cogeneration of electricity. In this scenario, the customer installs a generation system that utilizes both electrical as well as thermal (heat) outputs to supplement and reduce their dependence upon utility supplied electricity. Although cogeneration is not a new process, its use has become more

widespread as utility supplied electricity has become more costly. As can be seen, many electricity customers currently, or in the near future, will have options to typical utility supplied electricity. The question an electricity user will have to answer will be – which method of electricity purchasing is most cost effective? To answer this question, it is important to know what is available and how to most effectively utilize the best options. This publication will provide information needed by a customer to utilize the least expensive electricity available while assuring that supply integrity is maintained.

**Figure 1.2**  Potential Options for the Electricity User

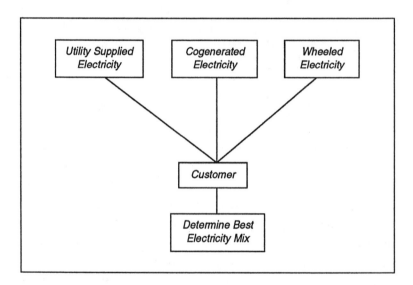

# Chapter 2

# Regulation of Electricity

## REGULATION IN GENERAL

Utilities, generally speaking, are considered to be regulated monopolies. A regulated monopoly is an entity that has no competition since no other provider of the same commodity can compete for the monopoly holder's customer. Since a position of no competition can lead to abuse in both cost and service, a check and balance system is in place that requires utilities to be held accountable for costs, services, etc. Utilities are regulated in at least two areas, "interstate" (between states) and "intrastate" (within states).

## INTERSTATE REGULATION

Interstate regulation in electricity is the responsibility of the Federal Energy Regulatory Commission (FERC). This agency was created in 1977 and has the responsibility for oversight and regulation of interstate transportation policies and rates concerning electricity. Since this agency has these responsibilities, it would be well to understand its impact on rates and transportation conditions.

Since electricity distribution from one state to and for use in another state is always interstate (between states), FERC has jurisdiction over the rules and regulations applying to it.

**Figure 2.1**   Regulation of Electric Utilities

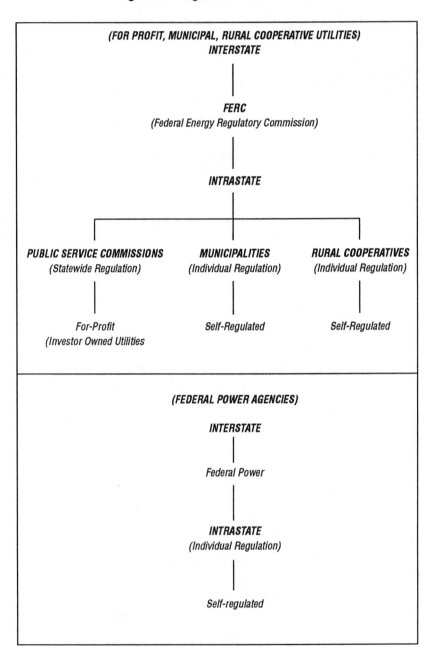

Members of FERC are appointed by the President of the United States with (5) commission positions being available. More and more the rulings of FERC meet with something less than enthusiasm on the part of the electric utilities it regulates, due primarily to its increasingly open access policies with relation to electricity.

Know what is happening at the Federal regulatory level so that as changes in electricity occur, you will have a strategy in mind. The following is the current address and telephone numbers of FERC:

Federal Energy Regulatory Commission
825 North Capitol Street, N.E.
Washington, D.C. 20426
Telephone (202) 208-0055
FAX (202) 208-2106
Bulletin Board (202) 208-8997

## AREAS REGULATED BY FERC

- Establishes and enforces rates and charges for electric energy transmission and sales for resale.
- Establishes and enforces conditions, rates and charges for electric energy interconnections.
- Certifies small power production and cogeneration facilities.
- Issues and enforces licenses for non-Federal hydroelectric power facilities.
- Issues and enforces certificates for construction and abandonment of interstate electricity transmission facilities.
- Establishes and enforces rates and charges for distribution and sale of natural gas.
- Establishes and enforces oil pipeline rates, charges and valuation.
- Establishes and enforces oil pipeline common carrier duties.
- Hears appeals from Department of Energy remedial orders and denials of adjustments.

### ENERGY POLICY ACT OF 1992
### House Rule 776, Report 102-1018
### Dated October 5, 1992

The Energy Policy Act of 1992 includes many energy related provisions pertaining to many kinds of energy sources including electricity, natural gas, alternative fuels, electric motor vehicles, renewable energy and coal to name a few. For any utility user, a copy of this Energy Policy Act is probably a wise investment. It can be obtained as follows:

Ordering Information:

    Energy Policy Act of 1992

    House Report 776

    Report 102-1018

    Date – October 5, 1992

    Cost $20.00

    Phone: (202) 782-3238

    Address:

        United States Government Printing Office

        Superintendent of Documents

        Washington, DC 20402

Of particular interest in this Act is the section on "Energy Efficiency By Electric Utilities" (Subtitle B - Utilities, Sec. 111, pp. 21-32).

This section outlines the steps all electric utilities must take to conserve electric energy usage (kWh) and demand usage (kVA/kW). Because of its application/impact on electric energy users, part of this section is quoted following:

### SUBTITLE B – UTILITIES

*SEC. 111. ENCOURAGEMENT OF INVESTMENT IN CONSERVATION AND ENERGY EFFICIENCY BY ELECTRIC UTILITIES.*

*(a) AMENDMENT TO THE PUBLIC UTILITY REGULATORY POLICIES ACT – The Public Utility Regulatory Policies Act of 1978 (P.O. 95-617; 92 Stat. 3117; 16 U.S.C. 2601 and following) is amended by adding the following at the end of Section 111(d):*

"(7) INTEGRATED RESOURCE PLANNING. – Each electric utility shall employ integrated resource planning. All plans or filings before a State regulatory authority to meet the requirements of this paragraph must be updated on a regular basis, must provide the opportunity for public participation and comment, and contain a requirement that the plan be implemented.

"(8) INVESTMENTS IN CONSERVATION AND DEMAND MANAGEMENT. – The rates allowed to be charged by a State regulated electric utility shall be such that the utility's investment in and expenditures for energy conservation, energy efficiency resources, and other demand side management measures are at least as profitable, giving appropriate consideration to income lost from reduced sales due to investments in and expenditures for conservation and efficiency, as its investments in and expenditures for the construction of new generation, transmission, and distribution equipment. Such energy conservation, energy efficiency resources and other demand side management measures shall be appropriately monitored and evaluated.

"(9) ENERGY EFFICIENCY INVESTMENTS IN POWER GENERATION AND SUPPLY. – The rates charged by any electric utility shall be such that the utility is encouraged to make investments in, and expenditures for, all cost-effective improvements in the energy efficiency of power generation, transmission and distribution. In considering regulatory changes to achieve the objectives of this paragraph, State regulatory authorities and nonregulated electric utilities shall consider the disincentives caused by existing ratemaking policies, and practices, and consider incentives that would encourage better maintenance, and investment in more efficient power generation, transmission and distribution equipment."

(b) PROTECTION FOR SMALL BUSINESS. – The Public Utility Regulatory Policies Act of 1978 (P.L. 95-617; 92 Stat. 3117; 16 U.S.C. 2601 and following) is amended by inserting the following new paragraph at the end of subsection 111(c):

*"(3) If a State regulatory authority implements a standard established by subsection (d) (7) or (8), such authority shall –*

*"(A) consider the impact that implementation of such standard would have on small businesses engaged in the design, sale, supply, installation or servicing of energy conservation, energy efficiency or other demand side management measures, and*

*"(B) implement such standard so as to assure that utility actions would not provide such utilities with unfair competitive advantages over such small businesses."*

*(c) EFFECTIVE DATE. – Section 112(b) of such Act is amended by inserting "(or after the enactment of the Comprehensive National Energy Policy Act in the case of standards under paragraphs (7), (8), and (9) of Section 111(d)" after "Act" in both places such word appears in paragraphs (1) and (2).*

*(d) DEFINITIONS. – Section 3 of such Act is amended by adding the following new paragraphs at the end thereof:*

*"(19) The term 'integrated resource planning' means, in the case of an electric utility, a planning and selection process for new energy resources that evaluates the full range of alternatives, including new generating capacity, power purchases, energy conservation and efficiency, cogeneration and district heating cooling application, and renewable energy resources, in order to provide adequate and reliable service to its electric customers at the lowest system cost. The process shall take into account necessary features for system operation, such as diversity, reliability, dispatchability, and other factors of risk: shall take into account the ability to verify energy savings achieved through energy conservation and efficiency and the projected durability of such savings measured over time; and shall treat demand and supply resources on a consistent and integrated basis.*

*"(20) The term 'system cost' means all direct and quantifiable net costs for an energy resource over its available life, including the cost of production, distribution, transportation, utilization, waste management, and environmental compliance.*

*"(21) The term 'demand side management' includes load management techniques.".*

*(e) REPORT. – Not later than 2 years after the date of the enactment of the Act, the Secretary shall transmit a report to the President and to the Congress containing –*

*(1) a survey of all State laws, regulations, practices, and policies under which State regulatory authorities implement the provisions of paragraphs (7), (8), and (9) of Section 111(d) of the Public Utility Regulatory Policies Act of 1978;*

*(2) an evaluation by the Secretary of whether and to what extent, integrated resource planning is likely to result in –*

*(A) higher or lower electricity costs to an electric utility's ultimate consumers or to classes or groups of such consumers;*

*(B) enhanced or reduced reliability of electric service; and*

*(C) increased or decreased dependence on particular energy resources; and*

*(3) a survey of practices and policies under which electric cooperatives prepare integrated resource plans, submit such plans to the Rural Electricification Administration and the extent to which such integrated resource planning is reflected in rates charged to customers.*

*The report shall include an analysis prepared in conjunction with the Federal Trade Commission, of the competitive impact of implementation of energy conservation, energy efficiency, and other demand side management programs by utilities on small businesses engaged in the design, sale, supply, installation, or servicing of similar energy conservation, energy efficiency, or other demand side management measures and whether any unfair, deceptive, or predatory acts exist, or are likely to exist, from implementation of such programs.*

SEC. 112. ENERGY EFFICIENCY GRANTS TO STATE REGULATORY
        AUTHORITIES.

(a) ENERGY EFFICIENCY GRANTS. – The Secretary is authorized
in accordance with the provisions of this section to provide grants to
State regulatory authorities in an amount not to exceed $250,000 per
authority, for purposes of encouraging demand side management including energy conservation, energy efficiency and load management techniques, and for meeting the requirements of paragraphs (7), (8), and (9)
of Section 111(d) of the Public Utility Regulatory Policies Act of 1978
and as a means of meeting gas supply needs and to meet the requirements of paragraphs (3) and (4) of Section 303(b) of the Public Utility
Regulatory Policies Act of 1978. Such grants may be utilized by a State
regulatory authority to provide financial assistance to nonprofit subgrantees of the Department of Energy's Weatherization Assistance
Program in order to facilitate participation by such subgrantees in proceedings of such regulatory authority to examine energy conservation,
energy efficiency, or other demand side management programs.

(b) PLAN. – A State regulatory authority wishing to receive a grant
under this section shall submit a plan to the Secretary that specifies the
actions such authority proposes to take that would achieve the purposes
of this section.

(c) SECRETARIAL ACTION. – (1) In determining whether, and in
what amount, to provide a grant to a State regulatory authority under
this section the Secretary shall consider, in addition to other appropriate
factors, the actions proposed by the State regulatory authority to
achieve the purposes of this section and to consider implementation of
the ratemaking standards established in –

(A) paragraphs (7), (8), and (9) of Section 111(d) of the Public
Utility Regulatory Policies Act of 1978; or

(B) paragraphs (3) and (4) of Section 303(b) of the Public
Utility Regulatory Policies Act of 1978.

(2) Such actions –

(A) shall include procedures to facilitate the participation of
grantees and nonprofit subgrantees of the Department of Energy's

*Weatherization Assistance Program in proceedings of such regulatory authorities examining demand side management programs; and*

*(B) shall provide for coverage of the cost of such grantee and subgrantees' participation in such proceedings.*

*(d) RECORDKEEPING. – Each State regulatory authority that receives a grant under this section shall keep such records as the Secretary shall require.*

*(e) DEFINITION. – For purposes of this section, the term "State regulatory authority" shall have the same meaning as provided by Section 3 of the Public Utility Regulatory Policies Act of 1978 in the case of electric utilities, and such term shall have the same meaning as provided by Section 302 of the Public Utility Regulatory Policies Act of 1978 in the case of gas utilities, except that in the case of any State without a statewide ratemaking authority, such term shall mean the State energy office.*

*(g) AUTHORIZATION. – There are authorized to be appropriated $5,000,000 for each of the fiscal years 1994, 1995, and 1996 to carry out the purposes of this section.*

Of particular interest in this extracted data on Subtitle B – Utilities, are the following items:

1. **Paragraph (7) INTEGRATED RESOURCE PLANNING –**

   This paragraph and following, through the end of Section 111, covers conservation which electric utilities must implement. Of interest to electricity users is the fact that electric utilities will be required to offer demand side management programs to customers to encourage them to reduce their demand usage, at least, during utility peak demand periods. Read this information carefully to determine whether a particular utility is offering such programs. Also, note that in subsection (e) REPORT – not later than (2) years after the date of this Act (October 5, 1994) a report to the President and Congress is due which describes the local electric utility service representative to determine their implementation plans/actions to comply with the requirements outlined in this Act.

2. **Sec. 112 – ENERGY EFFICIENCY GRANTS**

This section of the Act provides for the granting of not more than $250,000 per authority (state) for the purpose of encouraging demand side management including energy efficiency and load management techniques. This money is available for any state for uses as outlined in the Act. Check with your local utility regulatory agency to determine whether they have applied for available funds and if they have, how they are being utilized. It is always a good idea to have a copy of the Energy Policy Act or, at least, a copy of this extracted information to describe the program to the local regulatory agency representative since they may not be familiar with the Act or its provisions.

Now is the time to know how the interstate regulation of electricity process works since the rulings of FERC will increasingly affect the viability of retail wheeling of electricity.

## INTRASTATE REGULATION

Intrastate regulation occurs within the borders of a state and is the responsibility of one of at least three types of regulatory bodies. Who regulates what is determined by the type of electric utility that serves a customer. For-profit electric utilities are regulated on a statewide basis by a commission or group of individuals appointed or elected at the state level. All for-profit electric utilities, regardless of their geographic location within a given state, are regulated by this commission or group of individuals. Municipal electric utilities (utilities owned/operated by a city or county) are self-regulated. They are autonomous and structure their rates as they see necessary with minimal or no state supervision or legislation. Cooperative electric utilities are similar to municipal electric utilities in that they are self-regulated with little state oversight. Cooperative utilities often come into being when a for-profit utility does not provide service to a given area, generally because of a lack of a sufficient profit making opportunity. A cooperative utility is usually created when a group of potential users form their own utility to provide a commodity (electricity, natural gas or water/sewer) for themselves that otherwise would not be available. Both municipal and cooperative utilities are completely self-governing with little state intervention except with relation to rate case procedures and public notification guidelines. Ordinarily the state will require that normal rate case protocol is followed with relation to due process and input by affected customers (intervenor groups).

It is very important to know what is happening at the state regulatory level because of the impact of rate case decisions on customer costs. As a rule, at the federal (FERC) (interstate) level, electricity is more deregulated than at the state (intrastate) level. Since regulation at the intrastate level is generally more restrictive and in many instances results in tariff provisions that cause customer rates to be more costly than they could be, remain aware of pending rate cases in your intrastate electric utility so that you can develop a strategy based upon fact not hope.

## AREAS REGULATED BY INTRASTATE AGENCIES

■ Intrastate terms and conditions relating to tariff structures and pricing criteria.

In the case of electricity, the following areas are very important to the customer:

1. Types of service that should be available –

   A.  FIRM.

   B.  INTERRUPTIBLE.

   C.  NEGOTIABLE RATE.
       (Rates that compete with alternate sources of electricity.)

   D.  FIRM TRANSPORTATION.
       (Transportation of the retail customer's electricity through the serving utility's distribution system.)

   E.  INTERRUPTIBLE TRANSPORTATION.
       (Transportation of the retail customer's electricity through the serving utility's distribution system.)

   F.  MARKET SERVICE.
       (Acts as customer's agent for wheeled electricity.)

A "full service" electric utility would offer all of the options shown above but the sad truth is none do. At the time of this publication, most electric utilities offer only options A and B. It does no good to have deregulation at the interstate level (FERC) if at the intrastate level the advantages cannot be utilized because of restrictive tariff schedule provisions. There remains much to be done at the intrastate level before the true value of interstate deregulation will be recognized by many customers.

## THREE TYPES OF UTILITIES REGULATED ON AN INTRASTATE BASIS

### I.  FOR-PROFIT (INVESTOR-OWNED COMPANIES)

**Regulation –**

■  All for-profit investor-owned utilities that operate within state boundaries.

Regulation is on a statewide basis since (Intrastate regulation of utilities concerns the intrastate activities of a utility.) State agencies regulate the intrastate transportation and operation of electric utilities. Since electricity may be distributed from a location outside of the boundaries of the state in which the customer is situated, there are both federal and state regulations which apply. The state agencies usually take the form of Public Service Commission (PSC) or Public Utility Commissions (PUC). The functions of these entities are to regulate the intrastate distribution and operation of utilities. These agencies also determine and approve individual utility rates of return, grant franchises to utilities for specific areas of operation, and in general, regulate the operation of utilities which are within a given state. Although PSC or PUC structures are the most common forms of state regulation, other methods are used. In some states, these commissions regulate utilities only outside the incorporation limits of a municipality or city such as in Georgia, Texas, etc. There are rather strange situations which occur in a few states. For instance in the State of Texas, the Public Utility Commission regulates electricity outside of municipalities; however, outside of these same municipalities an entity called the "Railroad Commission of Texas" regulates natural gas. Generally, a retail customer will have more contact with the state regulatory agency than with the federal agencies. Since state agencies determine rate of return and approve or disapprove rate increase requests of utilities, the likelihood of involvement with these agencies will be greater. To remain informed on utility matters, a knowledge of the operation and function of the state agencies is required. To follow state regulatory matters can be very time-consuming and costly if done on an individual basis. One alternative to this is to become a member of a state energy users group commonly called a State Intervenor Group. These groups are comprised of numerous individuals which have common concerns, typically electricity and natural gas costs and regulations. Collectively these groups can accomplish much at the state regulatory level. Currently, at least the following states have intervenor groups as shown in Figure 2.2.

**Figure 2.2**  States With Intervenor Groups

| Alabama | Kentucky | Oklahoma |
|---|---|---|
| Arkansas | Louisiana | Oregon |
| California | Maryland | Pennsylvania |
| Colorado | Michigan | South Carolina |
| Connecticut | Missouri | Tennessee |
| Delaware | Montana | Texas |
| Florida | New Hampshire | Utah |
| Georgia | New Jersey | Virginia |
| Illinois | New Mexico | West Virginia |
| Indiana | New York | Wisconsin |
| Iowa | North Carolina | Wyoming |
| Kansas | Ohio | |

Any user or intervenor group is required to be registered with the appropriate State Regulatory Agency. Therefore, to determine whether a state has intervenor groups, contact the appropriate Regulatory Agency. Listed in Figure 2.2(a) are all know intervenor groups by state. Since the telephone numbers of contact persons in these groups change frequently, the State Regulatory Agency telephone number is shown. By contacting the appropriate Regulatory Agency, the current telephone number for a particular intervenor group can be obtained.

**Figure 2.2(a)**   State Intervenor Groups

**ALABAMA**
Alabama Industrial Group
Regulatory Agency   (205) 242-5209

**ARKANSAS**
Arkansas Electric Energy Consumers
Regulatory Agency   (501) 682-2051

**CALIFORNIA**
California Manufacturers Association
California Industrial Users
Regulatory Agency   (415) 557-0647

**COLORADO**
Colorado Multiple Intervenor Group
Regulatory Agency   (303) 894-2000

**CONNECTICUT**
Connecticut Industrial Energy Consumers
Regulatory Agency   (203) 827-1553

**DELAWARE**
Delaware Energy Users Group
Regulatory Agency   (302) 739-4247

**FLORIDA**
Florida Industrial Power Users Group
Regulatory Agency   (904) 488-3464

**GEORGIA**
Georgia Industrial Group
Regulatory Agency   (404) 656-4501

**ILLINOIS**
Illinois Industrial Energy Consumers
Illinois Industrial Utility Consumers
Regulatory Agency   (217) 782-5793

**INDIANA**
Indiana Industrial Energy Consumers, Inc.
Indiana Industrial Intervenors
Regulatory Agency   (317) 232-2801

**IOWA**
Iowa Industrial Intervenors
Iowa Energy Group
Iowa Mid-Size Industrials
Regulatory Agency   (515) 281-5979

**KANSAS**
Kansas Industrial Intervenor Group
Regulatory Agency   (913) 271-3100

**KENTUCKY**
Kentucky Industrial Utility Customers
Regulatory Agency   (502) 564-3940

**LOUISIANA**
Louisiana Energy Users Group
Regulatory Agency   (504) 342-4427

**MARYLAND**
Maryland Industrial Group
Regulatory Agency   (301) 333-6000

**MICHIGAN**
Association of Businesses Advocating
Tariff Equity
Regulatory Agency   (517) 334-6445

**MISSOURI**
Missouri Industrial Energy Consumers
Wolf Creek Industrial Intervenors
Regulatory Agency   (314) 751-3234

**MONTANA**
Montana Industrial Intervenor Group
Regulatory Agency   (406) 444-6199

**NEW HAMPSHIRE**
Business and Industry Association of
New Hampshire
Regulatory Agency   (603) 271-2431

**NEW JERSEY**
New Jersey Industrial Energy Users
Association
Regulatory Agency   (201) 648-2026

**NEW MEXICO**
New Mexico Industrial Energy Consumers
Regulatory Agency   (505) 827-6940

**NEW YORK**
Multiple Intervenors
Industrial Power Consumers Conference
Regulatory Agency   (518) 474-7080

**NORTH CAROLINA**
Carolina Industrial Group for Fair
Utility Rates
Carolina Utility Customers Association
North Carolina Industrial Energy
Consumers
Regulatory Agency   (919) 733-4249

**OHIO**
Ohio Power Industrial Energy Consumers
Ohio Industrial Electricity Consumers
Ohio Manufacturers Association
Ohio Retail Merchants Council
Regulatory Agency   (614) 644-8927

**OKLAHOMA**
Oklahoma Industrial Energy Users Group
Regulatory Agency   (405) 521-2261

**OREGON**
Industrial Customers of Northwest Utilities
Regulatory Agency   (503) 378-6611

**Figure 2.2(a)** State Intervenor Groups (Con't.)

**PENNSYLVANIA**
Industrial Energy Consumers of
Pennsylvania
The PENELEC Intervenor Group
Regulatory Agency    (717) 783-1740

**SOUTH CAROLINA**
South Carolina Energy Users Committee
Regulatory Agency    (803) 737-5100

**TENNESSEE**
Tennessee Associated Valley Industries
Tennessee Valley Industrial Committee
Regulatory Agency    (615) 741-5100

**TEXAS**
Texas Industrial Energy Consumers
Regulatory Agency    (512) 458-0100

**UTAH**
Utah Industrial Energy Consumers Group
Regulatory Agency    (801) 530-6716

**VIRGINIA**
Old Dominion Committee for Fair
Utility Rates
Virginia Committee for Fair Utility Rates
Regulatory Agency    (804) 786-3603

**WEST VIRGINIA**
West Virginia Energy Users Group
Regulatory Agency    (304) 340-0300

**WISCONSIN**
Wisconsin Industrial Electricity
Consumers Group
Regulatory Agency    (608) 266-2001

**WYOMING**
Wyoming Intervenor Group
Regulatory Agency    (307) 777-7427

## Public Utility Commission Periodic Reports

Periodically, all public utility commissions that regulate for-profit utilities are required to issue status reports. These reports are generally issued on a weekly basis and provide data on all currently pending rate cases within their jurisdictions. Copies of these reports are available to anyone who requests them. In most states there is no cost but even in those states where costs are incurred, they generally do not exceed $100 per year. If a customer's utility is regulated by a public utility commission, it is important to keep updated on what is going on at the commission level. Typically the following information is detailed in these reports:

1. Docket or case number of the proceeding being discussed.

2. Brief report concerning the status of the proceeding.

3. Identification of parties in the proceeding.

4. Timetable and place of next commission meeting concerning the proceeding.

For further information on how to receive commission reports, contact the commission involved.

**For-Profit Utility Regulation Synopsis**

**(Investor-Owned Utilities)**

1. *Intrastate regulatory body.*
   State regulatory agency.

2. *Utilities in this classification.*
   Any utility that is in business for the stated purpose of making a profit and is owned by investors through the purchase shares of stock.

3. *Regulation process.*
   Any rate changes must include at least the following items:

   A. Public notification of intent to change a rate.

   B. Adequate notification period prior to actual rate case presentation (this period defined by state law) to allow interested parties to study the merits of the change request.

   C. Presentation of rate request at a hearing open to the public before the appropriate regulatory agency.

   D. Allow input from interested customer groups (intervenors) relating to rate change requests. The state regulatory body, based upon testimony presented at rate case hearings, approves actual rates that will be put into effect.

## II.  MUNICIPALITIES

When municipalities regulate utilities, they are self-governing, that is, they are not subject to state regulatory rulings. Generally, when municipalities undertake the providing and regulation of utilities, they are purchasing the commodities at wholesale rates from a for-profit or federally regulated utility, and then retail these utilities to the public. This is especially true with electricity and natural gas. In the case of water and sewage, the municipality generally has control or jurisdiction over the entire process. Municipal utilities are self-regulated and generally are presided over by a utility commission or board of appointed or elected members. As in the case of all utility regulatory agencies, "due process" must occur before changes can be made with respect to rates and conditions under which utilities are provided. This means that public notice must be given and adequate time allowed for public input prior to a change being instituted. Typically, municipal utilities do not have as many rate classes or options as will for-profit investor-owned utilities since they generally do not have as diverse a class of customers. There are over 1,900 municipal utilities in the United States, but in terms of total energy supplied (electricity and natural gas), they constitute a minority when compared to the for-profit investor owned utilities. However, one area that is almost 100% municipal utility supplied is water and sewage services.

## Municipal Utility Regulation Synopsis

1. *Regulatory body.*

   Self-regulated by the body or agency selected by the municipality to oversee utility matters. Can be separate for each utility regulated.

2. *Utilities in this classification.*

   Any utility controlled and regulated by a municipality on a not-for-profit basis.

3. *Regulation process.*

   Similar to for-profit investor-owned utilities.
   
   A. Public notification.
   
   B. Adequate notification period.
   
   C. Presentation of rate request.
   
   D. Allow input from interested customer groups.

## III. RURAL ELECTRIC COOPERATIVE UTILITIES

Cooperative utilities are formed generally when a for-profit investor-owned utility elects not to serve a geographic area or customer base. Cooperative utilities generally serve rural areas where there is not a large customer load base. Generally, power is purchased at wholesale from a for-profit utility and distributed by the cooperatives' lines and/or pipes to the individual customers' locations. These utilities are like municipal utilities in that they are self-regulated but also are required to provide "due process" before instituting changes in the utility rate base. They are also very different from any other type of utility since they are classified as a "cooperative" entity. The term "cooperative," as far as utilities are concerned, literally means that each customer is a part owner of the utility and as such, at least in theory, has their proportionate say in how the utility is operated. They are similar to all other types of utilities in rate change cases. They propose rate changes, hear customer input and allow all other "due process" practices before actually instituting rate changes. Cooperative utilities are smaller in terms of total energy supplied, than are municipal utilities and in general are located in rural types of service areas.

### Cooperative Utility Regulation Synopsis

1. *Intrastate regulatory body.*
   Self-regulated. All customers are part owners of the utility and as such have their proportionate say or vote based upon their usage in relation to other customers. In practice many times, a board of overseers is appointed to represent customer interests with respect to the utility operation.

2. *Utilities in this classification.*
   Any utility defined as cooperative and that is owned and operated by the customers served.

3. *Regulation process.*
   Similar to other types of utilities and includes:
   A. Public notification.
   B. Adequate notification.
   C. Presentation of rate request.
   D. Allow input from customers.

### FEDERAL ENTITIES

These types of utilities are of Federal origin and regulation. Generally, intrastate regulation is not applicable since these types of utilities are operated on an interstate basis. The Federal Government has the overall responsibility of regulation and operating procedures. Generally, these utilities wholesale the majority of their power to for-profit investor owned companies, municipalities and cooperatives who in turn are regulated by their respective regulatory bodies. When direct sales are made to customers, regulation parameters are by Federal guidelines.

1. Alaska Power Administration
   Juneau, AK – (907) 586-7405

2. Bonneville Power Administration
   Portland, OR – (503) 230-3000

3. International Boundary & Water Commission
   U.S. and Mexico
   El Paso, TX – (915) 534-6700

4. Southeastern Power Administration
   Elberton, GA – (706) 283-9911

5. Southwestern Power Administration
   Tulsa, Ok – (918) 581-7474

6. Tennessee Valley Authority
   Knoxville, TN – (615) 632-2101

7. U.S. Army Corps. of Engineers
   Washington, DC – (202) 272-0001

8. U.S. Bureau of Indian Affairs
   Mission Valley Power
   Polson, MT – (406) 883-5361

9. U.S. Bureau of Indian Affairs
   San Carlos Irrigation Project
   Coolidge, AZ – (602) 723-5439

10. U.S. Bureau of Reclamation
    Washington, DC – (202) 208-4662

11. Western Area Power Administration
    Golden, CO – (303) 231-1513

## THE INFLUENCE INTRASTATE REGULATION HAS ON UTILITY COSTS

State agencies regulate the intrastate distribution of electricity. And electricity utilizes a combination of "inter" (between states) and "intra" (within a state) components, and therefore both federal and state regulation occurs.

Since state agencies provide the predominate day-to-day regulatory functions concerning electricity, it is important to know that they function in a manner that benefits the customer. One of the most discouraging factors in intrastate regulation is the number of regulatory agencies that allow the utilities they regulate to not offer truly "Cost Of Service" tariff schedule rates. It does a customer no good to have interstate access to retail wheeling of electricity if the intrastate utility does not allow retail wheeling of that electricity through their transmission system. To be better able to visualize the flow of electricity through electric utilities, Figure 2.3 is shown following:

**Figure 2.3**  Flow of Electricity

```
          ┌─────────────────────────────────┐
          │   GENERATION OF ELECTRICITY     │
          │  (Intrastate – State Regulation)│
          └─────────────────────────────────┘

          ┌─────────────────────────────────┐
          │  TRANSMISSION OF ELECTRICITY    │
          │    (Interstate and Intrastate)  │
          │   (FERC and State Regulation)   │
          └─────────────────────────────────┘

┌──────────────────────────────┐   ┌──────────────────────────┐
│ INTRA UTILITY DISTRIBUTION   │   │   RETAIL CUSTOMER        │
│  (Interstate and Intrastate) │   │     (Intrastate)         │
│  (FERC and State Regulation) │   │   (State Regulation)     │
└──────────────────────────────┘   └──────────────────────────┘
```

# Chapter 3

# Developing a Strategy for Reducing Electricity Costs

The first step in understanding anything is the obtaining of accurate information relating to the subject being investigated. In the case of electricity, the first step in understanding begins with the obtaining of data that relates to the pricing on a unit basis of the commodity (electricity) being purchased. Since all utilities are regulated in one way or another, written records of usage and pricing data as it relates to customers must be available to any interested party that requires it.

## ITEMS NEEDED FROM THE UTILITY AND STATE

Listed following are the mandatory basic informational items that must be obtained before any understanding of electricity rates will be realized. All of these items are a matter of public record and must be made available to any one who requests them. They are typically available from at least three sources – (1) the utility itself, (2) regulatory agencies, and (3) university libraries. Generally, the most logical place to obtain this information is from the utility or the utility regulatory agency themselves. If a request is received by a utility from one of its customers, there generally is no problem or cost involved. However, if a request is received from a non-customer, some problems may arise both with respect to availability as well as the potential for a cost being assessed for the material.

Remember, all utility rate information that is approved by a regulatory body for use in determining rates and conditions to which a customer is subject, must be a matter of public record; and, as such, available for public inspection. Typically, the utility service representative responsible for the customer involved is contacted and a request is made for the information needed. Generally, a telephone or face-to-face request is most productive from the requester's point of view. Normally, a utility will not charge one of its own customers for this information but may assess a "copy" charge to a non-customer. This charge should be reasonable and reflect the time and material required to furnish the information. The importance of obtaining the following information cannot be overstated since these items are basic to understanding utility costs.

With relation to information that is required from the state, the best way to proceed is to contact the state agency involved directly. Generally, there will be no problems in obtaining either sales tax or economic development/enterprise zone information from the state. It is always best to contact the proper state agency directly by telephone since letters seem to get lost or misplaced rather frequently.

In Figures 3.1 and 3.5 following is shown the various items needed prior to analyzing any electricity billing. Figure 3.1 lists the items that are normally obtained from the service representative of the utility involved. Figure 3.5 lists the items that are obtained from the state where the customer is located. If all of the items described in these two figures are obtained, a thorough comprehensive analysis of the specific utility involved can be done.

## RECAP OF FIGURE 3.1 (UTILITY DATA NEEDED)

### I.  COMPLETE TARIFF OR RATE SCHEDULE

A complete tariff or rate schedule covers all rates, terms and conditions that were approved in a rate case. All classes of customers are addressed – residential, commercial and industrial. These tariffs or schedules can range from several sheets to several hundred sheets in length. Contained in this information will be all data relating to customer rates, costs, terms for service, etc. The importance of this source document cannot be overemphasized since it is absolutely mandatory for

**Figure 3.1** Basic Utility Data Needed

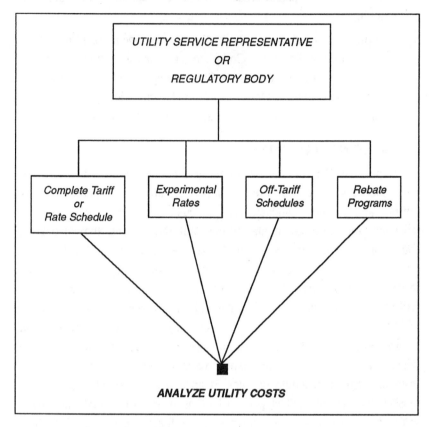

an understanding of utility costs. Make certain that the request is made for a "complete" tariff or rate schedule since utilities tend to provide only a particular schedule that currently applies to the customer making the request. It is important that the "complete" schedule be available since only then can comparisons between different rates and options be made. A typical complete tariff or rate schedule will contain the following items:

1. Complete list and explanation of all customer rates available.

2. Complete list of all items or riders that modify or change rate costs.

3. Alternative rates that may be available on a "customer request" basis for certain customer classes.

4. Information on "special" rates that may be available in certain geographic areas.

5. Complete explanation as to how all cost components of utility usage are measured and applied. Complete tariff or rate schedules remain in effect until a new rate case is filed and approved by the appropriate regulatory agency. Only one complete schedule is required for a given utility since all customer classes are addressed therein.

## II. EXPERIMENTAL RATES

Experimental rates are not normally contained in complete tariff or rate schedules since they are developed on an experimental basis by utilities and are not mandated for any customer class. These types of rates are not available in all utilities, but if they are, they can be a source of cost reduction potential. These types of rates are developed by the utility and approved on an experimental basis initially. The experimental category allows the utility to evaluate the potential for a different type of rate structure. Experimental rates are never mandated and are used only on a customer voluntary basis. Also, if a customer chooses an experimental rate and it results in an increased cost, typically the utility will not assess any cost more expensive than what would have resulted from the regular schedule of rates. If an experimental rate proves successful, the typical next step is to include it as an optional rate in the base tariff/rate schedule and not mandatory for any customer class. The final step is to change the optional classification to "mandatory" for a certain customer class in the base tariff/rate schedule. An example of what an experimental real time pricing electric rate could look like is shown in Figure 3.2 following.

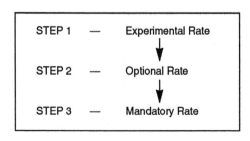

Keep up-to-date on experimental rates since long term they have a way of becoming mandatory for some customer classes. The most common experimental rate structure currently being used in electricity seems to be the "real time pricing" structure. Ask your utility service representative if experimental rates are available; and if they are, obtain a copy and determine the immediate applicability as well as the long term implications if they are later included in the base tariff/rate schedules as mandatory for your customer class.

**Figure 3.2**  Example of an Experimental Real Time Tariff Schedule

---

1. **SCHEDULE** – *EX-RPT-3 (Experimental Real Time Pricing)*

2. **APPLICABILITY** –

   *Applicable to any general service customer with service delivered at a voltage level of 4, 160 to 69,000 volts. To qualify for this rate, the customer must have maintained a monthly billing demand level of at least 200 kW for the last 12 month period.*

   *This rate is available on an experimental basis and the minimum term is for a one year period.*

3. **BASE MONTHLY RATES** –

   | | | |
   |---|---|---|
   | A. | Customer Charge | $250.00 |
   | B. | Demand Charge – per kW | (None) |
   | C. | Energy Charge: | |
   | | (1) Base Energy Charge – per kWh (Fuel Cost) | $   .0023 |
   | | (2) Energy Charge – per kWh | (Variable) ($0216 – $.2371) |

4. **COST DATA** –

   *Cost data shall be calculated on an hourly basis every day. No later than 8:00 A.M. every day the next day's hourly rates beginning at 12:01 A.M. will be provided to the customer via a telecommunication link with the customer mandatory dedicated telephone line. This data will provide the (24) hourly variable energy charge components for the next billing period. This data will be provided every day of the year. The energy charge components will reflect the utility's actual costs as detailed in the Public Utility Commission approved rate filing 427-AF dated 07-06, pages 476-A through 493-C.*

5. **VARIABLE ENERGY CHARGES** –

   *Variable energy charges will range from a minimum of $.0216/kWh to a maximum of $.2371/kWh per hourly measurement period.*

6. **MINIMUM BILLING** –

   *The minimum monthly billing shall consist of the following item:*

   | | | |
   |---|---|---|
   | A. | Customer Charge | $250.00 |

7. **MISCELLANEOUS PROVISIONS** –

   A. *There shall be no demand (kW) charges applied to this rate.*
   B. *The utility will provide and maintain the appropriate metering and related equipment to accurately measure the kWh consumption on an hourly basis, at no cost to the customer.*
   C. *The utility retains the right to limit the number of customers on this rate.*
   D. *The utility retains the right to withdraw this rate upon one month's notice.*

## ANALYSIS OF FIGURE 3.2

This experimental rate allows a customer to purchase electricity on an hour-by-hour basis paying only for usage (kWh). The problem with a rate of this type is that usage (kWh) charges will probably be more expensive at times when the customer's usage will be the greatest. For example, in the experimental rate shown in Figure 3.2, it is likely that the $.2371/kWh charge will occur from about 11:00 A.M. through 3:00 P.M. on normal work days (Monday-Friday). If this is true, very costly electricity will be consumed during most customers' largest usage period. Generally, this type of rate will be of benefit only to the customer that can shift the electrical usage to the utility's normal off-peak periods which would generally be during the evening, night, early morning, weekends and holidays. Most electricity users do not have the flexibility to shift usages to the extent needed to benefit from this type of rate. However, if the customer can adjust the usage patterns on a daily/hourly basis, a rate of this type can be very cost effective. An item-by-item analysis of this rate follows:

1.  **SCHEDULE** – *EX-RPT-E (Experimental Real Time Pricing)*

    This schedule number (EX-RPT-3) designates the rate case tariff schedule identification number assigned to this rate by the utility/regulatory agency as a result of the utility's rate case concerning this rate. If a customer wanted to examine all pertinent data presented in this rate case filing, this could be accomplished by requesting the data from either the utility or the regulatory agency by schedule number (EX-RPT-3).

2.  **APPLICABILITY** –

    This section addresses the type of customer that can be served on this rate. In this particular rate, the customer must be served at a primary voltage level of from 4,160 to 69,000 volts. Also, the customer must have maintained a minimum billing demand level of 200 kW monthly for the last 12 months. Generally, applicability provisions are instituted because the utility has determined that this minimum voltage/demand threshold would be required by a customer to benefit from the rate. Also sometimes, especially on a rate of this type (experimental), the utility may want to test the rate's validity or applicability only to a certain type or class of customers.

3. **BASE MONTHLY RATES –**

   A. *Customer Charge – ($250.00).*

   This is the minimum monthly charge, in the absence of other rate imposed minimums, that an individual customer would have to pay to be served on this rate. This charge covers the utility's cost of maintaining and reading the meter and miscellaneous other monthly billing cost items.

   B. *Demand Charge – (None/kW).*

   This particular type of rate has no demand charge as such. Nevertheless, demand costs are calculated and included in the energy charges associated with this rate. Although a rate with no demand (kW) charge may seem to be a very "cost effective" type of rate, the truth of the matter is that demand costs are calculated and included in the energy charge portion of this rate. In fact, a rate of this type actually would probably be more expensive for most customers that could not shift usage patterns on a daily/hourly basis, which is very difficult to do. Just because demand is not included as a specific billing item does not mean that its impact on the utility's costs has not been considered. It has, and in this particular type of rate, is included in the variable energy charge portion of the billing.

   C. *Energy Charge:*

   (1) *Base Energy Charge – per kWh (Fuel Cost) $.0023.*

   This energy charge of $.0023/kWh represents the utility's fuel cost to operate their generation equipment. This charge is sometimes called fuel cost adjustment and it is always applied to the energy (usage, kWh) portion of the billing. All customers of a utility are assessed the same charge on each kWh used. All of these charges are approved by the appropriate regulatory agency.

(2) *Energy Charge – per kWh – (Variable) ($.0216 – $.2371)*
This charge represents the variable usage (kWh) charges by the utility on a daily/hourly basis. The extremely wide range of variability, over $.2100 per kWh ($.2371 – $.0216 = $.2155) is due to the cost of electricity that is experienced by the utility based upon its generation load/utilization at various times of the day. Since this type of rate has no specific demand charge, it is part of and included in the energy charge shown here. Since this rate is variable and is priced by the day and hour, it actually can change on a daily basis. To see what a daily usage cost printout from the utility might look like, the following example, Figure 3.3, is shown:

**Figure 3.3**  Example of a Daily Usage Cost Printout

| RATE – EX-RPT–3<br>DATA FOR – Tuesday, 09-17 | | | |
|---|---|---|---|
| **Time of Day** | **Hourly kWh Cost** | **Time of Day** | **Hourly kWh Cost** |
| 12:01 AM – 1:00 AM – | $.0216 | 12:01 PM – 1:00 PM – | $.1743 |
| 1:01 AM – 2:00 AM – | .0216 | 1:01 PM – 2:00 PM – | .2371 |
| 2:01 AM – 3:00 AM – | .0297 | 2:01 PM – 3:00 PM – | .1420 |
| 3:01 AM – 4:00 AM – | .0297 | 3:01 PM – 4:00 PM – | .1420 |
| 4:01 AM – 5:00 AM – | .0321 | 4:01 PM – 5:00 PM – | .1376 |
| 5:01 AM – 6:00 AM – | .0321 | 5:01 PM – 6:00 PM – | .1011 |
| 6:01 AM – 7:00 AM – | .0796 | 6:01 PM – 7:00 PM – | .0710 |
| 7:01 AM – 8:00 AM – | .0810 | 7:01 PM – 8:00 PM – | .0600 |
| 8:01 AM – 9:00 AM – | .0910 | 8:01 PM – 9:00 PM – | .0327 |
| 9:01 AM – 10:00 AM – | .0910 | 9:01 PM – 10:00 PM – | .0251 |
| 10:01 AM – 11:00 AM – | .1176 | 10:01 PM – 11:00 PM – | .0216 |
| 11:01 AM – 12:00 PM – | .1312 | 11:01 PM – 12:00 AM – | .0216 |

As illustrated in this hourly kWh cost data is the cost of electricity during the hours of normal operation for most customers. The kWh cost from 7:01 A.M. through 6:00 P.M. ranges from $.0810 to $.2371. If a customer uses the majority of the electricity during these hours, then the cost for the electricity will be very high. If, however, a customer has the majority of the usage between the hours of 12:01 A.M./7:00 A.M. and 6:01 P.M./12:00 A.M., then the cost per kWh would range from $.0216 to $.0796 which could result in savings when compared to a typical tariff schedule rate for this same type of usage pattern. Basically a real time pricing rate is generally only cost effective if a customer can vary their electrical loads on a daily time related basis, or if they typically operate during periods of low utility load demand intervals of time – typically evening, night, early morning and weekends. If a customer was served on this rate, they would receive a daily printout of data similar to the one shown here for every day of the month including weekends and holidays.

4. **COST DATA –**

This section explains how the hourly kWh charges will be calculated.

5. **VARIABLE ENERGY CHARGES –**

This section simply restates the information shown in Item 3.C.(2) previously.

6. **MINIMUM BILLING –**

This section details what will constitute a minimum monthly customer bill. Basically the minimum charge will consist of the customer charge ($250).

7. **MISCELLANEOUS PROVISIONS –**

This section enumerates miscellaneous provisions associated with this tariff schedule rate. As can be seen from analyzing the provisions of this example of a real time pricing rate, it is not a rate for all customers. Generally, a rate of this type will not be cost effective for customers who operate on a one shift basis during normal daytime hours between 7:00 A.M. and 6:00 P.M. However, if a customer operates hours other than these, or can shift their usage on a daily and hourly basis, or can work many hours on weekends (typically Saturday and Sunday), then a rate of this type may prove to be very cost effective. Before changing to a rate of this type, always have the utility do an analysis of the past year for the facility/operation in questions to determine the cost effectiveness of a change.

### III.  OFF-TARIFF SCHEDULES

Off-tariff schedules differ from both base tariff as well as experimental rates in the way they are developed and applied. Off-tariff schedules are rates that are negotiated generally between a utility and a specific customer. They, at least initially, are generally discriminatory in nature and typically apply to larger customers. Rates of this type are negotiated between a utility and a specific customer and must be approved by the appropriate regulatory agency. Generally, off-tariff rates are developed for large user customers that have either extremely large loads or unusual use characteristics that are not addressed adequately in base tariff structures. Most off-tariff schedules occur in larger utilities with diverse customer bases. To establish an off-tariff schedule is at best a drawn out procedure. First, the utility as well as the regulatory agency has to be convinced of the need for a rate of this type – no easy task in itself. Second, other utility customers may protest a discriminatory rate since it could impact their utility costs unfavorably – someone could have to pay for the lost revenue that generally results from an off-tariff schedule. Off-tariff schedules in the past have not been widely used or applicable to a large user base, but this is changing with the potential of electricity retail wheeling becoming a reality. Evaluate the base tariff schedule in terms of usage characteristics and if large differences appear between actual usage patterns and those specified in the base schedule, the potential for an off-tariff schedule may exist. To determine whether off-tariff schedules are available, contact the utility service representative and request a copy of any off-tariff schedules that are currently available. An example of what an off-tariff schedule might look like is shown in Figure 3.4 following:

**Figure 3.4**  Example of an Off-Tariff Schedule Developed to Encourage a Customer to Greatly Expand Their Usage of Electricity

1.  *SCHEDULE – A OTS-B (Extra Large Power Service Rider)*

2.  *APPLICABILITY –*

    *Applicable to any large power service (Schedule LPS-1) customer who establishes a minimum demand of 5,000 kVA in at least 6 consecutive billing months out of the previous 12 billing months. Also, available to any large power service customer (Schedule LPS-1) who adds a minimum demand of 4,000 kVA and who can document to the utility's satisfaction that this demand will continue to exist for at least 6 consecutive billing months out of the next 12 billing months. This rate rider is available at the utility's discretion as approved by the P.U.C. in rate case Docket No. E07/GR-94-067.*

3.  *CHARACTER OF SERVICE – ac; 60 hertz 3 phase at 128,000 volts or higher.*

4.  *RATE –*

    A.  *Customer Charge– Schedule LPS-1 charge plus $750.00*

    B.  *Demand Charge  – 1,500 kVA – As provided for in Schedule LPS-1*
        *All over 1,500 kVA – $3.50 per KVA demand*

    C.  *Energy Charge:  – All kWh up to 1,000,000 kWh as provided for in Schedule LPS-1*
        *All kWh over 1,000,000 kWH  – $.013 per kWh*

5.  *MINIMUM BILL – Total charges applicable in Schedule LPS-1 plus $750.00 customer charge for this rate rider.*

6.  *FUEL COST ADJUSTMENT – Same as provided for in Schedule LPS-1.*

7.  *TAXES – Same as applicable to Schedule LPS-1.*

8.  *BILLING DEMAND – The billing demand shall be the greatest of the following and be in addition to any demand charges established in Schedule LPS-1 for the billing month.*

    A.  *The highest measured 15-minute demand established during the billing month;*

    B.  *95% of the highest demand established during the immediately preceding 11 months;*

    *OR*

    C.  *4,000 kVA.*

9.  *MISCELLANEOUS PROVISIONS –*

    A.  *This utility in a general rate case is allowed to seek recovery of the difference between the Standard Tariff Schedule Rate (LPS-1) and this Rider (A OTS-B), times usage level of the customer's utilizing this rider during a test year period if it is found that rate (A OTS-B) yields less revenue than rate (LPS-1) would have yielded for the last year if rate (A OTS-B) was not available.*

    B.  *The maximum possible kVA demand available for this rider shall be no more than 100,000 kVA.*

    C.  *The term of service of this rider will be no less than one year and no longer than 5 years.*

## ANALYSIS OF FIGURE 3.4

This example of an off-tariff schedule is typical of the types of rates/riders established on an off-tariff basis for the benefit initially of probably only one specific customer. In this example, the rider rate established is to supplement a regular tariff schedule currently in effect (LPS-1). Its purpose is to retain current extra large (LPS-1) customers as well as to encourage the addition of electrical usage by these customers. This rider rate basically supplements the current (LPS-1) rate through the institution of a full-blown rate case application rather than developing this off-tariff rate rider. However, a complete rate case is a very expensive and lengthy process, so the off-tariff schedule route is probably the most cost effective means of fulfilling this particular need. Probably the need for a rate rider of this type was necessitated because the (LPS-1) rate structure did not address the need for extra large electrical usage rates. Possibly because at the time the (LPS-1) rate was designed, industrial growth was not anticipated to the extent that it has actually occurred, or to the extent that the utility would like for it to grow.

1.  **SCHEDULE** – *A OTS-B* –

    This schedule number (A OTS-B) designates the rate case tariff schedule identification number assigned to this rate by the utility/regulatory agency as a result of the utility's rate case requesting this rate. If a customer wanted to examine all pertinent data presented in this rate case filing, they could do so by requesting the data from either the utility or the regulatory agency by schedule number (A OTS-B).

2.  **APPLICABILITY** –

    This section addresses the types of customers that can apply/qualify for this rate rider. In this particular case, a customer must currently be served by the (LPS-1) tariff schedule rate and have either a current demand of at least 5,000 kVA or add at least 4,000 kVA to their existing load. The reason for the institution of this rate was probably because of a very large customer(s) threats to leave this utility's service territory if their electricity costs were not reduced. Also, a very large customer(s) could have requested rate concessions to add new load at their facilities. The utility in either of these scenarios evidently determined that they had the required additional capacity to fulfill the customer's needs, at least up to a total system level of 100,000 kVA (See 9. B. following). Generally, a rate concession of this type is good for both the utility as well as the customers since it allows the utility to sell more of its electricity; and, if the additional capacity is available, the incremental cost to the utility per unit of electricity generated should be less, which should benefit all utility customers.

3. **CHARACTER OF SERVICES –**

This section addresses the type of electricity service, voltage/hertz (cycles), at which a customer receives their electricity from the utility. This character of service designation is probably the same as required in the LPS-1 rate since the A OTR-B rate is a rider to the regular LPS-1 rate.

4. **RATE –**

A. *Customer Charge – ($750.00)*
This is the additional customer charge applicable to this rate rider. The total customer charge would be the LPS-1 rate customer charge plus this customer charge. Customer charges cover the utility's cost of maintaining and reading the meter and miscellaneous other monthly billing costs items.

B. *Demand Charge – ($3.50 per kVA over 1,500 kVA)*
This section details the demand charge per kVA. Notice that this charge occurs only over 1,500 kVA. This is an unusual demand requirement but it is structured in this manner because this rate is a rider to the regular LPS-1 rate.

C. *Energy Charge – ($.013 per kWh over 1,000,000 kWh)*
This electricity usage or energy charge is structured in much the same way as the demand charge is. It is applicable only over 1,000,000 kWh. This charge pays for actual electricity usage during the billing month.

5. **MINIMUM BILL** – *(LPS-1 Charges Plus $750.00 Customer Charge)*

   This section details the minimum customer cost to utilize this rider on a monthly basis.

6. **FUEL COST ADJUSTMENT** – *(Same as for LPS-1)*

   The applicable fuel cost for any electricity used in this rider will have a fuel cost adjustment applied in the same manner as does the LPS-1 rate.

7. **TAXES** – *(Same as for LPS-1)*

   Whatever taxes (Federal, State, Municipal, etc.) that are applicable to the customer in rate LPS-1 will be equally applicable to this rider.

8. **BILLING DEMAND** – *Ratchet Method*

   The billing demand on this rider is calculated in one of three methods with the method that is utilized resulting in the highest billing demand. This method is call "Ratcheting." Either (A) the actual highest 15-minute demand, (B) 95% of the highest demand established in the immediately preceding 11 months, or (C) 4,000 kVA, whichever results in the highest demand figure will be utilized as the customer billing demand. Also, notice that the demand billed for in this rider is in addition to that billed for in the LPS-1 rate.

9. **MISCELLANEOUS PROVISIONS** –

   A. This utility has filed for and had approved a rate case that allows them to recover any lost revenue that might result through the utilization of this rate rider. It would be unlikely that this rider would ever result in lost revenue to the utility since it would, by definition, only be applicable to extra large usages which might not occur if this rider was not available. A rider like this generally will result in more revenue than would occur in a normal tariff schedule rate. The reason for this is, if the utility has the excess energy available and does not have to construct or enlarge current generation and/or distribution equipment, the more electricity sold results in lower incremental (kVA/kWh) costs for the utility. At this time, most electric utilities have excess base load (kWh) available all during the year and most have excess demand (kVA) at least during part of the year. Any of this excess (kVA/kWh) that can be sold for at least a small profit to the utility over its actual cost will result in additional revenue that helps to spread various utility cost factors over more units sold reducing the utility's incremental cost per unit and, at least in theory, result in a more profitable bottom line for the utility.

B.  The utility is limiting its overall exposure by stating that total kVA available in this rider is limited to no more than 100,000 kVA. Probably this limit represents the utility's available excess power available without additional expenditures for generation and/or distribution facilities.

C.  A customer that wants to utilize this rider must agree to remain on this rider for at least (1) year and no longer than (5) years. This is a normal provision for a rate of this type and any customer that would want to utilize this rider should be certain that their usage requirements will remain such that this rider will be of benefit for the time that they commit themselves.

## IV.  REBATE PROGRAM SCHEDULES –

Some electric utilities currently have peak power demand (kVA/kWh) deficits. This means that even though a utility may not have a base load (kWh) problem, they may experience a generation capacity shortfall during some periods of a 24 hour day. To compensate for this generation capacity shortfall, the utility can do several things. They can construct new generation plants *(supply side planning)* that are very expensive or they can offer their customers financial incentives to reduce demand during the utility's generation shortfall periods *(demand side planning)*. Many utilities offer rebate programs that encourage customers to reduce their demand needs by paying for or providing rebates for those items that favorably impact the utility's demand shortfall problems. Rebate programs range from, "not worth much" to "extremely beneficial." These programs change frequently and sometimes a specific amount of money is allocated for a program which means that when the money is gone, the program is ended. If a utility has a rebate program, they will also generally have an in-house rebate specialist that can be utilized for an onsite evaluation of a facility to determine the applicability of the utility program to a particular situation. The utility service representative can provide rebate program information as well as arrange for an onsite evaluation by the utility rebate specialist.

These programs typically include the following items/processes although not all items are included in all rebate programs:

1. Utility audits for rebate applicability.
2. Fluorescent lighting.
3. High Intensity Discharge lamping.
4. Electronic ballasts.
5. Efficient magnetic hybrid ballasts.
6. Reflectors.
7. Occupancy sensors.
8. Miscellaneous lighting controls.
9. Rooftop air conditioning.
10. Window air conditioning.
11. Electric chillers.
12. Gas-fired air conditioning.
13. Heat pumps.
14. Boiler/water heaters.
15. Cool storage - thermal storage.
16. Energy management systems (EMS).
17. Energy efficient motor drives.
18. Power factor correction capacitors.
19. Thermal insulation and window film.
20. Custom rebate programs structured to individual customer requirements. These programs are individually negotiated on a customer/utility basis.

**Figure 3.5** Basic State Data Needed

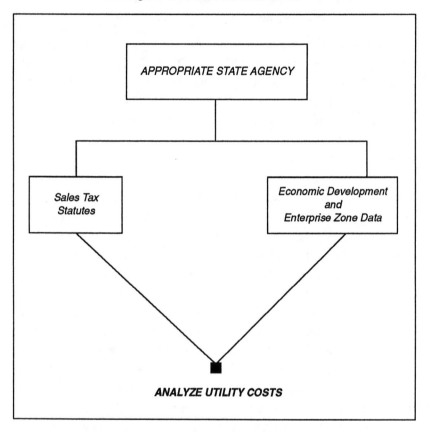

## RECAP OF FIGURE 3.5 – BASIC STATE DATA NEEDED

### Sales Tax Statutes

Generally most people would not consider sales tax to be a utility cost but many states tax utilities, especially for commercial and industrial customers, at whatever their regular rate of taxation is, normally 4-7%. Also, the majority (32) of the states offer some type of credit or offset for certain classes of customers. In most cases, this credit or offset is related to whether a customer is manufacturing a product. What is considered to be classified as manufacturing is subject to wide and varying interpretation by the various states but generally the two following items have to be present or take place in a process:

1. A change in form of the product or process has to occur.
2. A furthering or adding to a product or process has to occur.

Although these two items have to be present, there is considerable latitude in interpretation as to when they are present. For example, it has been accepted that the inputting of information on a computer floppy disc constitutes manufacturing even though there is no physical or perceptible change in the disc. It is also widely accepted that a restaurant can be considered to be manufacturing if it processes its food on the premises but if the restaurant purchases its food in the prepared frozen state and only heats or cooks it, no manufacturing occurs. Also, within a given state different interpretations concerning a given situation can be obtained simply by consulting different state taxation department employees. The best strategy to follow is – if you think that you have a sales tax exemption situation, contact the State Department of Sales Tax and obtain a copy of the applicable sales tax statute. When you read the statute, you may find considerable latitude in the interpretation of what can be exempted and what cannot be exempted from sales tax. If at this point you feel that your situation qualifies for a sales tax exemption, process an application. The worst that can happen is that the application will be rejected – but a rejection can be appealed and won. The best that can happen is that your application will be approved and you will have reduced your overall utility costs. In general, if your company or organization is paying state sales tax and is in one of the following categories, and is sited in one of the (32) states that allow exemptions (See Figure 3.6, Item 1. following), process a sales tax exemption.

1. Manufacturing operation.
2. Not-for-profit organization.
3. Municipal, state or federal organization.

If your company or organization is approved for sales tax exemption, you can also recover sales tax paid in the past up to the state statute of limitation time period – generally 3 to 5 years in the past.

## Information to Obtain from the State

To determine if exemptions are available, it will be necessary to contact the state involved so that copies of regulations, laws or statutes concerning exemptions can be obtained. Generally, one of the following state agencies can provide the information needed:

1. State Department of Taxation
2. State Department of Revenue

When contact has been made with the proper authority, ask for the following items:

1. Copies of taxation exemption regulations, laws or statutes.
2. Copies of taxation exemption forms to be completed to qualify for exemption.
3. Copies of retroactive refund regulations, laws or statutes.
4. Copies of retroactive refund forms to be completed to qualify for retroactive refunds.

Once this information is available, the difficult part starts. Unless there is a familiarity with the way in which legal documents are written or worded, the process of determining eligibility for exemption can be confusing, to say the least. Do not hesitate to call a state taxation or revenue officer for assistance. Once the exemption forms are submitted to the state, you can normally expect to have a waiting period of six to nine months before the petition for exemption will be ruled on. This process may seem complicated, but if the state guidelines are followed and the exemption forms are completed as instructed, exemption approval will be received if eligibility is approved. To assist you in becoming familiar with what various states allow with regard to exemption, following is Figure 3.6 – a listing of all 50 states and their current state sales tax regulations relating to utility exemptions.

**Figure 3.6**  Listing of all 50 states, the District of Columbia and their current state sales tax regulations relating to utility exemptions

1. The (32) States that, in general, allow sales tax exemptions on utility purchases: (Specific exemption conditions vary widely by State)

| | |
|---|---|
| Alabama ............Limited exemption | New Jersey .........General exemption |
| California ............General exemption | New York |
| Colorado | North Carolina ......Lower rate |
| Connecticut | Ohio ..................General exemption |
| District of Columbia | Oklahoma |
| Florida ...............Limited exemption | Pennsylvania |
| Idaho ..................General exemption | Rhode Island |
| Indiana | South Carolina |
| Iowa | Tennessee .........Lower rate |
| Kentucky | Texas |
| Maine ...............Limited exemption | Virginia |
| Maryland | Washington .........General exemption |
| Massachusetts | West Virginia |
| Michigan | Wisconsin ............Offset on other |
| Minnesota | state fees |
| Mississippi | Wyoming |
| Nevada ...............General exemption | |

2. The (14) States that, in general, allow no exemption on utility purchases.

| | | |
|---|---|---|
| Arizona | Kansas | North Dakota |
| Arkansas | Louisiana | South Dakota |
| Georgia | Missouri | Utah |
| Hawaii | Nebraska | Vermont |
| Illinois | New Mexico | |

3. The (5) States that do not have sales tax.

| | | |
|---|---|---|
| Alaska | Montana | Oregon |
| Delaware | New Hampshire | |

## ECONOMIC DEVELOPMENT AND ENTERPRISE ZONE DATA

At least 35 of the 50 states/District of Columbia currently have economic development/enterprise zone designations within their jurisdictions. In addition, two states have pending legislation to create such zones and two other states have incentive job credit programs. Economic development/incentive zones are created to stimulate the economy in a given geographic area of a state. These zones have nothing to do with utilities specifically, but in their effort to stimulate the economy, they generally allow credits for new or increased usage of utilities in the enterprise zone areas. Typically the utility incentives take the form of credits or concessions on new or increased utility usages with the credit or concession gradually disappearing over a period of time, generally 5 years. An example would be as follows:

| | |
|---|---|
| 1st year | 80% credit or concession |
| 2nd year | 60% credit or concession |
| 3rd year | 40% credit or concession |
| 4th year | 20% credit or concession |
| 5th year | 0% credit or concession |

These credits or concessions are directly deducted from the monthly billing for the utility involved. All utilities are generally included – natural gas, electricity, water/sewer, fuel oils, propane, etc. These credits or concessions do not cost the utilities since they are allowed a corresponding offset on their state tax liability. To determine what economic development/enterprise zones programs exist in a particular state, contact your state government offices and request "Economic Development/ Enterprise Zone" information including geographic boundaries and specific credits or concessions available.

Following in Figure 3.7 is shown all states and the District of Columbia and their specific economic development/enterprise zone data. Also, included is the respective telephone numbers by state where information can be obtained concerning these zones. NOTE: The telephone numbers shown were in effect at the time this publication was written. Since these telephone numbers are subject to change at any time, they may not all be up-to-date by the time this publication is printed.

**Figure 3.7**   State Breakdown of Economic Development/Enterprise Zones

| STATES | ZONES | TELEPHONE NUMBERS |
|---|---|---|
| Alabama | 27 | 205-263-0400 |
| Alaska | None | 907-465-2017 (Economic Dev.) |
| Arizona | 11 | 602-280-1307 |
| Arkansas | 456 | 501-682-2555 |
| California | 10 | 916-322-5665 |
| Colorado | 16 | 303-450-5106 |
| Connecticut | 11 | 203-258-4203 |
| Delaware | 30 Targeted areas | 302-739-4271 |
| District of Columbia | 3 Development zones | 202-727-6600 |
| Florida | 30 | 904-488-5507 |
| Georgia | 2 Enterprise & Industrial zones | 404-656-3556 |
| Hawaii | 24 | 808-586-2355 |
| Idaho | None | 800-842-5858 (Economic Dev.) |
| Illinois | 88 | 312-814-2354 |
| Indiana | 15 Urban zones | 317-232-8800 |
| Iowa | None | 515-242-4725 (Economic Dev.) |
| Kansas | 255 | 913-296-3483 |
| Kentucky | 10 | 502-564-7140 |
| Louisiana | 1,000 | 504-342-5402 |
| Maine | 4 | 207-289-3153 |
| Maryland | 17 | 410-333-6985 |
| Massachusetts | Pending legislation to create zones | 617-727-3206 |
| Michigan | 1 Benton Harbor | 517-373-7230 |
| Minnesota | 16 | 612-297-1291 |
| Mississippi | No zones. Incentives offered under Economic Development Reform Act, 1989 | 601-359-3449 |
| Missouri | 40 | 314-751-4241 |
| Montana | None | 466-444-3797 (Economic Dev.) |
| Nebraska | None | 402-471-3111 (Economic Dev.) |
| Nevada | 2 | 702-687-4325 |
| New Hampshire | None | 603-271-2591 (Economic Dev.) |
| New Jersey | 10 | 609-292-7751 |
| New Mexico | None | 505-827-0300 (Economic Dev.) |
| New York | 19 | 518-474-4100 |
| North Carolina | None | 919-733-4977 (Economic Dev.) |
| North Dakota | None | 701-223-8583 (Economic Dev.) |
| Ohio | 263 | 614-466-2317 |
| Oklahoma | 89 | 405-843-9770 |
| Oregon | 30 | 530-373-1200 |
| Pennsylvania | 43 | 717-787-6500 |
| Rhode Island | Pending Legislation | 401-277-2601 |
| South Carolina | Job credit program, no specific zones | 803-737-0400 |
| South Dakota | None | 605-773-5032 (Economic Dev.) |
| Tennessee | 1 North Memphis area | 615-741-3282 |
| Texas | 101 | 512-472-5059 |
| Utah | 15 | 801-538-8708/801-538-8804 |
| Vermont | 3 | 802-828-3221 |
| Virginia | 18 | 804-371-8100 |
| Washington | None | 206-753-5630 (Economic Dev.) |
| West Virginia | None | 304-348-0400 (Economic Dev.) |
| Wisconsin | 12 | 608-256-4567 |
| Wyoming | None | 307-777-7284 (Economic Dev.) |

## WHY IS REDUCING ELECTRICITY COSTS SO COMPLICATED?

As with anything new, unfamiliarity makes the process or procedure seem more difficult that it really is. The base data collection portion of reducing your electricity costs is probably the most important part of the undertaking. Once you begin the process of getting the information outlined in this chapter, you will realize that basically you only have two sources that you have to contact – the utility and the state. To assist you in obtaining utility information, Figure 3.8 following is shown. With relation to getting state information, I would suggest (from experience) that data be requested by telephone and that you always note the day, hour and person's name with whom you spoke.

**Figure 3.8**  Sample Letter For Requesting Information From the Utility Company

Dear (Service Representative of Utility Company):

As part of an ongoing program in our company to reduce operating costs, we are evaluating areas for investigation. One of these areas is (insert commodity name – electricity, natural gas, water or sewer). Please provide the following information as soon as possible:

1. Complete tariff schedule including riders, attachments, etc.
2. Experimental rates, if applicable.
3. Off-tariff schedules, if applicable.
4. Rebate programs, if applicable.

We appreciate your attention in this matter and thank you in advance for your help.

Sincerely,

(Utility Customer)

Figure 3.8 shows a sample of a utility data request form. This sample, if utilized, may assist in the obtaining of utility data that will be needed to analyze utility costs. This form is presented only as a sample but it does contain the basic elements that should be present in any request. The request should be submitted by the customer of the utility company to the customer's own utility service representative.

## WHO IS ULTIMATELY RESPONSIBLE FOR UTILITY COSTS?

The Federal Regulatory Commission together with all state regulatory agencies agree that the customer is ultimately responsible for being on the most cost effective rate. There are no state statutes that require a utility to ensure that a customer is served under the most economical or least costly rate available. Neither are there any requirements that a utility refund any excess monies paid by a customer if they are on a correct rate even if it is not the most cost effective. It is the customer's responsibility to select the least costly rate schedule. The customer cannot rely upon or accuse the utility of not being fair and equitable if the customer allows the utility to make the decision concerning the rate on which they should be served. Due to the vast number of customers most utilities serve, and the changes and revisions their customers are constantly experiencing, it would be impossible to assure that any customer is at all times on the most economical rate available. Each customer is responsible for the cost effectiveness of the rate under which they are served. Unfortunately, most utility customers know very little about the rate that forms the basis of their utility billing. Through information provided in this publication, the correct approach to reducing electricity costs can be understood.

With this knowledge, the customer can determine the steps needed to be assured their electricity costs are what they should be.

# SECTION II

## *Electricity Retail Wheeling – The Process Involved*

### Chapters 4 – 6

# Chapter 4

# Electricity Retail Wheeling Basics

## RETAIL WHEELING OF ELECTRICITY

Retail wheeling of electricity is simply the purchasing of electricity by a retail customer from a source other than their own serving utility. The process is very similar to retail customer purchase of natural gas; however, the effect on the electric utility is very different from that on the natural gas provider. In the purchase of electricity from a utility, the commodity (electricity) being purchased is generally originated or generated by the electric utility. In the purchase of natural gas, in the majority of instances, the commodity (natural gas) being purchased does not originate within the provider but is simply purchased by the provider and resold to the retail customer. Although these differences between electric and natural gas may seem to be of little importance to a retail electricity customer, they actually are critical to the utilities/providers and their differing attitudes towards the customer's direct purchase of the commodities they sell. Since most natural gas providers purchase the commodity they sell from someone else, it does not disrupt their operation or profitability to any great extent whether their customers purchase "provider" natural gas or arrange for their own natural gas and simply utilize provider pipes, meters and services. If the provider charges are based upon true cost of service principles, most natural gas providers would probably rather retail customers obtain their own natural gas since it would result in less headaches for the provider. An electric utility, however, takes a very different view of direct purchase of electricity by its retail customers since generally the serving electric utility generates the electricity it sells to retail customers. When an retail electricity customer purchases their electricity from some source other than the serving utility, the lost electricity sales for the serving utility result in lost revenue. The lost revenue in theory, at least, may not be capable of being replaced by the serving utility. If this is true, as retail customers choose to purchase their electricity from sources other than the serving utility, the utility will be required to increase electricity incremental rates to offset the reduced electricity sales. As this happens, more and more retail customers might opt to obtain their electricity from other than the serving utility. This scenario has a name which electric utilities call the "Death Spiral." This means that as less and less electricity is purchased by retail customers from their serving utilities, the incremental electricity cost will continue to rise. Ultimately, the serving electric utility's incremental rates will become prohibitively expensive, resulting in financial disaster for the utility involved. Is this scenario realistic and will wholesale electric utility bankruptcies result if retail wheeling becomes widespread? Probably, as has happened in many industries when competition has presented itself, the affected entities find ways to compete. The question at this point might be – what happens if my electric utility declares bankruptcy? If a utility bankruptcy occurs, an interim administrator would be appointed by the courts until a purchaser for the utility assets could be located. Utility bankruptcies, while not a common occurrence, have happened recently with the results being that the utilities declaring bankruptcy have been purchased and continue to operate. Retail wheeling of electricity is inherently neither good nor bad, but depending upon your prospective, a valid case can be made both for and against the process. From a customer's viewpoint, due to the large variation in electric utility rates caused by a lack of true competition and inefficiencies, retail wheeling of electricity would seem to be a welcomed option. From an electric utility viewpoint, someone has to pay for its investment in materials and generation capacity; and, if customers can purchase their electricity anywhere on the distribution grid, the utility has no way to recoup its costs. Both of these views have some validity, but what will ultimately determine the reality of the process will be the retail customers causing it to happen. If retail electricity customers take a "wait and see" attitude, then retail wheeling will probably never be widely available since most electric utilities are not going to push for a process that will ultimately force them to compete for their customer base. Retail wheeling of electricity is not something that is technologically impossible to do since almost all electric utilities currently "wholesale" wheel electricity between themselves on a daily basis. The real problem electric utilities have with retail or customer wheeling of electricity is that it will require them to obtain and keep their retail customer base through competition, not through regulatory commission mandated service territory boundaries. It is best to keep the lines of communication open between the retail customer and the electric utility, seeking the utility's opinion regarding retail wheeling of electricity and asking your electric utility's service representative such questions as –

1.  Does your utility recognize that retail wheeling will have a dramatic effect on how utilities operate?

2.  When and how does your utility think retail wheeling of electricity will effect them and the way they market electricity?

3.  Does your utility feel that retail wheeling will increase or reduce their customer base?

4.  What customer retention strategies has your utility developed to cope with or to utilize retail wheeling of electricity?

5.  Does your utility currently have any experimental or off-tariff schedules that have been developed to address retail wheeling? If any of these types of rates are currently available, ask the service representative for copies of them.

Retail wheeling will effect each electric customer whether they ever wheel electricity themselves or not. Know what is going on in this area of electricity retail sales.

## HOW WILL RETAIL WHEELING EVOLVE?

One of the real questions concerning retail wheeling of electricity is how will the wheeled electricity get from the point of generation to the point of use over various transmission grids. The stated problem is one of logistics – how to get the electricity from the point of generation to an individual specific retail customer that is perhaps located on a distribution grid different from the one on which the electricity is generated. A good overview of some of the potential problems relating to retail wheeled electricity is found in the publication "Overview of Issues Relating to the Retail Wheeling of Electricity," published by "The National Regulatory Research Institute," dated May, 1994, pages 59-67 and 69, as follows: (Note: Information on how to receive a copy of this publication can be found in Appendix "D".)

### *OVERVIEW OF ISSUES RELATING TO THE RETAIL WHEELING OF ELECTRICITY*

#### *Parallel Path and Loop Flow Problems*

*The actual path taken by electric power wheeled across transmission systems is difficult to predict and impossible to measure. Electric current moves according to Kirchoff's Laws and essentially flows on the path of least electrical resistance. As a result of these physical laws, power moves across many parallel lines in often circuitous routes.*

*For example, assume that four utilities (A, B, C, and D) are interconnected to each other through a tie-line between each of them. If utility A plans to wheel power to utility D, one might assume that the power will flow over transmission line AD which connects utility A to utility D. Realistically, the current may flow from utility A over line AB to utility B and then line BD to utility D. Alternatively, the current may also flow from utility A over line AB to utility B, then down to line BC to utility C and then over CD to utility D. In actuality, the current has numerous possible paths it can take depending on the loads on the individual transmission lines at the time. Most likely though, a portion of the wheeled current traveling over each transmission line would hinge upon trans-*

*mission loads on those lines at the time. In sum, the actual flow of power may, and typically does, diverge widely from the contract path. As a result, the supposed economics of the contract path frequently have little to do with the actual costs of the power transfer. Furthermore, these loop flows can affect third parties distant from the intended power flows, and these third parties may, and often do, incur costs without compensation. Most utilities, however, consider the parallel path problem as a cost of interconnection and generally prevent other utilities from wheeling only if the additional transmission system loads cause capacity overload problems on portions of their transmission grid.*

### *Network Congestion and Line Capacity*

*If the transmission network is heavily loaded, bottlenecks may lead to congestion that will prevent full use of the cheapest plants. Often referred to as "out-of-merit" dispatch, the constrained use of the plants frequently can create a significant opportunity cost that can be assigned to consumers causing the congestion.*

*The congestion limitations arise in two principal forms. The first is the limit on the flow of power on an individual line. The thermal capacity of a transmission line sets an upper limit on the flow of power on that line. Through the interactions of Kirchoff's laws, a line limitation affects every other flow in the network. A change in generation or load at any buss will have some effect on the flow on the constrained line; hence, the constraint can affect the loading profile at each buss. A second major source of congestion in a power network arises from voltage magnitude constraints at busses. In normal operations or as an approximation of the more complicated worst-contingency analysis, voltage constraints define operating bounds that can limit the amount of power flowing on transmission lines. Even when power flows do not approach the thermal limits of the system and the transmission lines appear to have excess capacity, voltage limits can constrain the transfer capacity.*

*Voltage constraints inevitably require attention to both the real and reactive power loads and transfers in the alternative current (AC) transmission system. Recall that real power (the power that lights out lamps) is measured in watts or megawatts (MWs) and reactive power is measured in voltage-reactive or VARS and megaVARS (MVARS). Power generation, load, and flow in an AC system are divided into both real and reactive power components. Without voltage constraints, the only matter of concern is the real power flow; it is common practice to ignore the associated reactive power analysis. But voltage can be affected by both real and reactive power loads, and the interaction between the two is critical in determining the induced limits on real power flows.*

*In reality, voltage limitations and the associated reactive-power compensation are prevalent. For example, the power shortages in New England and New York in 1988 were largely attributed to voltage and reactive power problems. Consequently, accounting for the congestion limits created by thermal limitations on transmission lines may not by itself prevent losses of real power flows. Any new regime for transmission access must address the congestion problem created by reactive power and voltage constraints. The most direct method is to account for both real and reactive power when designing wheeling prices.*

*Existing transmission and distribution lines are capable of providing electrical service to all electric customers currently with a utility's service territory. Today's transmission and distribution system was primarily designed and constructed to transmit electricity from a utility's on-system generators at specific locations to its customers within its territory, and secondarily to transmit electricity from interconnection points for reliability and economy power transactions. This same transmission system may therefore be incapable of transmitting large quantities of power from outside sources to its retail customers or to other utilities. Additionally, every transmission line is designed to carry a certain maximum amount of electric current. If this maximum current is exceeded, then the transmission line will be damaged. Consequently, a wheeling transaction may overload and damage the line.*

## Line Losses

*Even if a wheeling transaction does not cause transmission line damage, it can increase transmission line power losses. Transmission line power loss can be defined as the loss of power, in the form of wasted heat, associated with transmitting electrical current over a transmission line. Line loss is generally unavoidable and is directly proportional to the mathematical square of the current. Therefore, doubling the current on a transmission line would cause quadrupled line losses. Line losses also are directly proportional to transmission distance – the greater the distance of electrical transmission over the same size transmission line, the greater the line losses associated with the flow of power. Wheeling transactions can increase transmission line losses substantially.*

### Metering Problems

*The electricity requirements of a system constantly fluctuate. The actual power supplied to the system is dependent upon its load requirements at any given time. Thus, the party selling power must be sensitive to these load fluctuations. Two different methods are commonly used to handle this problem. The first and most efficient method focuses on the use of meters at the purchaser's delivery point(s). The amount of power delivered to the delivery points is instantaneously summed and telemetered to the generation dispatch center of the utility selling the power. In this way, the seller is constantly aware of the purchaser's instantaneous power requirements. In the second method, the seller of power provides scheduled allocations of power to the purchaser on a day-to-day basis. The party wheeling the power is responsible for providing the actual power requirements to the purchaser and for load fluctuations on the purchaser's system. Since metered delivery points are a requirement of any party purchasing off-system power, the exact amount of power supplied to the purchaser is known. The meters are read on a periodic basis (usually monthly) and the actual power supplied to the party purchasing off-system power is determined. The amount of actual power supplied is compared to the amount of scheduled power provided and the difference is calculated. If more power was actually supplied during the period than was scheduled, the seller would reimburse the party wheeling the off-system power for the previous month's deficiency in its following month's schedule power.*

*The metering problems associated with retail wheeling could be complex and cumbersome. In order to accurately track customer's load, a network of meters and telemetering would have to be installed from retail customers to the parties generating and supplying their power. Since the system load is adjusted automatically, the computer would instantaneously sum the demands of the retail customers and automatically adjust for the increase or decrease in load.*

### Distribution System Concerns

*Certain technical problems associated with wheeling of electricity are intertwined with legal issues. If a consumer decided to purchase off-system power, he would have to purchase the distribution services from his host's utility grid or construct his own distribution grid. If he purchases the service, the wheeled power would in most cases be distributed to him easily as long as it is within the distribution system limits. If he opts to construct his own grid, a whole host of legal issues would likely arise.*

### Generation and Transmission Planning

*If a customer in a utility's service area contracts for off-system power and wheeling, does that utility still have the responsibility to plan for generation and transmission capacity to serve that customer? Must the utility stand ready to service a former customer during system emergencies experienced by this customer's current supplier? Must the utility resume service to a former customer who wishes to again become that utility's customer at some future time? These are questions that will require answers before capacity planning can be done efficiently.*

*Retail wheeling could certainly harm a utility's ability to forecast future generating capacity requirements. A utility's load would now depend, among other things, upon the difference between the utility's own retail rates and the market price of electricity. Retail wheeling would also create transmission planning problems for utilities. Utilities wishing to provide service to off-system retail customers could require costly transmission line and system improvements. As a utility added and lost different off-system retail customers, changes in that utility's transmission system could be required.*

### Construction of New Lines

*Although a utility's transmission and distribution systems are capable of serving customers within its service area, existing trans- mission systems were not built with wheeling in mind. In particular, the points of interconnection between utilities were not designed for retail wheeling. Thus, in order to make retail wheeling possible, in some instances improvements to the current transmission systems may be necessary. Construction of new transmission lines presents a large obstacle for retail wheeling. Utilities face many barriers in constructing new transmission lines. Construction of a transmission line is a lengthy and expensive project. Before construction of the transmission line begins, the required land must be purchased. Transmission lines are restricted to certain areas. Consequently, the proposed transmission-line construction must meet the requirements and obtain the approval of different federal and state agencies. The next section briefly illustrates how to improve the capabilities of the transmission and distribution network.*

### Technical Measures to Correct For Wheeling Impediments

*To make wheeling and competition possible, the previously dis- cussed technical impediments have to be carefully handled. Legal, administrative, and pricing policies could correct for loop flow, metering, planning, and distribution problems. Line limitations and losses represent physical problems that could be solved only by either expanding or improving the networks physical capabilities. Because of environmental concerns and regulatory delays, electric utilities are now seeking practical alternatives to constructing high- voltage and ultra-high-voltage transmission lines. A recent utility trend is to more effectively use existing transmission lines and rights-of-way. For example, the power transfer capability of lines not operating at their thermal limits can be increased by the addition of series, shunt compensation, or the use of phase shifting transformers. Rights-of-way also can be made to carry more power by (1) raising the voltage on existing lower voltage lines, (2) converting AC lines to DC (direct current), (3) using hybrid lines where AC and DC lines occupy the same tower or the same right-of-way, or (4) by compacting the lines where more circuits are permitted in a given space. High-phase order transmission is one promising form of compaction that has been investigated.*

*High-voltage DC (HVDC) transmission is an area of particular importance. Thyristor converters rated 500 kV, 2,000 A have been developed using both air and liquid cooling. Several areas of development have made HVDC systems more cost effective over time and have greatly improved their performance. They include direct light firing of thyristors, the development of higher voltage cells that lead to lower losses, greater control flexibility through the use of microprocessors and sophisticated new control functions (for example, multiterminal operation, real and reactive power control, and damping of subsynchronous oscillations), the reduction of converter transformer losses, and better protection of equipment against overvoltages with the development of zinc oxide arresters. HVDC should play an increasingly important role in enhancing the capability of the transmission network to accommodate increased wheeling and competitive activities.*

*An economical way to increase the power transfer capability of an AC line is to install capacitors in series with the line to reduce its electrical impedance. Using zinc oxide discs with high-energy handling capability, series capacitors can be reliably protected against overvoltage by connecting series-parallel arrays of discs directly across the capacitors. The protection of turbine generators against subsynchronous oscillations, which may arise when series capacitors are used, has been accomplished using either passive filters or active thyristor dampers.*

*Another means of increasing the power transfer capability of existing transmission lines is the addition of shunt compensation of the form of switched capacitor banks or static VAR controls. Static VAR controls were initially applied to control the voltage flicker produced by electric arc furnaces. More recently, static VAR controls were applied to control rapid voltage fluctuations on power transmission systems and to improve the stability of large networks. Static VAR controls consist of thyristor switches, sometimes in conjunction with mechanical switches, to regulate the amount of inductance or capacitance connected to the transmission line for purposes of voltage regulation and increased power transfer.*

*These measures should significantly enhance the overall reliability and capability of electric power systems to comply with the new competitive regime. They have limitations and costs, however. In a recent study, the enhancement potential and installation costs of five options of different technical measures were compared. These options, proposed to enhance the network transfer capabilities, are (1) fixed series capacitors and static VAR compensators (SVCs); (2) adjustable series and SVCs, plus and parallel paths controlled; and (5) the fourth option plus rapid response generation. The study concludes that power transfer could be increased by 35 percent, 50 percent, 60 percent, 70 percent, and 90 percent with the adoption of options 1 through 5, respectively. Assuming option 1 is the bench mark, the study found that the installation of option 2, 3, 4, and 5 are approximately 100 percent, 150 percent, 500 percent, and 800 percent more expensive than the installation cost of option 1. The savings that would result from the transfer of cheap and remove power by the enhanced network should be accounted for when conducting a cost/benefit analysis. The question remains whether utilities would be willing to invest in such measures if the economic benefits and rewards accrue mainly to consumers.*

### Final Comments

*Society has limited tolerance for actions which may disrupt electric service over a wide area. If numerous players are encour-*

*aged to engage in any sort of competition in the electric network, some workable enforcement procedure should be established to ensure that variances from the rigorous and unforgiving nature of operations on the grid are not compromised because of competitive pressure. Unlike natural gas transmission, electric wheeling can affect the reliability and stability of service over a wide area. Because electric utilities are interconnected and operate in parallel, the actions of one utility affect other utilities.*

## 6. ECONOMIC/POLICY CONSIDERATIONS

### General Effects of Retail Wheeling

*Retail wheeling would undoubtedly advance the competition that is evolving in the electric power industry. Along with EPAct and emerging market pressures, retail wheeling would move the future path of the industry toward a more balanced mix of market factors and regulation in determining performance and structure.*

*Allowing retail customers the right to purchase power from competing generators would affect the electric power industry in five major ways. First, by weakening a utility's monopoly power, it would directly enhance competition in retail markets. Second, it would eventually cause a change in the rate-making practices of state regulators. Third, it would stimulate vertical disintegration of the industry where some utilities may decide to exit the generation business. Fourth, it would reshape the "regulatory compact" by changing the service obligations of utilities and their status as the sole supplier of power within their franchise areas. Fifth, it would cause the industry to become more cost conscious and accommodating to the needs of individual customers.*

Another good evaluation of retail wheeling of electricity is found in the publication "Retail Competition In The United States Electricity Industry", published by the Electricity Consumers Resource Council (ELCON), dated June, 1994. This publication outlines eight principles for achieving competitive, efficient and equitable retail electricity markets. The eight principles as listed are as follows: (Note: Information on how to receive a copy of this publication can be found in Appendix "D".)

- **PRINCIPLE NO. 1 –**

  *Market forces can do a better job than any government or regulatory agency in determining prices for a commodity such as electricity.*

- **PRINCIPLE NO. 2 –**

  *Laws and regulations that restrict the development of competitive electricity markets should be rescinded or amended. The need for burdensome regulation will be reduced where competitive electricity markets are allowed to flourish.*

- **PRINCIPLE NO. 3 –**

  *The benefits from competition will never fully materialize unless and until there is competition in both wholesale and retail electricity markets. But not all retail electric services are natural monopolies and therefore they should not be regulated as such.*

- **PRINCIPLE NO. 4 –**

  *The owners and operators of transmission and distribution facilities, and the providers of coordination and system control services, should be required to provide access to those facilities and services to any buyer or seller on a nondiscriminatory, common-carrier basis.*

- **PRINCIPLE NO. 5 –**

  *Rates for the use of transmission and distribution facilities should reflect the actual cost of providing the service. If the facility is a natural monopoly, those rates should be based on actual costs and the services provided on a nondiscriminatory and comparable basis to all users.*

- **PRINCIPLE NO. 6 –**

  *Resource planning is not a natural monopoly. The types and market shares of generation and end-user technologies that will be supplied in wholesale and retail markets should be decided in the marketplace.*

- **PRINCIPLE NO. 7 –**

  *Legitimate and verifiable transition costs that develop as a result of competition should be recovered by an equitable split amount ratepayers, shareholders and taxpayers. The costs of assets that were uneconomical in the existing regulatory regime are not transition costs.*

- **PRINCIPLE NO. 8 –**

  *The potential for transition costs should not be used as an excuse to prevent or delay the onset of a competitive electricity market.*

As can be seen, there are both obstacles to and advantages in retail wheeling of electricity. When and whether retail wheeling occurs to any great extent will depend upon how involved potential retail wheeling customers become involved in the process. Although there are many questions on how the process will work, I feel that in all practicality the process will or should evolve as follows:

1. Retail wheeling of electricity will, at least initially, occur internally on each of the nine (9) North American Electric Reliability Council Regions (NERC) in the contiguous United States. Currently there are (9) regions in the contiguous United States. Following are the geographic areas served by each of these regions together with each region's name.

| REGION NAME | GEOGRAPHIC AREA SERVED |
|---|---|
| 1. **Western Systems Coordinating Council (WSCC)** | Arizona<br>California<br>Colorado<br>Idaho<br>Montana (partial)<br>Nevada<br>New Mexico (partial)<br>Oregon<br>Utah<br>Washington<br>Wyoming |
| 2. **Mid Continent Area Power Pool (MAPP)** | Iowa<br>Minnesota<br>Montana (partial)<br>Nebraska<br>North Dakota<br>South Dakota |
| 3. **Southwest Power Pool (SPP)** | Arkansas<br>Kansas<br>Louisiana<br>Mississippi (partial)<br>Missouri (partial)<br>New Mexico (partial)<br>Oklahoma<br>Texas (partial) |
| 4. **Electric Reliability Council of Texas (ERCOT)** | Texas (partial) |
| 5. **Mid American Interpool Network (MAIN)** | Illinois<br>Missouri (partial)<br>Wisconsin |

| <u>REGION NAME</u> | <u>GEOGRAPHIC AREA SERVED</u> |
|---|---|
| 6. **East Central Area Reliability Coordination Agreement (ECAR)** | Indiana<br>Kentucky (partial)<br>Maryland (partial)<br>Michigan (partial)<br>Ohio<br>Pennsylvania (partial)<br>Virginia (partial)<br>West Virginia |
| 7. **Southeastern Electric Reliability Council (SERC)** | Alabama<br>Delaware<br>District of Columbia<br>Florida<br>Georgia<br>Kentucky (partial)<br>Missouri (partial)<br>North Carolina<br>South Carolina<br>Tennessee<br>Virginia (partial) |
| 8. **Northeast Power Coordinating Council (NPCC)** | Connecticut<br>Maine<br>Massachusetts<br>New Hampshire<br>New York<br>Rhode Island<br>Vermont |
| 9. **Mid Atlantic Area Council (MAAC)** | Maryland (partial)<br>Michigan (partial)<br>New Jersey<br>Pennsylvania (partial) |

**Figure 4.1**   Maps of North American Electric Reliability Council Regions
for the Contiguous United States

*1. Western Systems Coordinating Council*

**Figure 4.1**   (Continued)

### 2. Mid Continent Area Power Pool (MAPP)

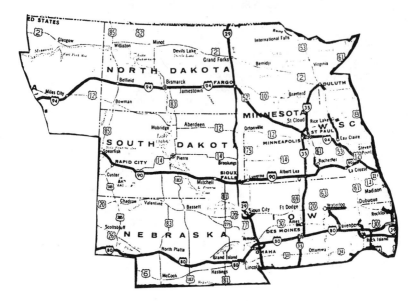

### 3. Mid Continent Area Power Pool (SPP)

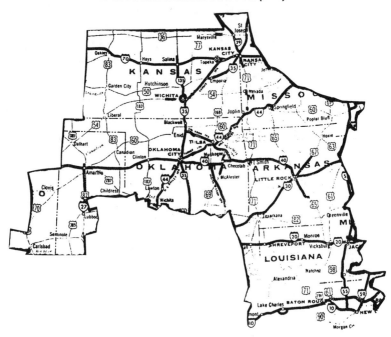

**Figure 4.1** (Continued)

*4. Electric Reliability Council of Texas (ERCOT)*

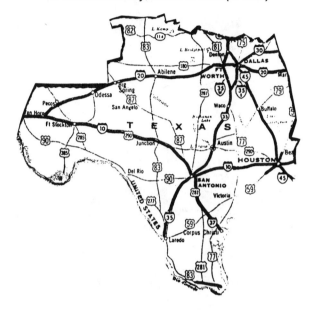

*5. Mid American Interpool Network (MAIN)*

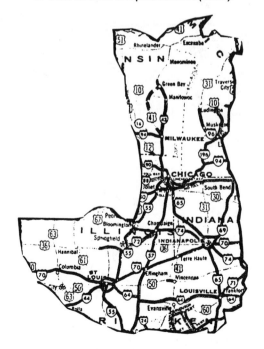

**Figure 4.1**   (Continued)

*6.  East Central Area Reliability Coordination Agreement (ECAR)*

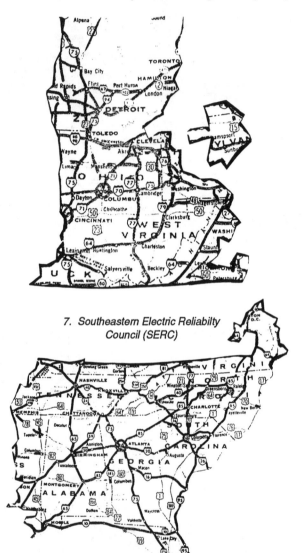

*7.  Southeastern Electric Reliabilty*
*Council (SERC)*

**Figure 4.1** (Continued)

*8. Northeast Power Coordinating Council (NPCC)*

*9. Mid Atlantic Area Council (MAAC)*

**Figure 4.2**  Chart Showing Typical Generation (GWH), Production Costs (¢/kWh), and
Retail Rates (¢/kWh) For Each of the (9) NERC Regions

| NERC REGION | ELECTRIC GENERATION (GWH) | *PRODUCTION COSTS (¢/kWh) | RETAIL RATES (¢/kWh) |
|---|---|---|---|
| WSCC | 39,800 | 1.7 | 7.9 |
| MAPP | 11,500 | 1.5 | 5.3 |
| SPP | 21,500 | 1.9 | 6.0 |
| ERCOT | 16,400 | 1.9 | 6.5 |
| MAIN | 17,900 | 1.9 | 6.5 |
| ECAR | 38,700 | 2.0 | 5.7 |
| SERC | 51,700 | 1.8 | 6.2 |
| NPCC | 14,800 | 2.2 | 10.7 |
| MAAC | 15,400 | 2.2 | 8.3 |
| Total Generation – 227,700 GWH | | | |
| Average Costs | | 1.9¢/kWh | 7.1¢/kWh |

**Note:** Electric generation/production costs/and retail rates for each of the NERC
regions varies each hour, day, week and month. The figures shown are
typical and are not intended to represent any actual month. This data is
presented only to provide insight to differences between the regions in
actual generation amounts, production costs and retail rates.

\*   Production Costs include fuel prices and nonfuel O & M costs.

It is this writer's opinion that logically intra NERC region retail
wheeling competition would be the first step in overall retail wheeling
of electricity. This would make sense both with respect to transmission
distribution (intra region only) and variations in specific utility production costs and retail rates. This type of competition, to a limited extent,
is already taking place in various parts of the United States. Although
there is very little retail wheeling competition currently, there is very
real concern within individual utilities about their costs/rates in comparison to an adjoining utility's costs/rates.

2.  A large portion of retail customers that could retail wheel electricity will never do so because their serving utility will negotiate a concessionary rate with the customer to retain their base load. It must be remembered that in a utility that generates the electricity, their good retail base load customers are critical to the profitability of that utility. I have personally been involved in negotiations with electric utilities in a client's behalf where the utility was willing to negotiate rates, project cost concessions and various other cost reductions with the client even where there was no opportunity for the client to leave the serving utility. Why do these types of negotiations occur? Because the serving utility really does want to keep their retail customers satisfied, if possible. We will address the negotiation of rates, terms and other cost concessions in Section III (Electricity Retail Wheeling Alternatives).

# Chapter 5

# The Retail Wheeling Transaction

## INTRODUCTION TO THE ELECTRICITY RETAIL WHEELING ENVIRONMENT

- Electricity Costs on a True Energy Cost Basis
- Categories of Retail Wheeled Electricity
- The Retail Wheeling Process

## ELECTRICITY COSTS ON A TRUE ENERGY COST BASIS

Frequently, electricity competes with other energy sources for various uses – heating, cooling, processing, etc. Both electricity and other energy equipment providers tend to favor their own particular equipment to the exclusion of other types or processes that result in the same process or product. As a user of either electricity or other energy sources, it is important to evaluate different sources of the energy that might be available for use. When evaluating electricity versus other energy sources for a process, one of the most important cost considerations is the energy cost. The only accurate way electricity can be compared with other energy sources is on a uniform cost basis. Since electrical (kWh) and the measurements used in other energy sources are not comparable, another unit of measure must be used. This unit is the British Thermal Unit (Btu). If the true (Btu) value of both electricity and other energy sources are known, then an accurate comparison between the cost differences of the two processes can be determined.

Shown here are the various factors that need to be known to accurately evaluate electricity versus other energy source costs.

**Figure 5.1**  Energy Btu Comparisons

| ENERGY Btu COMPARISONS | | |
|---|---|---|
| ENERGY SOURCE | UNIT OF MEASURE | TOTAL Btu |
| Electricity | (1) Kilowatthour (kWh) | 3,412 |
| Natural Gas | (1) Dekatherm (Dth) | 1,000,000 |
| Fuel Oil #2 | (1) Gallon (Gal) | 140,000 |
| Fuel Oil #6 | (1) Gallon (Gal) | 150,000 |
| Propane | (1) Gallon (Gal) | 91,500 |
| Coal | (1) Ton (2,000 lb) | 24,000,000 |

Using the information shown in Figure 5.1, the true cost of electricity per the Btu standard of measure of (1,000,000 Btu) is as follows:

> (1) kWh  = 3,412 Btu
>
> Number of kWh in 1,000,000 Btu –
> (1,000,000 Btu ÷ 3,412 Btu)  =  293.08 kWh
>
> There are 293.08 kWh per 1,000,000 Btu.

True electricity costs, when stated in cost per 1,000,000 Btu, is as follows:

| COST OF ELECTRICITY (Cost per KWh) | COST PER 1,000,000 Btu |
|---|---|
| $.01 | $ 2.93 (293 kWh X $.01) |
| .02 | 5.86 |
| .03 | 8.79 |
| .04 | 11.72 |
| .05 | 14.65 |
| .06 | 17.58 |
| .07 | 20.51 |
| .08 | 23.44 |
| .09 | 26.37 |
| .10 | 29.30 |
| .11 | 32.23 |
| .12 | 35.16 |
| .13 | 38.09 (293 kWh X $.13) |

## EXAMPLES OF ELECTRICITY COSTS TO OTHER FORMS OF ENERGY

### 1.  ELECTRICITY vs NATURAL GAS –

| | |
|---|---|
| Electricity Cost – | $.07/kWh |
| Natural Gas Cost – | $3.50 / 1,000,000 Btu |
| | |
| Electricity Cost – | $20.51 (1,000,000 Btu) |
| Natural Gas Cost – | $ 3.50 (1,000,000 Btu) |

True cost comparisons can be calculated for any energy source if the true Btu value of the source can be obtained. When doing cost comparisons, always consider efficiency of the energy source being considered. All natural gas, fossil fuel and/or petroleum distillates are less than 100% efficient. In the extracting of energy from these sources typically, combustion must occur which releases a waste stream of products of combustion that contains heat value or Btu's. Usually, efficiencies for these energy sources are between 60%-90%. Also, electricity can be more than 100% efficient in some applications. For example, an electric heat pump application can be 200% to 400% efficient since heat or (Btu) value can be extracted from the air, ground, water, etc. Always consider true efficiency when doing cost comparisons between energy sources.

An example of a comparison between an electric heat pump application that is 200% efficient with a natural gas fired application that is 75% efficient follows:

---

**ELECTRIC COST** (kWh) $.06 = $17.58/1,000 Btu
True Energy Cost at 200% Process Efficiency –
$17.58 ÷ 2 = $8.79/1,000,000 Btu

**NATURAL GAS COST** (1,000,000 Btu) = $3.75
True Energy Cost at 75% Process Efficiency –
$3.75 ÷ .75 = $5.00/1,000,000 Btu

---

As can be seen in this example, the initial cost difference between electricity and natural gas true energy cost appears to be very large. However, when the two processes are calculated utilizing their true efficiencies, the cost differential becomes much less.

---

**Apparent Cost Differences:**

| | |
|---|---|
| Electricity Cost – | $17.58 / 1,000,000 Btu |
| Natural Gas Cost – | $ 3.75 / 1,000,000 Btu |
| Apparent Difference – | $13.83 / 1,000,000 Btu |

**True Cost Difference:**

Electricity Cost –
(200% efficient)    $17.58 ÷ 2   =  $8.79 / 1,000,000 Btu

Natural Gas Cost –
(75% efficient)     $ 3.75 ÷ .75 =  $5.00 / 1,000,000 Btu

          ACTUAL DIFFERENCE        $3.79 / 1,000,000 Btu

---

## 2.  ELECTRICITY vs #2 FUEL OIL –

---

| | |
|---|---|
| Electricity Cost – | $0.06 / kWh |
| Fuel Oil #2 Cost – | $0.48 / gallon |

| | |
|---|---|
| Electricity Cost – | $17.58 (1,000,000 Btu) |
| Fuel Oil #2 Cost – | $ 3.43 (1,000,000 Btu) |

(Fuel Oil = 140,000 Btu/gal)

1,000,000 Btu ÷ 140,000 Btu/gal = 7.143 gal

7.143 x $0.48 = $3.43 / 1,000,000 Btu

---

## CATEGORIES OF RETAIL WHEELED ELECTRICITY

This section addresses the two classes of retail wheeled electricity that will probably be available. An understanding of these classes of wheeled electricity is necessary to be able to cost effectively retail wheel electricity from other than the serving utility sources.

## Firm Service

Electricity that is purchased under this category is the type that is typically purchased from the serving utility and has the highest priority of delivery. If any electricity is available, it will flow to firm service customers. Generally firm service customers have no back-up generation capability and as a result, pay the highest tariff rate applicable. Depending upon the serving utility's tariff schedules, firm category customers may or may not be eligible for other than firm service electricity. Probably a retail wheeling customer, if they require an uninterrupted flow of electricity, will purchase firm distribution capacity from the serving utility or back themselves up with onsite generation capacity.

## Interruptible Service

This category of service is the type that probably will be most widely available to retail wheeling customers. Those retail wheeling customers who can accommodate interruption of electric service on short notice, generally in peak load seasons or situations, will benefit from this class of service. This category of service is less expensive than firm service. A customer who chooses this type of service will probably either have a type of business than can withstand interruption or will have a back-up generation source to supplement a disruption of electricity service. Most electricity retail wheeled through other than the normal serving utility transmission grids will be interruptible. Many times the cost differential is such that a back-up generation supply can be obtained with the savings realized. And, if this can be done, the end result is increased customer flexibility with respect to electricity supply sources. This type of service is becoming widely available from serving electric utilities even without the advent of retail wheeling. Investigate your serving utility's tariff schedules to determine the availability and applicability of interruptible electric service to a particular situation.

## Who will most probably utilize the retail wheeling process? Will there be other options available?

The most probable "first" customers for retail wheeling will be large electricity users where electricity costs have considerable impact on their product/processes. Since true retail wheeling of electricity will or could negatively effect the serving utility's profitability, there will probably be much pressure on the customer to not wheel or at least to consider other options that cause them to remain with the serving electric utility. As has happened in natural gas, electric utilities will probably be inclined to be responsive to customers' needs to keep them as satisfied users of the serving utility electricity. These utility efforts will probably take many forms to help their customers reduce their electricity costs – e.g. negotiated incremental rates and/or financial assistance to customers. Serving electric utilities will begin to operate more on a competitive rather protected monopolistic basis. This change will not come easily since competition is not something any company likes to have to contend with. Many negative things are said about retail wheeling with relation to overall electricity system reliability and utility "stranded" investment costs if currently captive customers leave their serving utility. But the fact is that competition in the electricity industry is here to stay and grow. Electric utilities will either adopt and grow or resist and fail – there will be no middle ground. Change is not easy but resistance is fatal.

Not all potential retail customers will choose to or financial find it prudent to wheel their own electricity. However, these customers will find in many cases, that they will be able to negotiate less costly electricity rates with their serving utility. As with any situation that involves competition, even those not directly affected will in many cases find that they too can benefit from the process. One thing that electric utilities say will happen if retail wheeling becomes widely available, is that some customer's rates will have to increase as a result of lost utility revenue. This would be true if the utilities were to continue to operate in the same method that they currently do. What will happen in all likelihood is that electric utilities will take either one of two possible positions – view retail wheeling as a new opportunity for growth or resist and fight the process and see their market share continue to erode. Those that see it as an opportunity will grow and all of their customers will benefit from the process. Those that resist will ultimately fail, go bankrupt or be purchased by a company that through vision sees opportunities rather than disaster. Retail wheeling will come regardless of what electric utilities want, there will be problems and failures but once the transitional period is over, electricity will become a commodity rather than a protected monopolistic service regardless of individual feelings about the process.

Following in Figure 5.2, in flow chart form, is shown the various steps that probably will be present in the retail wheeled electricity process. Remember that the process shown here is the one envisioned by the author and may not be completely accurate with what may actual come to pass when retail wheeling becomes commonplace. Utilize this data only as a guide to the probable incremental steps that will be required in a retail wheeling transaction.

**Figure 5.2** Retail Wheeled Electricity Flow Chart

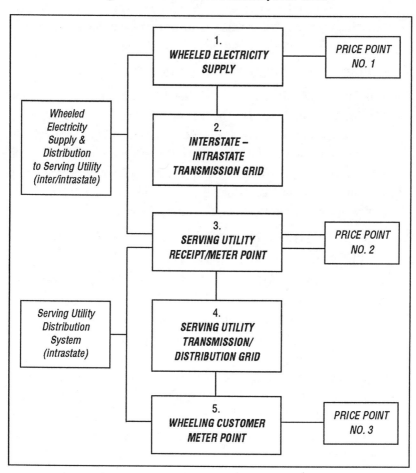

## EXPLANATION OF FIGURE 5.2 –
## WHEELED ELECTRICITY FLOW CHART

1. **WHEELED ELECTRICITY SUPPLY** – *(Price Point No. 1)*

   This will be the utility that is supplying the retail customer wheeled electricity. This utility will have to be physically connected to the electricity transmission/distribution grid that the customer's serving utility utilizes. The wheeling utility may be adjacent to the customer's serving utility or it may be in a different state so long as both the wheeling and wheeled-to parties have access to a common transmission grid. The costs accumulated at this point include the actual wheeling utility charges for the electricity. These costs will probably include both demand (kW/kVA) and usage (kWh) charges. Also, the customer being wheeled to will probably have a choice of either firm or interruptible service (kW/kVA and kWh).

2. **INTERSTATE – INTRASTATE TRANSMISSION GRID** –

   This is the transmission grid that links the wheeling utility to the wheeled customer's utility. This transmission grid may be interstate or intrastate depending upon where the wheeling utility is physically located in relation to the wheeled customer's utility. Generally, the grid will be governed by the Federal Energy Regulatory Commission. It is likely that the wheeled customer will have a choice of firm or interruptible transmission service.

3. **SERVING UTILITY RECEIPT/**
   **METER POINT–** *(Price Point No. 2)*

   This point will be where the wheeled customer's utility receives, meters and takes title to the wheeled electricity. The costs at this point will include the wheeled electricity costs as accumulated in Price Point No. 1, plus the transmission grid costs to deliver the wheeled electricity to the wheeling customer's utility. Included in the transmission costs will be line loss factors due to the resistance of flow of electrons through the transmission grid. Generally, it will be advantageous for the wheeling customer to utilize as high of a transmission voltage as is possible since there is less line loss at higher voltages.

4. **SERVING UTILITY TRANSMISSION/DISTRIBUTION GRID–**

   This portion of the transmission/distribution system is intrastate and is part of the customer's serving utility grid. It is regulated on an intrastate basis by the appropriate regulatory agency. As retail wheeling of electricity evolves, it is the intrastate portion of the wheeling transaction that will be subject to the most regulatory change or (deregulation). Both the utilities as well as the regulatory agencies will have to perceive a real customer desire for retail wheeling before any major deregulation will occur. It is likely that line loss factors will effect this portion of the transaction much the same as occurred in the transmission/distribution grid between the wheeled electricity supply and the serving utility receipt point.

5. **WHEELING CUSTOMER METER POINT–** *(Price Point No. 3)*

   This is the point at which the wheeled electricity passes through the retail customer's onsite electricity meter. Remember, the electricity the retail customer actually receives will probably never include any of the actual wheeled electrons that were transported to the serving utility. The reason for this is that the retail customer's wheeled electricity is co-mingled with all other electricity that is present in the transmission/distribution grid, both between the wheeled electricity supply and the serving utility receipt point, as well as between the serving utility receipt point and the retail customer's meter point. There is no problem with this since actual electrons of electricity are all the same. The actual electrons of electricity that the customer will receive in the retail wheeling transaction will in all likelihood be the same as prior to the wheeling arrangement, much like the natural gas transportation process. The wheeled electricity received and metered at the serving utility receipt point will be recorded and credited to the retail wheeling customer much like a deposit in a bank savings account. During the billing month, the retail wheeling customer will have these deposits available to utilize as determined by the retail wheeling agreement. The exact electrons deposited in the wheeling customer's account will probably not be the same electrons that are utilized by the wheeling customer, but so long as there are not more withdrawals than deposits, the overall system will remain in equilibrium. This may sound inordinately complicated, but basically this same process goes on daily where utilities wheel among themselves on a wholesale basis. It would be very difficult to trace a given electron from generation point to use point, but the system works and remains in balance as long as the same quantity of deposits of electricity are available as there are withdrawals made. Since electricity cannot be practically stored, this electricity generation, transmission/distribution, use system must be essentially balanced all of the time – no small feat given the complexies of electricity generation/distribution in the United States. Physically, retail wheeling will work. The problem will be all of the metering and related billing calculations concerning – line losses (under or over), usage of electricity by the customer, and many other cost items that will need to be addressed by all of the entities involved.

The total retail wheeled electricity cost to the using customer will be the sum of the costs accumulated in Price Points Nos. 1 and 2 and totaled in Price Point No. 3.

In most scenarios, the retail wheeling customer will probably utilize interruptible electricity and transmission up to the serving utility receipt point because of the probable differentials between firm and interruptible electricity costs to these points. If a retail wheeling customer requires firm or noninterruptible electricity, there will probably be a back-up arrangement negotiated with the serving utility for supplemental electricity in the event of interruption of the customer's wheeled electricity. Although retail wheeling of electricity is nothing like customer transportation of natural gas in technical and operational characteristics, it will appear similar in the process to the natural gas transportation transaction.

**Figure 5.3**   Retail Wheeled Electricity Cost Flow Chart

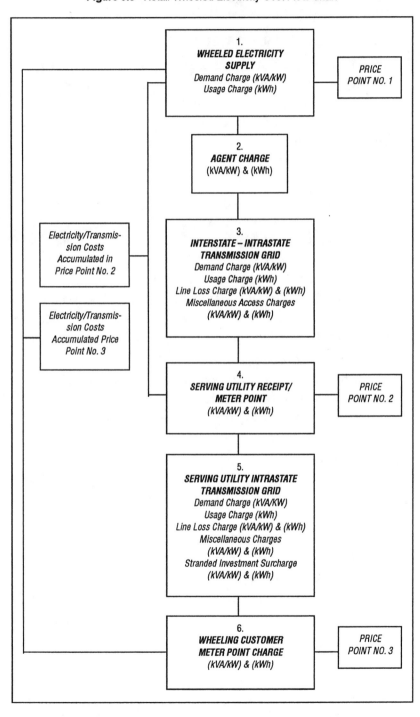

## EXPLANATION OF FIGURE 5.3 – RETAIL WHEELED ELECTRICITY COST FLOW CHART

1. **WHEELED ELECTRICITY SUPPLY** – Price Point No. 1

   Costs that are incurred in this area include the charges that the wheeling utility assesses for the electricity that is being wheeled to the retail wheeling customer. These charges will include both demand (kVA/kW) costs as well as usage (kWh) costs. Additionally, there may be other charges based upon various factors which may affect either or both demand and usage costs. These wheeling customer charges could include items as follows:

   A. *Demand Measurement* – (kVA/kW)

   Demand is utilized on a daily basis and is normally measured in intervals (15 or 30 minute periods, 24 hours a day); and, if the wheeling customer requires their demand during the wheeling utility's high demand periods, more expensive demand charges may occur. Alternately, interruption of wheeled demand over a certain "base" threshold may occur as contractually agreed to by both the wheeling and wheeled parties.

   B. *Available Rate Options* –

   There may be various options available to the wheeling customer similar to typical electricity tariff schedule rates that will require evaluation to determine the most advantageous rate structure to utilize.

   C. *Usage Penalties* –

   There may be power factor penalties when the wheeling utility measures demand in kW if the wheeling customer's efficiency falls below a certain level (80-90%). This type of penalty will not be present if the wheeling utility measures their demand in (kVA) since (kVA) does not require power factor correction factors.

   D. *Miscellaneous Charges* –

   There may be various wheeled utility cost factors such as fuel cost adjustments, regulatory fees and taxes that could be passed through to the wheeling customer.

2.  **AGENT CHARGES –**

Probably most wheeling customers will utilize the services of a third party to initiate and follow-up on the wheeling process much as is generally done in customer transportation of natural gas. These third parties, whether brokers, marketers or producers, are technically known as agents since they act in the customer's behalf. These entities will probably perform at least the following functions for the retail wheeling customer:

A.  Select an appropriate wheeled electricity supply source.

B.  Select an appropriate interstate/intrastate transmission grid to move the customer's wheeled electricity from its origination point to the customer's serving utility meter/receipt point.

C.  Negotiate the least expensive wheeled electricity and transmission rates for the customer.

D.  Assist the wheeling customer in the contractual agreements that will be required. Probably there will be at least (3) different contracts required. One contract will be between the wheeled electricity supplier and the wheeling customer. A second contract will be between the transmission grid utilized between the wheeled electricity supply and the serving utility meter/receipt point, and the wheeling customer. And, a third contract will be required between the customer's serving electric utility for the transmission and other services that they provide to the wheeling customer. These contracts in a flow chart form will look as follows:

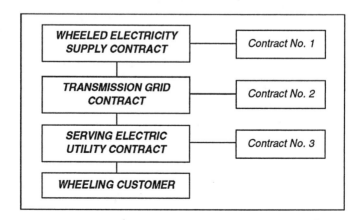

3. **INTERSTATE/INTRASTATE TRANSMISSION CHARGES –**

   These charges will include the cost to move the customer's wheeled electricity from the generation point of the wheeling utility to the meter/receipt point of the wheeling customer's serving utility. Charges in this area will probably include both demand (kVA/kW) as well as usage (kWh) charges. Also, transmission line loss costs will be calculated in this transaction. Other charges may occur such as transmission and access fees, FERC and/or state regulatory fees, and demand variability penalties or fees.

4. **SERVING UTILITY CHARGES –**
5.
   The serving utility charges will include probably both demand (kVA/kW) as well as usage (kWh) costs. Also, line loss costs may be calculated in this area for the serving utility's transmission grid losses. Miscellaneous other charges that will probably be present may include state regulatory fees, state and/or local taxes, and rental/lease fees on meters and/or equipment that the wheeling customer requires to utilize their electricity and that is provided by the serving utility. Also, included in this section will probably be a charge for the serving utility's stranded investment costs. These stranded investment charges will be what the serving utility considers to be its investment in generation/distribution facilities for the wheeling customer. These facilities are not being utilized when the customer elects to purchase their electricity from a source other than the serving utility. Whether these charges are justified or not is open to debate but at least initially expect to see these types of charges present on any retail wheeling transaction you initiate.

6. **WHEELING CUSTOMER METER POINT –**

   The total wheeled electricity charges will include all costs listed in items 1-5. The total of these costs will be compared to non-wheeled electricity costs to determine the viability of utilizing retail wheeling.

Following in Figure 5.4 is shown the probable incremental steps in retail wheeled electricity. This outline is the author's best estimate as to the various incremental costs that will be present in a typical retail wheeling transaction. Do not necessarily expect all retail wheeling trans-

**Figure 5.4**  The Probable Incremental Steps in Retail Wheeled Electricity

Total peak demand required per month _____

Total usage required per month _____

| INCREMENTAL PRICING OF WHEELED ELECTRICITY | Cost Per kVA/kW | Cost Per kWh | Monthly Charge |
|---|---|---|---|
| 1. Wheeled electricity generation point. *(Price Point #1)* | $_____ | $_____ | $_____ |
| 2. Fuel cost adjustment. | $_____ | $_____ | $_____ |
| 3. Agent charges. | $_____ | $_____ | $_____ |
| 4. Interstate transmission grid charges: | | | |
|     A. Firm. | $_____ | $_____ | $_____ |
|     B. Interruptible. | $_____ | $_____ | $_____ |
| 5. Interstate transmission losses. | $_____ | $_____ | $_____ |
| 6. FERC mandated charges. | $_____ | $_____ | $_____ |
| 7. Miscellaneous charges: | | | |
|     _____ | $_____ | $_____ | $_____ |
|     _____ | $_____ | $_____ | $_____ |
| 8. Intrastate receipt point.  *(Price Point #2)* | | | |
|     (Total of Items #1 through #7) | $_____ | $_____ | $_____ |
| 9. Intrastate transmission grid charges: | | | |
|     A. Firm. | $_____ | $_____ | $_____ |
|     B. Interruptible. | $_____ | $_____ | $_____ |
| 10. Intrastate transmission losses. | $_____ | $_____ | $_____ |
| 11. State regulatory agency mandated fees. | $_____ | $_____ | $_____ |
| 12. Intrastate utility charges including. (Transformation, Switchgear, Meter, etc. charges) | $_____ | $_____ | $_____ |
| 13. Miscellaneous charges: | | | |
|     _____ | $_____ | $_____ | $_____ |
|     _____ | $_____ | $_____ | $_____ |
| 14. Customer meter point.  *(Price Point #3)* (Total of Items #1 through #7 and Items #9 through #13) | $_____ | $_____ | $_____ |

actions to contain the exact incremental steps as shown here. This outline is provided only as a tool to provide insight to what will probably happen on an incremental basis in retail wheeling transactions. When retail wheeling actually becomes available on a wide spread basis, the various utilities involved will have their own individual incremental cost steps much the same as they now have different types of tariff schedules.

To better understand how costs might look in an actual retail wheeling transaction, Figure 5.5 is provided. The actual incremental costs shown in this figure are the author's best estimate as to how these costs will be structured. The author has no hard facts to serve as a basis for the costs shown other than his insight to the way electric utility costs occur in general. This cost data should be utilized only as an example of what will be involved in a typical retail wheeling transaction. For the purpose of this figure, the following assumptions will be made:

1. Peak demand required on a monthly basis – 1,250 kVA.

2. Usage on a monthly basis – 850,000 kWh.

3. Customer will utilize interruptible demand and usage for the wheeled electricity and transmission to the serving utility's meter/receipt point (#8).

4. Customer will utilize serving utility (intrastate) firm transportation so that back-up demand and usage is available if there is an interruption of wheeled power.

5. The rate structure will be a standard rate type with no (on-, shoulder- or off-peak) demand designations. Also, the usage will be a standard single cost non-ratcheted structure.

6. The wheeling customers power factor will be 95%+ so that no power factor penalty will occur on the serving utility's system where demand will be measured in kW, not kVA.

## RECAP OF DATA OF FIGURE 5.5

This is a recap of the information shown in Figure 5.5. It is shown to provide an illustration of how a cost comparison could be done between retail wheeled and serving utility provided electricity.

**Figure 5.5**   The Probable Incremental Steps in Retail Wheeled Electricity –
(Filled Out Form)

Total peak demand required per month ___**1,250 kVA**___

Total usage required per month ___**850,000 kWh**___

| INCREMENTAL PRICING OF WHEELED ELECTRICITY | Cost Per kVA | Cost Per kWh | Monthly Charge |
|---|---|---|---|
| 1. Wheeled electricity generation point. **(Price Point #1)** | $ 4,500 | $ .0111 | $ |
| 2. Fuel cost adjustment. | $ | $ .0100 | $ |
| 3. Agent charges. | $ | $ .0010 | $ |
| 4. Interstate transmission grid charges: | | | |
|     A. Firm. | $ | $ | $ |
|     B. Interruptible. | $ | $ .0300 | $ |
| 5. Interstate transmission losses.   (1%) | $ .0450 | $ .0002 | $ |
| 6. FERC mandated charges. | $ | $ .0001 | $ |
| 7. Miscellaneous charges: | | | |
|    (Grid access charges) | $ | $ .0001 | $ |
| | $ | $ | $ |
| 8. Intrastate receipt point.                **(Price Point #2)** | | | |
|     (Total of Items #1 through #7) | $ 4.5450 | $ .0255 | $ |
| 9. Intrastate transmission grid charges: | | | |
|     A. Firm. | $ .2500 | $ .0030 | $ |
|     B. Interruptible. | $ | $ | $ |
| 10. Intrastate transmission losses.   (1%) | $ .0480 | $ .0003 | $ |
| 11. State regulatory agency mandated fees. | $ | $ .0001 | $ |
| 12. Intrastate utility charges including. | | | |
|     (Transformation, Switchgear, Meter, etc. charges) | $ | $ | $ 200.00 |
| 13. Miscellaneous charges: | | | |
|    (Customer charge) | $ | $ | $ 100.00 |
|    (Stranded investment cost adjustment | $ | $ .0010 | $ |
| 14. Customer meter point.                **(Price Point #3)** | | | |
|     (Total of Items #1 through #7 | | | |
|     and Items #9 through #13) | $ 4.8430 | $ .0299 | $ 300.00 |

---

### WHEELED ELECTRICITY COST PER MONTH

| | | | | |
|---|---|---|---|---|
| 1,250 kVA | X | $4.843/kVA | = | $ 6,053.75 |
| 850,000 kWh | X | $ .0299/kWh | = | $25,415.00 |
| Customer/equipment Charge ($300.00) | | | = | $    300.00 |
| | | TOTAL | = | $31,768.75 |

**COST PER KWH $.0374**

### SERVING UTILITY PROVIDED ELECTRICITY COST PER MONTH

| | | | | |
|---|---|---|---|---|
| 1,250 kVA | X | $6.00/kVA | = | $ 7,500.00 |
| 850,000 kWh | X | $ .0420/kWh | = | $35,700.00 |
| Customer/equipment Charge ($200.00) | | | = | $    200.00 |
| | | TOTAL | = | $43,400.00 |

**COST PER KWH $.0510**

**SAVINGS** = $11,631.25
**% SAVINGS** = 27%

---

## EXPLANATION OF FIGURE 5.5

### 1. WHEELED ELECTRICITY GENERATION POINT–
*(Price Point #1)*

| | | |
|---|---|---|
| *Cost per kVA* | – | *$4.5000* |
| *Cost per kWh* | – | *$0.0111* |

Shown here is the cost of the generated electricity for both demand (kVA/kW) and usage (kWh). These are the costs for the wheeled electricity at the point of generation. These costs do not include any distribution of the electricity. These costs will be negotiated between the seller (wheeling utility) and the purchaser (wheeling customer). These costs will probably be negotiated monthly or fixed for a certain period such as 6 to 12 months. A spot market pricing index will probably be established to be utilized as a guide to wheeled electricity costs at point of generation. This spot market pricing index will probably be similar to what is now used in the natural gas industry. In all probability, these electricity costs will be based upon an interruptible basis. The wheeling customer will "firm up" the transaction on either the serving utility's distribution grid or by the installations of onsite back-up generation capacity.

2. **FUEL COST ADJUSTMENT –**

   *Cost per kWh    –    $0.0100*

   The fuel cost adjustment allows the wheeling utility to recover their actual cost of fuel to operate their generation facilities. These costs apply to all utility customers equally without regard to usage size. The cost shown here would apply to retail customers of this utility the same as it would to those wheeling electricity. The fuel cost adjustment always occurs where the electricity is generated. Also, this cost only applies to usage (kWh) not to demand (kVA/kW).

3. **AGENT CHARGES –**

   *Cost per kWh    –    $0.0010*

   This charge is to compensate the wheeling customer's agent for their services. These services would generally include the following items:

   A. Evaluate and obtain the lowest cost electricity for the wheeling customer.

   B. Arrange for and initiate required contracts in behalf of wheeling customer.

   C. Evaluate and obtain the best, least costly distribution path for the wheeling customer's electricity.

   D. Provide special services for the wheeling customer such as firm pricing for a fixed period of time, providing assurance that the wheeled electricity will be distributed to the customer's serving utility receipt point (see item #8 following). Assure that the customer will be held harmless (legally not liable) for any wheeling customer serving utility penalties or other charges relating to non-delivered electricity to serving utility receipt point.

   E. Negotiate discounted interstate transmission rates because of the volume of wheeled electricity they send through the grid on the behalf of multiple individual retail wheeling customers. These discounts should always be passed through to the individual retail wheeling customers represented by the agent.

The actual fee that is paid to the agent will be negotiable based both upon the volume of electricity the wheeling customer utilizes, as well as negotiation abilities the wheeling customer possesses. Although it will probably be possible for a wheeling customer to perform the entire wheeling transaction without agent assistance, it probably will not be cost effective to do so.

4.  **INTERSTATE TRANSMISSION GRID CHARGES –**

    *Interruptible Cost per kWh        –        $0.0030*

This is the charge the wheeling customer pays to the interstate transmission grid owner to transport the wheeled electricity across this grid. Normally, these transmission grids will be interstate in nature – between or outside of individual states. The terms and conditions for transportation of wheeled electricity will be determined by the Federal Energy Regulatory Commission (FERC). Even though these transmission grids cross many individual states, they are considered to be interstate (between states) in nature. It is likely that these transmission grids will be required to transport wheeled electricity on a nondiscriminatory basis and generally offer at least two categories of service – firm and interruptible. Where possible, a wheeling customer should utilize all transmission grids available for transportation of their wheeled electricity. Doing this will provide increased flexibility in transmission grid capacity as well as the potential for lower transportation rates due to competition. If the wheeling customer utilizes an agent, they should provide this service without charge. Both firm (noninterruptible) and interruptible transportation will probably be offered to retail wheeling customers. It will probably be normally less expensive to utilize interruptible interstate transportation of wheeled electricity; and, if required, opt for firm serving utility transportation. It would be of no value to utilize firm wheeled electricity and firm interstate transmission grid transportation only to have the electricity interrupted on the serving utility's distribution grid. If firm wheeled electricity is required, only "firm up" the transaction in the serving utility's territory.

5. **INTERSTATE TRANSMISSION LOSSES (1%)** –

> *Cost per kVA/kW*    –    *$0.0450*
> *Cost per kWh*    –    *$0.0002*

These charges are for electricity losses on the transmission grid due to the resistance of flow of electrons across the grid. These losses are real and appear as generation capacity loss to the generating utility. The losses shown in this section will have been approved by the appropriate regulatory agency, in this case FERC. The losses indicated in this section will apply to all transmission grid users whether retail wheeling or not. These losses will probably be applicable to both demand (kVA/kW) as well as usage (kWh).

6. **FERC MANDATED CHARGES** –

> *Cost per kWh*    –    *$0.0001*

Since FERC will probably be in charge of the retail wheeling transaction across the interstate transmission grid, they may assess some retail wheeling customer charges. These charges will be structured to return the costs FERC incurs in their oversight of the retail wheeling transaction. These charges, if they exist, will probably be assessed on the usage portion of the transaction (kWh). Whatever form these fees take, they will be uniformly assessed across all retail wheeling customers.

7. **MISCELLANEOUS CHARGES** – *(Grid Access Charges)*

> *Cost per kWh*    –    *$0.0001*

As this item indicates, any charges/costs that occur on a random or inconsistent basis are itemized/accumulated in this miscellaneous section. In this particular example, grid access charges are being assessed. Many utilities contend that when a retail wheeling customer wants to utilize their transmission grid, there should be a charge for doing so. Part of this reasoning is that when a retail wheeling customer utilizes the normally wholesale transmission grid, there are special metering, switching and other retail wheeling specific costs that occur. Whether this rationale is valid is open to conjecture. If retail wheeling across a transmission's grid is priced based upon true "cost of service" principles, there is no rationale for access charges. However, do not be surprised if these types of charges are present at least initially in the retail wheeling transaction, if for no other reason than "revenue enhancement."

8. **INTRASTATE RECEIPT POINT** – *(Price Point #2)*
   *(Total of Items #1 Through #7)*

   | | | |
   |---|---|---|
   | Cost per kVA/kW | – | $4.5450 |
   | Cost per kWh | – | $0.0255 |

   This receipt point cost includes all costs accumulated from the point of the electricity generation through its transmission to the wheeling customer's serving utility receipt or meter point. At this point, the costs incurred are primarily interstate and as such will probably be regulated by FERC.

9. **INTRASTATE TRANSMISSION GRID CHARGES** –

   | | | |
   |---|---|---|
   | Firm Cost per kVA/kW | – | $0.2500 |
   | Firm Cost per kWh | – | $0.0030 |

   This transmission cost reflects the wheeling customer's serving utility's charge to transport the wheeled electricity across this grid. The terms and conditions for this wheeling transportation charge will be regulated on an intrastate regulatory agency basis. If a retail wheeling customer cannot be interrupted, or if they have no onsite backup generation capacity, this will be the point to opt for firm transportation. Firm transportation of wheeled electricity across this grid simply means one of two things will occur based upon the serving utility's tariff schedule provisions relating to firm transportation as follows:

   A. The serving utility may consider firm transportation as being that they (the serving utility) will assure the wheeled electricity will arrive at the customer's meter point if they (the serving utility) receive it at their receipt point. In effect, this arrangement only assures delivery of the wheeled electricity if it is delivered to the serving utility's receipt point. The serving utility does not assure that any wheeled electricity will be delivered to the customer if the utility does not receive any of the customer's wheeled electricity from the interstate transmission grid. This type of firm transportation is not as desirable as the second type.

B. The serving utility may consider firm transportation as providing the wheeling customer assurance that electricity will be delivered to the customer's meter point even though the customer's wheeled electricity does not arrive at the utility's receipt point. In this arrangement, the serving utility will provide the wheeling customer with "system supply" electricity if the wheeled electricity is interrupted. Of the two types of firm transportation, this is the preferred interpretation. If the serving utility only assures delivery of the customer's wheeled electricity across their transmission grid, the customer may still have to provide onsite back-up generation if interruptability cannot be tolerated.

Also, remember firm transportation, even in its best form, is actually like term insurance – it accrues no value and ceases to exist if the required fee is not paid on a monthly basis. When evaluating firm transportation, always consider whether it would be more advantageous to utilize the firm transportation surcharges to construct an onsite back-up generation facility which would have real value.

10. **INTRASTATE TRANSMISSION LOSSES (1%)** –

*Cost per kVA/kW     –     $0.0480*
*Cost per kWh        –     $0.0003*

This item is similar to item #5 and compensates the serving utility for any transmission losses due to the resistance of flow of electrons across the intrastate transmission grid.

11. **STATE REGULATORY AGENCY MANDATED FEES** –

*Cost per kWh        –     $0.0001*

These fees are similar to those in item #6. Many states, because of difficult financial conditions, are requiring all state agencies that directly regulate or serve a specific public sector to obtain their revenue from that sector. In the past, many of these agencies received their funds from general state revenues. These fees are normally assessed on a unit basis, (kWh) in electricity and (Dth) in natural gas.

## 12. INTRASTATE UTILITY CHARGES INCLUDING –

*(Transformation, Switchgear, Meter, Etc. Charges)*
  *Monthly Charge    –    $200*

These charges would not normally appear as line-item entries on an electric utility billing since they would be included in other areas of the "bundled" charges. Since a retail wheeling customer will only be utilizing the serving utility's transmission grid and not normally be consuming serving utility generated electricity, these "equipment" charges must be itemized as separate entries.

## 13. MISCELLANEOUS CHARGES –

  *Monthly Customer Charge        –        $100*
  *Stranded Investment Cost Adjustment    –    $.0010/kWh*

These charges as indicated in the headings are miscellaneous in nature. This is a "catch-all" classification and may include many items not addressed in other areas of the transaction. In this particular example, two items are included – customer and stranded investment charges as follows:

A. *Customer Charges   –   $100*

These are charges that the utility assesses a customer just to be a customer. These charges generally are to compensate the utility for its cost to service the customer's account – meter reading, billing, etc. Customer charges range from nothing to many thousands of dollars per month. Customer charges, if present, are approved by the appropriate regulatory agency before they are implemented.

B. *Stranded Investment Cost Adjustment   –   $0.0010/kWh*

These charges, at least in theory, are to compensate the serving utility for its investment in various tangible assets for the retail customer's use. If the retail customer only utilizes the serving utility's transmission grid to retail wheel their electricity, then the utility's generation investment for the retail customer is stranded. When this happens, the serving utility reasons that it should be compensated for at least the unrecovered portion of such investment. In a regulated monopolistic environment, this reasoning can probably be rationalized. But if true open market pressures occur, serving utilities will find it difficult to win sur-charges like this. Do not be surprised if, at least initially, these types of charges are assessed to retail wheeling customers.

## 14. CUSTOMER METER POINT – *(Price Point #3)*

| | | |
|---|---|---|
| *Total Cost per kVA/kW* | – | *$4.8430* |
| *Total Cost per kWh* | – | *$0.0299* |
| *Total Monthly Charges* | – | *$300* |

This entry totals all of the various costs that have occurred in items #1 through #13. These costs represent the retail wheeling cus-tomer's total cost to retail wheel electricity to their meter point. As was outlined at the beginning of this billing analysis, don't expect a particular retail wheeling transaction to look exactly like this exam-ple. Use the information provided to obtain an overview of how the retail wheeling transaction may appear as well as an outline of the components that will be required in the procedure.

## ROADBLOCKS TO RETAIL WHEELING OF ELECTRICITY

Thus far, it might appear that there are few hindrances to the retail wheeling process; however, this is far from the truth of the matter. Technically, the process is possible but the problem is within the utility structure itself and its resistance to change. In defense of the utilities, it is and will be very difficult to make the transition. No one eagerly embraces competition – I certainly do not. To move from a highly regu-lated and vertically integrated structure with a virtual lack of true compe-tition is no easy task. It will happen, however, due to retail customer and general market pressures – some utilities will grow and become stronger and some will cease to exist. The reasons for these difficult transitions are many but some of the more prominent are described following.

The majority of the electric power market in the United States his-torically has been the responsibility of for-profit investor-owned utilities operating as a monopoly with regulation at both the federal and state levels. These "regulated monopolies", at least in theory, have the neces-sary checks and balances in place that preclude the problems normally associated with monopolistic entities. The problem is that potentially, from a cost point of view, the current system leaves something to be desired. True "cost of service" electricity rates, even when present, tend to be inflated due to operating cost pass-throughs that probably would not be tolerated in a deregulated environment. The simple fact is that with no direct competition, electric utilities, even with the current regulatory safeguards, tend to be cost plus operations, which from a purchaser's viewpoint may not result in the least costly electricity that could be provided. A monopolistic industry may provide many things, but generally efficiency and competitive costs are not included in the list of benefits. Currently, there are approximately 200 for-profit, 2,027 municipal, and 994 cooperative electric utilities in the United States that are all separately regulated. Each of these approximately 3,200+ utilities are separately regulated through federal, state and local regulatory bodies whose rate make policies sometimes defy logic. These are instances where electric utilities that are side-by-side have very different types of rates as well as substantial cost differences. These utilities may be on the same transmission grid, in the same state, and serve the same types of customers, yet have very different incremental cost structures. One of the first roadblocks that must be removed before electric utilities will be truly competitive is the overly complex and highly structured state regulatory process. Although dismantling or, at the very least, reducing the control state regulators have over the electric utilities would seem to be a logical step to take – there is much resistance to this. Both the regulators themselves, as well as the electric utilities they regulate, are for the most part very opposed to any such tinkering with their systems. Each of these groups has a vested interest in preserving its power, resources and prestige; and, each may attempt to camouflage their real concern (competition) with well written rhetoric. Politically active, well organized and well financed, they could cause electricity users to pay more for electricity than could probably result in a less regulated, more competitive environment. Another roadblock to some extent is self-interest. State Regulatory Commissioners who serve in utility regulatory capacities could be at least indirectly affected if electricity should become more deregulated – they could find themselves out of a job.

Another voiced concern is that of the degradation of service to small consumers who cannot take direct advantage of the competitive environment. Will utilities leave the marginally or less profitable market segment without dependable service? What about safety or integrity of the electricity generation system – will competition force utilities to lower costs by keeping older marginal equipment in service? Will they be forced to reduce system maintenance which could result in massive power outages? What will happen if some electric utilities cannot compete – will they go out of business; and, if they do, what will happen to their customers? What about the transmission grid capacity – will it fail because of all of the retail customers that will choose to wheel their electricity if given the opportunity? What about an electric utility's stranded investment in capital equipment that would not be utilized if retail customers elected to wheel their electricity – who would pay for this investment – the customers that are captive to the utility, or the utility stockholders?

I do not pretend to be able to answer all of these questions, but the same types of questions could be asked in any industry that would be faced with competition. No one that is in business (myself included) likes competition because it is more difficult to be profitable if someone else can offer the same product or service to a customer I now have. I personally do not feel that the electric utilities are the "bad guys." Change is difficult, especially as dramatic a change as is currently being thrust upon the electric utilities. Probably there has never been a more radical change taking place in the electric utility industry than there now is. Electricity is going to be more a commodity than a service in the future and when any product or service is reduced to this status, it becomes more difficult to make or provide it at a profit. Customer retail wheeling of electricity will occur whether the arguments for or against it are valid or not because the electricity customer wants it. It will be neither all bad nor all good, but it will change forever the way in which the electric utilities operate. As a retail electricity customer, if you want to keep your costs as low as they can be, you need to understand the impact this change will have on you in particular and the industry in general.

A good pro and con argument about retail wheeling of electricity can be had from the following sources:

## PRO Retail Wheeling

"Retail Wheeling – Expanding Competition in the Electric Utility Industry", (April, 1991)
    Authors: Jay B. Kennedy, Richard A. Baudino
        (202) 383-0151

## CON Retail Wheeling –

"The Cast Against Retail Wheeling", (July, 1992)
Edison Electric Institute
Authors: Staff of Edison Electric Institute with assistance of
        Joe D. Pace and William W. Lindsay of Putnam,
        Hayes & Bartlett, Inc.
        (202) 508-5425

# Chapter 6

# The Retail Wheeling Contract Process

## THE AGENTS THAT WILL BE USED FOR OTHER THAN SERVING UTILITY SUPPLIED ELECTRICITY

This section details the various agents for retail wheeled electricity. This information will provide the background necessary to be able to intelligently determine which method should be used to provide the electricity you will need at the reliability required. The information given herein provides the foundation for doing retail wheeling transactions.

## RETAIL WHEELING INFORMATION

Generally, retail wheeling (direct purchase) will be provided by at least three different entities – (1) brokers, (2) marketers, and (3) producers. The three entities are explained following:

1. **BROKERS** –

   Most retail wheeled electricity that will be available to customers will not be obtained from the serving utility. Other parties like brokers will actively market electricity to retail customers. The main and most important distinction between brokers and producers will be the fact that brokers will not take or assume title to the electricity they will market. These brokers will act only as third party facilitators. They, in effect, will sell for someone else. Brokers will act as agents, but will not actually take title to the electricity they will sell. Brokers will be paid a fee for their services by either the buyer or seller. This is not to say broker retail wheeled electricity will be unreliable or in anyway different from purchasing from a titled source. The thing to remember is that since title will not pass to the brokers, their warranty as to availability will be no better than their source will provide. In general, the fewer steps required to arrive at the actual electricity generation source, the more reliable the supply. Do not disregard broker supplied electricity but remember they will be able to provide no better title to the electricity they will market than what they will have – which is none. If a broker will be used, make sure (1) their source will be identified, (2) the supply will be assured for the duration of the contract, and (3) their source will have title to the electricity that they will provide to you. In general, it will probably be better, both on long-term cost and availability, if you contract with either a marketer or an electricity producer.

2.  **MARKETERS –**

Marketers will differ from brokers in that they will take title to the electricity they will sell the wheeling customer. A marketer will take title to the electricity but will probably not have or own the generation facilities. Marketers, or marketing affiliates, will probably also be known in the electric industry as "traders." While all of this may seem confusing, remember the difference between this category and the broker category will be that title to the electricity will pass with the marketer where it will not with the broker. The difference between marketers and producers, will be that producers will own electricity generation facilities and marketers will not.

The marketer category will probably be the largest supplier of retail wheeled electricity. As with any group of individual entities, there will be good and bad available, so be certain that any contracts to be negotiated will conform in general to the one that will be described in this section.

3. **PRODUCERS** –

Producers will have title to and will also own electricity generation facilities. They will be the original owners of the electricity and will be responsible for its generation and distribution to an interstate transmission grid. Some producers will probably market their own electricity directly to the retail wheeling customers. And most likely, several generators will join together to form a cooperative that will in turn market the electricity to retail wheeling customers. Producers, as such, probably will not be a dominate force in the retail wheeling market. They, in general, will sell their product to either a transmission grid, serving utility, or marketer, who in turn will supply the retail wheeling customer.

## BASIC DIFFERENCES BETWEEN BROKERS, MARKETERS AND PRODUCERS

1. **BROKERS** –

Will not take title to or will not own generation facilities.

2. **MARKETERS** –

Will take title to but probably will not own generation facilities.

3. **PRODUCERS** –

Will have title to and will own generation facilities.

## SYNOPSIS

Generally, there will be no reason to limit the choice of your supplier strictly on the basis of the category (broker, marketer or producer). The criteria for selecting a supplier will be based upon data such as –

1. Reliability of supply.
2. Price.
3. Transmission distribution routing.
4. Contract language.
5. Retail wheeling customer service.
6. Congeniality between buyer and seller.

Making these evaluations will be no simple matter. Sometimes reliance upon the broker, marketer or producer for help will be possible; however, they will be primarily motivated by a desire to sell their service, not necessarily to satisfy the needs of the customer. The surest method to follow will be to have a set of guidelines like the ones previously described, and evaluate any potential supplier in terms of these guidelines.

## *How To Structure An Electricity Retail Wheeling Contract*

### THE CONTRACT PROCESS

Figure 6.1 outlines the contract process and the items that a contract should contain which will be fair to both parties (buyer and seller). The outline shown here will be able to be used as a guide in any retail wheeling transaction; and, its provisions should cause no problems to either the seller or buyer. The contract is simple and straight forward.

**Figure 6.1** Retail Wheeled Electricity Sale Agreement

## RETAIL WHEELED ELECTRICITY SALE AGREEMENT

*Between*

_____

_____

*And*

_____

_____

Date_____    Contract No._____

Page 1

**Figure 6.1**   Retail Wheeled Electricity Sale Agreement (Continued)

***INDEX***

**Figure 6.1** Retail Wheeled Electricity Sale Agreement (Continued)

## RETAILED WHEELED ELECTRICITY SALE AGREEMENT

THIS AGREEMENT, made and entered into this _____ (day) of _____ (month), _____ (year).

By and Between: _____

With principle offices at:_____

_____

[Hereinafter referred to as "BUYER" (Customer).]

Who agree as follows:

1. **Definitions.**

   1.1 **"DEMAND"** will be in kVA/kW.

   1.2 **"USAGE"** will be in kWh.

   1.3 **"EXPIRATION DATE"** refers to 8:00 A.M. on the date which is one (1) year after electricity is first delivered by SELLER to BUYER hereunder.

   1.4 **"SERVING UTILITY"** refers to transmission grid of retail wheeling BUYER's (Customer's) serving electric utility.

   1.5 **"POINT OF USAGE"** is the location at which BUYER will consume or otherwise use said wheeled electricity.

2. **Purchase and Sale.**

   2.1 SELLER agrees to sell to retail wheeling BUYER (customer) and BUYER agrees to purchase from SELLER up to (Maximum Monthly Volume) kVA/kW and kWh of electricity ("Maximum Monthly Volume" hereinafter) each month during the term of this Agreement. Said wheeled electricity will be ordered by BUYER as provided for in this Section. Delivery and acceptance shall be at Point of Delivery (as defined hereinafter).

   2.2 BUYER may order any volume up to the "Maximum Monthly Volume" for any specific month or months by written notice (or FAX) thereof which is received by SELLER at least eighteen (18) days prior to the commencement of the next month of delivery. Such BUYER orders in monthly volume shall become "Ordered Volume". If BUYER does not change monthly volume for a succeeding month, the volume of the prior month shall be the "ORDERED VOLUME" for such succeeding month.            Page 3

**Figure 6.1**   Retail Wheeled Electricity Sale Agreement (Continued)

*2.3   BUYER and SELLER may <u>mutually</u> agree, at any time, to increase the delivery of additional quantities of wheeled electricity (over and above the "Maximum Monthly Volume") if SELLER has such additional quantities available.*

*2.4   During the term of the Agreement, BUYER may accept or purchase wheeled electricity from its serving electric utility or any other source.*

*2.5   If in any month SELLER fails to tender an amount of wheeled electricity equal to the "Maximum Monthly Volume"; or, if in any month the SELLER fails to tender the volume nominated by the BUYER up to the "Maximum Monthly Volume" for that month, BUYER may at its sole option elect to terminate this Agreement.*

*2.6   SELLER warrants that it has permanent title to wheeled electricity for the entire term of this Agreement hereunder and the right to sell same.*

**3.   Term of Agreement.**

*This Agreement shall become effective upon execution and shall remain in effect for an initial term of twelve (12) months after wheeled electricity is first delivered hereunder.*

**FIXED PRICE METHOD** *(Option #1)*

*4A.* **Price of Wheeled Electricity – Fixed Price for ( _____ ) Month Period.**

*4A.1   The purchase price shall be _____ per kVA/kW and _____ per kWh delivered at Point of Delivery during the initial ( _____ ) month period.*

*4A.2   The SELLER shall provide to the BUYER a new purchase price at least forty-five (45) days prior to expiration of the initial ( _____ ) month period (or of any extended period). Any such new price shall be evidenced by a written amendment to this Agreement executed by both parties. Failure to agree upon a price per kVA/kW and kWh shall permit either party to cancel this Agreement effective at the end of the then current ( _____ ) month period, by providing thirty (30) days prior written notice of such cancellation to the other.*

**Figure 6.1**   Retail Wheeled Electricity Sale Agreement (Continued)

---

*4A.3  BUYER will (in addition to paying the prices established in 4A.2 above) pay all state and local sales, use and public utility taxes (associated with the sale contemplated by this Agreement) and all other costs associated with the transportation, handling, ownership, sale, distribution and use of wheeled electricity after acceptance by BUYER at Point of Title Transfer as set forth herein.*

*4A.4  BUYER shall have no responsibility to pay generation or other taxes, or to make royalty or other payments due out of generation revenue.*

*4A.5  The prices established in 4A.1 above, shall apply to all wheeled electricity delivered pursuant to this Agreement (whether over or under the "Maximum Monthly Volume").*

*Page 5*

---

## HOW TO ESTABLISH A FIXED PRICE FOR WHEELED ELECTRICITY

Generally, the fixed price method will be more costly than the spot market method that will probably be established because the supplier will have to guess or speculate on what the cost of wheeled electricity will be at some point in the future. Fixed price contracts will probably be for 3,6,9 or 12 months. The longer the term, the more speculative will be the cost of wheeled electricity. Unless, for some reason, a known wheeled electricity cost will be required on a month-by-month basis for some future period of time, it will probably be less costly to utilize the spot market or monthly pricing scenario for wheeled electricity purchases. If a fixed wheeled electricity price will be required, then it will be best to utilize some benchmark to at least make the process logical and not pure speculation.

At this time, the New York Mercantile Exchange (NYMEX) is anticipating the establishment of a futures contract market in electricity. When this information becomes available, it would be wise to utilize the data to at least establish a benchmark for establishing a fixed wheeled price.

**Figure 6.1**    Retail Wheeled Electricity Sale Agreement (Continued)

## ALTERNATE FORM OF ITEM #4

*SPOT MARKET METHOD (Option #2)*

*4B.*  **Price of Wheeled Electricity – Spot Market Pricing.**

*4B.1 The purchase price shall be determined by the Spot Market Pricing Guide chosen, per kVA/kW and kWh in effect on date of nomination.*

*4B.2 Not used with spot market pricing.*

*4B.3 BUYER will (in addition to paying the prices established 4B.1 above) pay all state and local sales, use and public utility taxes (associated with the sale contemplated by this Agreement); and, all other costs associated with the transportation, handling, ownership, sale, distribution and use of wheeled electricity after acceptance by BUYER at Point of Title Transfer as set forth herein.*

*4B.4 BUYER shall have no responsibility to pay generation or other taxes or to make royalty or other payments due out of generation revenue.*

*4B.5 The prices established in 4B.1 above shall apply to all wheeled electricity delivered pursuant to this Agreement (whether over or under the "Maximum Monthly Volume").*

*5.*  **Deliveries.**

*Deliveries shall commence by no later than fifteen (15) days after execution of this Agreement and of all transmission grid transportation and delivery agreements required for transmission of said wheeled electricity to Point of Usage. If deliveries do not so commence, BUYER may terminate this Agreement.*

*6.*  **Billing and Payment.**

*6.1 Billings shall be rendered monthly. The monthly billing period ("Billing Period" hereinafter) shall end on the last day of each calendar month. The first Billing Period will end on the last day of the month in which deliveries commence, whether or not a full month of deliveries is involved. BUYER will be required to accept and to pay each month for the ordered monthly volume, pursuant to Section 2 above, (prorated for billing periods of less than one month) and for all additional quantities of wheeled electricity ordered and delivered by mutual agreement of the parties pursuant to Item 2.3 above.*

*Page 6*

**Figure 6.1** Retail Wheeled Electricity Sale Agreement (Continued)

6.2    Monthly billings will be made based on the monthly quantities ordered by BUYER pursuant to Section 2 and corrections to billings (if any) will be reflected in the next billing rendered after the need for correction is discovered. Payment (or credit) for corrected monthly billings will be made or reflected in the next due payment. Corrections will not be made more than one (1) year after the original billing date.

6.3    BUYER shall pay all amounts due less any penalties incurred by SELLER'S incorrect order quantities which would result in serving utility company penalties, surcharges and/or supplying of tariff electricity at a cost in excess of wheeled electricity that could have been purchased under provisions of this contract.

Payments shall be made by wire transfer, within five days after receipt of a billing from SELLER or by the fifteenth (15th) day following the month of delivery, whichever shall last occur. SELLER's billing may be submitted by FAX, telegram or other written instrument.

Payments will be made into an Escrow Account at (any bank selected by SELLER). BUYER agrees to execute any necessary instructions to the Escrow Bank (as directed by SELLER) so long as said instructions do not change or enlarge any obligation of BUYER under this Agreement.

6.4    The interest equal to prime rate at the Escrow Bank plus two percent (2%) per annum shall be paid on all late payments. BUYER shall, in addition, be responsible for paying for collection costs and reasonable attorney fees incurred by SELLER in its efforts to collect delinquent payments.

6.5    If failure to pay shall continue for ten (10) days after receipt of a billing by BUYER, SELLER may, in addition to any other remedies available, suspend further deliveries to BUYER until all amounts due are paid.

6.6    It is contemplated that credit circumstances and requirements of the BUYER will be determined after execution of this Agreement. Item 6.6 is reserved for any mutually satisfactory provisions which may result from said determination. In the event no mutually satisfactory credit arrangements are made, SELLER may terminate this Agreement without further obligation hereunder.

**Figure 6.1** Retail Wheeled Electricity Sale Agreement (Continued)

---

### 7. *Transmission Grid Transportation Agreements.*

*Point of Usage is identified in Exhibit "A" hereto. SELLER, as directed by BUYER, will negotiate and arrange all transportation and delivery contracts with transmission grid companies and with serving utility companies. BUYER recognizes it may be called upon to aid and assist SELLER in the negotiation of said transmission grid and serving utility Agreements. BUYER recognizes that it will be a required signatory party to such transportation and/or delivery agreements and agrees to execute same.*

### 8. *Title to Wheeled Electricity.*

*8.1    Title to wheeled electricity sold pursuant to this Agreement will pass to BUYER at Point of Delivery. Point of Delivery is identified in Exhibit "B" hereto, which is incorporated herein by reference.*

*8.2    SELLER may change Point of Delivery and will negotiate and arrange all necessary transmission grid and delivery contracts.*

*8.3    In the event of such change in Delivery Point, the then current price of wheeled electricity (established in Section 4) will be changed to a price which, when added to the new total of transmission grid and delivery costs (from said new Point of Delivery to the location identified in Exhibit "A" hereto), exactly equals the price plus all transmission grid and delivery costs (from old Point of Delivery) of wheeled electricity delivered during the prior monthly billing period.*

*8.4    Price adjustments (if any) during months subsequent to the establishment of new Point(s) of Delivery will be made as provided for in Section 4A. or 4B. above.*

### 9. *Force Majeure.*

*9.1    All obligations of the parties to this Agreement (except for the payment of money for wheeled electricity delivered) shall be suspended while and for so long as compliance is prevented in whole or in part by an act of God, strike, lockout, war, civil disturbance, explosion, breakage, accident to machinery or transmission grid, failure of sources of wheeled electricity generation, Federal or State or local law, inability to secure materials or right of way, or permits or approvals or licenses, binding order of a Court or Governmental Agency, the failure, inability or refusal of any transmission grid or serving utility to accept wheeled electricity for delivery, or otherwise transport, the default of any part to Other Contracts (other than BUYER or SELLER), or by any other cause beyond the reasonable control of BUYER or SELLER.*

*Page 8*

**Figure 6.1** Retail Wheeled Electricity Sale Agreement (Continued)

*9.2 No part of this Force Majeure clause shall be construed to provide for the discontinuance of wheeled electricity delivery by the SELLER due to wheeled electricity not being available at a favorable cost to the SELLER. The SELLER shall be obligated to provide wheeled electricity to the BUYER, subject to other provisions of the Agreement, at the agreed-to price, without regard to the wheeled electricity cost to the SELLER. Ability of the SELLER to realize a profit on the wheeled electricity transaction shall not be considered as a Force Majeure condition providing for suspension of the obligation of the SELLER to provide wheeled electricity to the BUYER.*

*10.* **Notices.**

*Any notice or other communication required or desired to be given to any party under this Agreement shall be in writing and shall be deemed given when: (a) delivered personally to that party, or (b) delivered by the United States mail, certified postage prepaid, return receipt requested, or delivered by overnight delivery, FAX, or courier return receipt requested, addressed to that party at the address specified for that party earlier in this Agreement or at any other address hereafter designated by that party by written notice.*

| **SELLER** | **BUYER** |
|---|---|
| *Payments* | *Payments* |
| *Name* _____ | *Name* _____ |
| *Address* _____ | *Address* _____ |
| _____ | _____ |
| *Attention* _____ | *Attention* _____ |
| *Correspondences* _____ | *Correspondences* _____ |
| _____ | _____ |
| _____ | _____ |
| _____ | _____ |
| _____ | _____ |
| _____ | _____ |

*Page 9*

**Figure 6.1**   Retail Wheeled Electricity Sale Agreement (Continued)

---

*11. **Miscellaneous.***

*11.1  If any provision of this Agreement is found to be invalid or unenforceable (other than the requirement concerning payment for wheeled electricity delivered), it is intended that the balance of this Agreement remain in full force and effect.*

*11.2  This Agreement is intended for the exclusive benefit of the parties to this Agreement and their respective heirs, successors, and assigns and may not be assigned without written approval of the nonassigning party. Nothing contained in this Agreement shall be construed as creating any rights or benefits in or for any third party.*

*11.3  BUYER shall use its best efforts to order up to the Maximum Monthly Quantity of wheeled electricity specified in Section 2.1 above but shall have no obligation to order any specific quantity of wheeled electricity in any specific month. SELLER shall use its best efforts to deliver the quantity of wheeled electricity ordered by BUYER pursuant to this Agreement but shall have no obligation to deliver any minimum quantity of wheeled electricity regardless of the amount ordered. BUYER shall never be obligated to pay for wheeled electricity which has not been delivered.*

*11.4  The obligation of BUYER(S), if more than one (1), shall be joint and several.*

*11.5  This document (including Exhibits and Addenda, if any) contains the entire Agreement between the parties and supersedes all entire Agreements between the parties and supersedes all prior or contemporaneous discussions, negotiations, representations, or agreements relating to the subject matter of this Agreement. No change to this Agreement shall be made or be binding on any party, unless made in writing and signed by each party of this Agreement.*

*11.6  This Agreement shall be binding upon and shall inure to the benefit of the parties hereto, their respective heirs, successors and assigns.*

*Page 10*

---

**Figure 6.1**   Retail Wheeled Electricity Sale Agreement (Continued)

*11.7 This contract is expressly made subject to all present or future valid rules, orders or regulations of duly constituted governmental authorities having jurisdiction over the subject matter hereof.*

*11.8 The failure, by either party hereto, to act in the event of default shall not constitute a waiver of the right to so act unless otherwise provided herein.*

*EXECUTED this _____ (day) of _____ (month, _____ (year).*

**SELLER**

*By_____*

*Title _____*

**BUYER**

*By_____*

*Title _____*

*Page 11*

**Figure 6.1**  Retail Wheeled Electricity Sale Agreement (Continued)

---

# ACKNOWLEDGMENTS

## SELLER

STATE of_____ COUNTY of_____

Executed and acknowledged by _____,as
the act and deed of_____.
Before the undersigned Notary Public this _____ (day)
of _____ (month), _____ (year).



_____

Notary Public In and For

_____County,

_____ State

My Commission Expires_____

---

## BUYER

STATE of_____ COUNTY of_____

Executed and acknowledged by _____,as
the act and deed of_____.
Before the undersigned Notary Public this _____ (day)
of _____ (month), _____ (year).



_____

Notary Public In and For

_____County,

_____ State

My Commission Expires_____

Page 12

Figure 6.1  Retail Wheeled Electricity Sale Agreement (Continued)

---

## EXHIBIT "A"

## POINT OF USAGE

COMPANY NAME – _____

FACILITY ADDRESS TO RECEIVE WHEELED ELECTRICITY –

_____

_____

_____

SERVING UTILITY –_____

_____

---

## EXHIBIT "B"

## POINT OF DELIVERY

## (To be completed by SELLER)

**RECEIVING TRANSMISSION GRID –**

_____ Transmission Grid

**POINT OF DELIVERY –**

All interconnect points on:

_____ Transmission Grid

_____

_____

Page 13

**Figure 6.1**   Retail Wheeled Electricity Sale Agreement (Continued)

---

## EXHIBIT "C"

## AGENT'S CHARGE


*AGENT'S fees per unit of wheeled electricity delivered under terms enumerated in this contract shall be as follows:*


1.   *Fee per unit delivered from generation point, will*

    *be _____ per kVA/kW,*

    *_____ per kWh.*


*No profit will be realized on the difference between posted FERC interruptible interstate transmission grid rates and actual FERC approved discounted interruptible interstate transmission grid rates AGENT is able to negotiate. AGENT will utilize their best efforts to negotiate a discounted interruptible interstate transmission grid rate on the behalf of the BUYER.*

---

## EXPLANATION OF FIGURE 6.1 CONTRACT TERMS
## RETAIL WHEELED ELECTRICITY SALE AGREEMENT

This Retail Wheeled Electricity Sale Agreement outlines the parties to the Agreement, the effective dates and the addresses of both the SELLER (agent) and the BUYER (customer).

1. **DEFINITIONS** –

   1.1 **"DEMAND"**

   This item identifies the measurement criteria to be used for delivery of the electricity. Demand is measured in kVA/kW.

   1.2 **"USAGE"**

   This item identifies the measurement of electricity in kilowatt hours and is a function of connected electrical load, times hours in use. Usage is measured in kWh.

   1.3 **"EXPIRATION DATE"**

   This determines the date upon which this contract becomes null and void.

   1.4 **"SERVING UTILITY"**

   This refers to the BUYER'S (customer's) serving utility that will be delivering the wheeled electricity.

   1.5 **"POINT OF USAGE"**

   This identifies the end location of the actual consumption of the wheeled electricity.

2. **PURCHASE AND SALE** –

   The six paragraphs contained in this section constitute the Agreement between the SELLER and BUYER (retail wheeling customer) in its entirety. It outlines the conditions for acceptance of wheeled electricity and limits the BUYER'S responsibility to the SELLER.

   2.1 **Agreement setting forth maximum quantities of wheeled electricity the SELLER is obligated to provide.**

   This does not obligate the BUYER to any specific volume purchases.

**\*2.2 Agreement setting forth the BUYER's options relating to wheeled electricity volumes ordered.**

The BUYER has the right to purchase from zero to the maximum quantity of wheeled electricity set forth in 2.1 above. This item also determines the lead time the BUYER must provide to the SELLER for wheeled electricity purchases. (Always have this provision in the contract.)

**2.3 Additional quantities of wheeled electricity.**

This item outlines an Agreement between the SELLER and BUYER that allows the BUYER to purchase quantities of wheeled electricity in excess of the maximum amount stated in 2.1 if the SELLER can obtain this excess amount.

**\*2.4 BUYER'S rights to purchase "foreign" wheeled electricity.**

This paragraph allows the BUYER to purchase wheeled electricity from sources other than the SELLER during the contract period. A provision like this gives the BUYER additional latitude in their options. (Always have this provision in the contract.)

**2.5 SELLER'S failure to tender (deliver) wheeled electricity.**

This item allows the BUYER to terminate the contract if the SELLER cannot or does not deliver the quantity of wheeled electricity ordered. (Always have this provision in the contract.)

**\*2.6 Title to wheeled electricity.**

Title to wheeled electricity is important since actually taking title is the only way to assure that the specified quantities will be available when needed.

NOTE: The descriptive words "Permanent" and "For the Entire Term of This Agreement." These are important since the term "Title to Wheeled Electricity" may not extend to the entire length of the Agreement. Permanent title does not guarantee deliverability of wheeled electricity, but it does assure that interruption will not occur for other than actual physical supply or transmission constraints. (Always have this provision in the contract.)

3. **TERM OF AGREEMENT –**

This section defines the Agreement time boundaries both beginning and ending.

4A. **PRICE OF WHEELED ELECTRICITY –**
(**FIXED PRICE METHOD**)

Two pricing methods are provided – "Fixed Price" and "Spot Market Price." The Fixed Price Method will be detailed here.

4A.1 **Wheeled electricity price per specified quantity (kVA/kW/kWh).**

This item sets the agreed upon price for the wheeled electricity during the term of the Agreement.

*4A.2 **New purchase price notification by SELLER to BUYER (used only with Fixed Price method).**

This item sets forth the details of negotiating of a new purchase price at the end of the agreed-to period.

NOTE: That either the SELLER or BUYER can cancel the contract if agreement cannot be reached on a new price. Do not sign a contract if a clause such as "SELLER shall have the right to match the price and term of any contracts offer(s) to the BUYER for such subsequent periods" appears. What this says is that the current SELLER has the right to match any wheeled electricity prices you might receive. If a SELLER cannot arrive at a competitive price on their own, then you, in all probability, do not want them as a supplier. (Always have this provision in the contract.)

4A.3 **BUYER assumed taxes and other costs.**

Since the SELLER is selling only wheeled electricity, it is not their responsibility to pay any sales, local, utility or other taxes. Also, it is not the seller's responsibility to pay for any transmission handling or distribution charges after transfer of title to the BUYER occurs. (Title transfer is detailed in 8.1.)

4A.4  **SELLER assumed taxes and other costs.**
The SELLER assumes responsibility for all taxes and other costs so long as they have title to the wheeled electricity. Simply put, the information in 4A.3 and 4A.4 means that whoever has title to the wheeled electricity assumes the costs related to that wheeled electricity whether they are in the form of taxes or other expenses.

*4A.5  **Applicability of wheeled electricity price established in 4A.1.**
The price established in 4A.1 applies to all wheeled electricity delivered by the SELLER whether under or over the specified "Maximum Monthly Volume." This clause is important since the SELLER cannot increase the wheeled electricity charges because of monthly order volume variations. (Always have this provision in the contract.)

4B. **PRICE OF WHEELED ELECTRICITY –
(SPOT MARKET METHOD)**

4B.1  **Wheeled electricity price per month per specified quantity (kVA/kW/kWh).**
This item names the agreed upon spot price for the wheeled electricity during the month of delivery. When the "spot pricing guide" method is utilized for wheeled electricity, the wheeled electricity cost will probably vary every month. There will probably be several spot pricing guides from which to choose as there are currently in natural gas. This method of wheeled electricity purchasing will probably result in the lowest cost electricity for the BUYER. The primary reason for this is that it will be difficult for either the SELLER or the BUYER to determine accurately that the price of wheeled electricity will be 3,6,9 or 12 months in the future. This uncertainty will probably lead to higher priced wheeled electricity. To realize the lowest cost wheeled electricity figure on a monthly basis, the spot price guide method will be the system to utilize. The only advantage to the fixed price method is that a known wheeled electricity cost can be determined to some point into the future. If a retail wheeling cus-

tomer must know their wheeled electricity incremental costs for some future period of time, the fixed price method will have to be utilized. In any other situation, if true lowest cost electricity is the goal, the spot pricing guide method should be utilized.

4B.2 **Not used with spot market pricing.**

4B.3 **BUYER assumed taxes and other costs.**

Since the SELLER is selling only wheeled electricity, it is not their responsibility to pay any sales, local, utility or other taxes. Also, it is not their responsibility to pay for any transmission handling or distribution charges after transfer of title to the BUYER occurs. (Title transfer is detailed in 8.1)

4B.4 **SELLER assumed taxes and other costs.**

The SELLER assumes responsibility for all taxes and other costs so long as they have title to the wheeled electricity. Simply put, the information in 4B.3 and 4B.4 means that whoever has title to the wheeled electricity assumes the cost related to that wheeled electricity whether they are in the form of taxes or other expenses.

4B.5 **Applicability of wheeled electricity established in 4B.1**

The monthly price established in 4B.1 applies to all wheeled electricity delivered by the SELLER whether under or over the specified "Maximum Monthly Volume." This clause is important since the SELLER cannot increase the wheeled electricity charges because of monthly order volume variations. (Always have this provision in the contract.)

5. **DELIVERIES –**

This section outlines the SELLER'S responsibilities for beginning initial deliveries and the BUYER'S remedies if delivery does not begin as outlined.

6. **BILLING AND PAYMENT –**

6.1 **Billing periods.**

This item sets forth the billing periods, in this case and normally, monthly.

6.2 **Monthly billing amount computation.**

This item details what shall constitute a monthly billing amount.

*6.3 **Payments of amounts due by BUYER.**

This item outlines the time parameters agreed to by both the SELLER and BUYER for payment of monthly billings by the SELLER. Also, identified are those items that the BUYER may deduct from the payment due, caused by the SELLER'S incorrect nomination procedures. (Always have this provision in its contract.)

6.4 **Delinquent payment charges.**

The interest penalty amount and the SELLER'S legal recourse in the case of delinquent payments by the BUYER are outlined here.

6.5 **Suspension of delivery for delinquent payments.**

Detailed here is the SELLER'S recourse in the event of non-payment in excess of a specified period of time by the BUYER.

6.6 **Determination of credit worthiness of BUYER.**

This item covers any special provisions that might be necessitated due to an unusual credit circumstance of a BUYER. Before any provisions can be attached to this item, they must be mutually agreeable to by both parties.

7. **TRANSMISSION GRID AGREEMENTS –**

This section covers where the BUYER wants the wheeled electricity delivered and outlines the BUYER'S responsibility in assisting the SELLER in obtaining the transmission grid transportation agreement.

*8. **TITLE TO WHEELED ELECTRICITY –**

8.1 **When title passes to BUYER.**

This item defines when title passes to the BUYER. Also, when the BUYER becomes responsible for taxes and other costs (when title passes from SELLER to BUYER). Title will be able to pass at 3 distinct locations (1) electricity generation meter point, (2) serving utility receipt meter point, and (3) BUYER'S electricity usage meter point. Generally, the best place for title to pass from the BUYER'S viewpoint will be at the electricity generation meter point. This is because normally state sales tax will probably not be charged on the portion of the transaction from the electricity generation to the serving utility receipt meter point if title passes to the BUYER at the electricity generation location. For BUYERS in states that levy sales tax on electricity purchases, title pass point is an important consideration. (Always have this provision in the contract.)

8.2 **Delivery point changes.**

This allows the SELLER to change delivery points when needed. Changes could be necessitated by wheeled electricity availability, transmission grid problems or severe weather conditions.

8.3 **Delivery point change affect on wheeled electricity price to BUYER.**

This item simply says that change in delivery points will not affect the delivered cost of the wheeled electricity to the BUYER.

8.4 **Price adjustments.**

If a point of delivery change results in higher costs to the supplier, the effect to the BUYER depends upon whether a spot market or fixed price for wheeled electricity is utilized. If the spot market method is utilized, any cost differentials will be passed through to the BUYER the month that the change is made. In the case of fixed pricing, any cost differentials will not be passed through to the BUYER until the fixed price period has expired. Naturally, if catastrophic or completely unforeseen circumstances occur that drastically affect the SELLER'S ability to sell wheeled electricity at the agreed-to price, it would be in the best interest of the BUYER to consider an adjustment in the purchase price with the SELLER. Reasonableness is the test that must prevail.

## *9. FORCE MAJEURE (SUPERIOR OR IRRESISTIBLE FORCE)–

9.1 **Responsibility limits.**

This item limits the responsibility of both parties for circumstances over which neither of them have control – acts of God, war, accident, etc. If the SELLER cannot deliver or the BUYER cannot accept wheeled electricity due to one of the reasons outlined in this item, neither of them have a legal responsibility to do so.

### 9.2 Non-Force Majeure items.

This item limits the SELLER'S ability to not deliver wheeled electricity due simply to the SELLER not being able to obtain wheeled electricity at a cost which will allow a profit to be realized. Force Majeure applies only to circumstances over which neither party has any control, as detailed in 9.1. (Always have this provision in the contract.)

## 10. NOTICES BY OR TO EITHER SELLER OR BUYER –

This section outlines the acceptable methods and forms of communication between the SELLER and BUYER. The information would only be used if either party wanted to amend or change provisions in the contract during its term. Specific addresses and names of individuals are designated in the section to be used as correspondence by either party.

## 11. MISCELLANEOUS PROVISIONS –

### 11.1 Unenforceability of contract provisions.

If any section of the contract is or becomes legally invalid or unenforceable, it does not negate the remainder of the Agreement. This is a common contract clause and protects both parties against unenforceable conditions.

### 11.2 Benefit of this contract.

This details the intended beneficiaries of the Agreement.

### 11.3 Best efforts clause.

This clause will be typical of all retail wheeled electricity purchase contracts or agreements. It says that the SELLER will use their "best efforts" to obtain wheeled electricity but will not be able to give a guarantee to do so. For this reason, it is important to check out the SELLER prior to signing and making any commitments. Although this provision may discourage many first-time BUYERS, it must be remembered that even utilities in their most expensive category of electricity have been know to curtail their BUYERS. The simple fact is that if either a nonutility SELLER or the utility itself cannot generate or obtain the electricity, it will not be delivered. By choosing a SELLER with multiple transmission grid connections, the likelihood of nondeliverability will be minimized.

### 11.4 Joint and several obligations of the BUYER(S).

All BUYERS who are party to the Agreement are equally liable. For example, if more than one company were to purchase and use wheeled electricity under this Agreement, either would be liable in the event of nonperformance (nonpayment) by the other.

### 11.5 Entirety of Agreement.

This item states that the Agreement as signed by the SELLER and BUYER is complete as written with no unattached side clauses or agreements.

### 11.6 Binding of parties to the Agreement.

This item protects both SELLER and BUYER in the event their company is sold or absorbed by another company. If this happens, then the successor company is obligated by the terms of the Agreement to the same extent as were the original party.

### 11.7 Contract validity clause.

This states that the Agreement was made subject to current rules by governmental bodies having jurisdiction over agreements of this type. If a governmental body would enact legislation that changed or restricted provisions in the Agreement, then the legislated changes would supersede the Agreement provisions.

### 11.8 Failure to act clause.

If either party would violate provisions of the Agreement and the other party fails to act, that failure will not constitute a waiver of the right to do so.

## ACKNOWLEDGMENTS PAGE –

Both parties are identified by company and name and the signatures of the responsible parties are notarized in the SELLER'S and BUYER'S individual locations. When this page is properly signed by both parties and notarized, the Agreement becomes binding upon both parties.

## EXHIBIT "A"

This exhibit identifies the point of use of the wheeled electricity contracted for and the serving utility who will deliver the wheeled electricity to the BUYER.

## EXHIBIT "B"

This exhibit identifies the points of delivery by the SELLER to the transporting transmission grid. It also identifies the receiving transmission grid that would deliver the wheeled electricity to the serving utility.

## * EXHIBIT "C"

This exhibit requires the SELLER (Agent) to list their fees per unit of electricity delivered to the BUYER. This is an important exhibit to the BUYER since the SELLER'S charge effects the overall cost of the wheeled electricity to BUYER. Many wheeled electricity SELLERS will probably not like this provision but should provide the required information if the BUYER is insistent. (Always have this exhibit as part of the contract.)

---

*   *Items indicated with an asterisk will be critical to the retail wheeled electricity BUYER. Always have these items in any contract that is utilized for retail wheeling of electricity.*

## HOW TO BE ASSURED THAT THE CONTRACT WILL SERVE THE NEEDS OF THE WHEELED ELECTRICITY BUYER

**Questions to ask a potential wheeled electricity seller and points to consider prior to the signing of a contract.**

1.  Is title to the wheeled electricity for the entire term of the agreement?

2.  How many electricity generation transmission grid entry points to the transporting transmission grid are available?

3.  Has nondelivery of wheeled electricity ever occurred, and if so, why?

4.  Always have a seller quote not only the wheeled electricity cost but also the total point-of-use cost. This point-of-use (commonly called "customer meter point") cost is what would be paid in total for the wheeled electricity delivered. It would include (1) electricity, (2) transmission grid transportation and line loss, and (3) serving utility transmission grid transportation and line loss. This would be the buyer meter point figure and would be the one to use in determining savings.

5.  Always obtain quotes and terms from more than one seller and compare them to see if one is more favorable than the other.

6.  Do not be afraid to negotiate on agreement terms or wheeled electricity cost since most, if not all sellers, will probably be willing to do this.

7.  After doing the other six steps in this questioning exercise, do what is probably the most important step – find a seller you will feel comfortable working with and one that will sincerely want your business. If the right seller is selected, they will be able to provide much insight and assistance in all steps of this wheeled electricity process.

## HOW TO HAVE A SELLER PROVIDE THE CONTRACT INFORMATION THAT A BUYER REQUIRES

Now that we have outlined a retail wheeled electricity contract, how will we have prospective sellers provide data in the form that we will need? One of the best ways will be to provide each seller that wants to quote an RFP (Request For Proposal), the same as any other vendor would be required to submit for their products or services. It will be very important for all sellers that quote to provide the same or uniform information to the buyer. If this is not done, accurate correlation of data from the various quotes will not be possible. A sample wheeled electricity purchase RFP is shown in Figure 6.2 following. You will note that this RFP can be utilized for both intrastate wheeled electricity (Item 3 – Pricing), as well as interstate wheeled electricity, (Item 4 – Pricing). This RFP example should be utilized as a guideline only and should be individually structured to a specific company's procedural requirements and needs.

**Figure 6.2**   Sample of a Retail Wheeled Electricity Purchase RFP

---

### GUIDELINE SPECIFICATIONS FOR RETAIL WHEELED ELECTRICITY PURCHASE CONTRACT

#### Request For Proposal

*Develop and submit for review, a contract document with appropriate attachments, to supply, retail wheeled electricity to:*

_____

*Please use format and include all applicable information listed in the attachments hereto.*

*All contract proposals must be submitted on or before –*

*Date_____*

*Please send all proposals to –*

_____

_____

_____

*Attention_____*

*Telephone_____*

Page 1

---

**Figure 6.2** Sample of a Retail Wheeled Electricity Purchase RFP (Continued)

---

### GUIDELINE SPECIFICATIONS FOR RETAIL WHEELED ELECTRICITY PURCHASE CONTRACT

1. **Type of Agreement –**
   A. *Spot Market.*
   B. *6 Month's Fixed Pricing.*
   C. *12 Month's Fixed Pricing.*

2. **Purchase Agreement –**
   A. *Maximum Monthly*
      *Buyer Commitment.*      $_____/kVA/kW  $_____/kWh
   B. *Minimum Monthly*
      *Buyer Commitment.*      $_____/kVA/kW  $_____/kWh

3. **Pricing –**
   *(For Intrastate Transmission*
   *Grid Wheeled Electricity Only)*
   *Itemize as follows:*

   A. *Generation Point.*       $_____/kVA/kW  $_____/kWh
      1. *Spot Market*
         *(Pricing Guide)*
      2. *Fixed Pricing.*
         *(For Term of Agreement)*

   B. *Agent's Fee.*           $_____/kVA/kW  $_____/kWh

   C. *Transmission Loss Amount/Cost.*
      *(Intrastate)*           $_____/kVA/kW  $_____/kWh

   D. *Miscellaneous Intrastate Charges.*
      *(List separately, e.g.)*
      *Regulatory Agency Fees*
      *Monthly Buyer Charge*
      *Equipment Costs, etc.*  $_____/kVA/kW  $_____/kWh

   E. *Serving Utility*
      *Transmission Grid*
      *Transportation Rate.*   $_____/kVA/kW  $_____/kWh

---

**TOTAL COST AT**
**BUYER METER POINT –**      $_____/kVA/kW  $_____/kWh

*Page 2*

**Figure 6.2**   Sample of a Retail Wheeled Electricity Purchase RFP (Continued)

---

### GUIDELINE SPECIFICATIONS FOR RETAIL WHEELED ELECTRICITY PURCHASE CONTRACT

4. **Pricing –**
   *(For Interstate Wheeled*
   *Electricity Only)*

   A. *Generation Point.*          $_____/kVA/kW $_____/kWh
      1. *Spot Market.*
         *(Pricing Guide)*
      2. *Fixed Pricing.*
         *(For Term of Agreement)*

   B. *Agent's Fee.*              $_____/kVA/kW $_____/kWh

   C. *Interstate Transmission*
      *Grid Charges.*
      *(Actual Agent's Cost)*     $_____/kVA/kW $_____/kWh

   D. *Transmission Loss Amount/Cost.*
      *(Interstate)*              $_____/kVA/kW $_____/kWh

   E. *Miscellaneous Interstate Charges.*
      *(List separately, e.g.)*
      *Regulatory Agency Fees*
      *Equipment Charges, etc.* $_____/kVA/kW $_____/kWh

   F. *Serving Utility*
      *Transmission Grid*
      *Transportation Rate.*      $_____/kVA/kW $_____/kWh

   G. *Transmission Loss Amount/Cost.*
      *(Intrastate)*              $_____/kVA/kW $_____/kWh

   H. *Miscellaneous Intrastate Charges.*
      *(List separately, e.g.)*
      *Regulatory Agency Fees*
      *Monthly Buyer Charges*
      *Etc.*                      $_____/kVA/kW $_____/kWh
      _____

   **TOTAL COST AT**
   **BUYER METER POINT –**        $_____/kVA/kW $_____/kWh

*Page 3*

**Figure 6.2**  Sample of a Retail Wheeled Electricity Purchase RFP (Continued)

---

### GUIDELINE SPECIFICATIONS FOR RETAIL WHEELED ELECTRICITY PURCHASE CONTRACT

5. **Definitions.**

   A.  Buyer obligations for maximum/minimum order quantities.

   B.  Lead time from execution of all agreements to first day delivery of wheeled electricity.

   C.  Terms and conditions relating to billing and payments.

   D.  List of agreements negotiated in Buyer's behalf. (Generation, Interstate & Intrastate Transmission Grid, etc.)

   E.  Title to wheeled electricity. (Where does it pass to Buyer.)

   F.  Force Majeure. (Specify conditions)

   G.  Buyer's remedy due to Seller's error in regard to:
       1.  Nominations. (Under/Over)
       2.  Balancing. (Interstate vs Intrastate)

   H.  Terms and payments of penalty amounts to Buyer due to Seller's errors. (G.1. and G.2.)

   I.  Procedures and obligations for nominations and verification of nominations.

6. **Attachments.**

   A.  Source of wheeled electricity.
       (Specifically identify.)
       1.  Location of wheeled electricity.
           (Generation point, etc.)
       2.  Specific contractual agreements, at/with generation points, Interstate and Intrastate transmission grids, etc. in Buyer's behalf.

7. **References.** (List using following guidelines)

   A.  Current clients with this Buyer's serving utility company.

   B.  Current clients with the same general usage characteristics as this Buyer.

   C.  Current clients that have been with Seller for at least a one (1) year period that are with this Buyer's serving utility company.

Page 4

## THE MONTHLY BILLING

After the wheeled electricity agreement is signed and wheeled electricity is flowing, monthly billings begin to arrive. In most instances, as many as three different bills will be received – (1) one from the wheeled electricity supplier, (2) one from the interstate transmission grid, and (3) one from the serving utility. When these bills first start arriving, it will probably seem that retail wheeling of electricity is very cumbersome. This section will be helpful to understand what these bills will mean. The bills will not be that complex if their terminology and use is understood.

The monthly billings will probably all arrive at different times. When these bills are received and paid, it will be wise to retain a copy of each so a record of what was purchased and transported is available. The bills will be generally self-explanatory and a little patience when first starting the retail wheeled electricity process will reap many dividends. The bills will be discussed in the following sequence:

1.  The Wheeled Electricity Purchase Billing Process.
2.  The Transmission Grid Transportation Billing Process.
3.  The Serving Utility Billing Processes.

## 1. THE WHEELED ELECTRICITY PURCHASE BILLING PROCESS –

The electricity charges will be included in the wheeled electricity purchase billing itself. This billing will probably be separate from either transmission grid transportation or serving utility billings. However, some electricity suppliers may be willing to assume responsibility for both wheeled electricity generation as well as transmission grid transportation billing processes in order to be competitive.

Since the purchase of wheeled electricity will generally be considered to be an interstate transaction, State taxes will not normally be applicable. The purchase of normal tariff serving utility electricity would be considered to be an intrastate transaction and as such could be subject to State tax. Depending upon the state and local taxes applicable, the savings in this category alone could amount to 3%-7% of the total bill.

## 2. THE TRANSMISSION GRID TRANSPORTATION BILLING PROCESS –

The transmission grid transportation billing will probably be a separate billing or it may be included with the wheeled electricity supplier billing, depending upon the particular situation. This billing will consist of transmission grid transportation charges based on the quantity of wheeled electricity delivered to it by the electricity generator. For example, if the electricity generator delivers 1,000 kVA/kW and 600,000 kWh to the wheeling transmission grid and the transmission grid loss is 1%, 990 kVA/kW and 594,000 kWh would be delivered to the serving utility's receipt point, and the billing for interstate transportation will be for 1,000 kVA/kW and 600,000 kWh. The monthly billing will include the total amount of the wheeled electricity requested.

## 3. SERVING UTILITY BILLING PROCESS –

The serving utility's billing process will remain much the same as it would be currently for tariff or retail wheeled electricity. In the case of retail wheeled electricity, the following items will be included:
A. The total quantity of wheeled electricity delivered to the retail customer.
B. The serving utility charge for this transmission grid transportation.

## THE RETAIL WHEELED ELECTRICITY NOMINATION PROCESS

The process of purchasing electricity by the retail customer through other than the serving utility sources is termed "retail wheeling." This expression is an apt one because if electricity is purchased in this manner, the serving utility will no longer be responsible for the actual electricity that the customer will use. As a retail wheeling customer, this responsibility will now be assumed by the buyer for determining these usages of electricity in the following month, or as it will be called "making nominations". This section contains an overview of what will normally be required and includes a "generic" sample of a nomination form. Due to widely varying policies that will probably develop, this particular form shown may not exactly fit every need and situation, but it does contain all of the information that should normally be required by any serving utility or transmission grid. Before a nomination will be processed, some key information will be required. This information will be obtained from the retail customer's own operations, the serving utility, and possibly, the transmission grid involved. The proper nomination will depend upon an accurate estimate of electrical usage for the coming month. To make this estimate, the following items will need to be considered:

1. **TYPE OF USAGE** –

   Consider what the usage for electricity will be – heating, cooling, processing, or a combination of all of these items. For heating/cooling loads, consult past records for the same months, or utilize degree day charts. For processing loads, consider the current usage adjusting for any planned production schedule changes.

2. **ELECTRICITY USAGE IMBALANCE PROCEDURES** –

   To determine usage patterns, consider the actual usages in past months compared to what will be nominated or ordered. Normally, the monthly serving utility billing will indicate actual usages together with any variations that exist. Probably a float amount of electricity will be allowed by the serving utility since exact nominations and actual usage will vary. Most serving utility companies will probably not charge a penalty if a minimum imbalance is not exceeded. If this is possible, the nomination process will be easier since the amount of electricity nominated will not have to be exactly what will be used in any given month. Also, if the majority of the load is heating and/or air conditioning, using a similar month in a past year may not be an accurate guide to what will be needed in the current month since weather changes can measurably affect usage rates. Generally speaking, it will be better to have a surplus of electricity available rather than having a deficit since any shortfall will be supplemented with normal tariff electricity, with the possibility of a serving utility penalty being charged.

Before determining how to structure the imbalance process, it will be necessary to check with your serving utility to determine their requirements and penalty conditions. In most instances, next month's electricity needs will be nominated prior to receiving the current month's usage figures, so it will be necessary to either estimate or to actually read the electric meter figures on a monthly basis. Normally, if the same person processes the nomination information each month, their ability to estimate will be accurate enough for most situations. If the electric meter(s) are actually read, read them at about the same time as the serving utility does and be sure to include all meters since many facilities have more than one metering location.

3.  **THE POLICIES OF THE SERVING UTILITY –**

    The next area to investigate will be the serving utility's policies, including the following items:

    A.  **Imbalance policies.**
        (1) What will be the maximum imbalance the serving utility will allow?
        (2) How much time will be allowed to adjust an imbalance?
        (3) What will be the changes or penalties for imbalance?

    B.  **Transmission grid losses.**
        This refers to that portion of the wheeled electricity that will be delivered but which will be lost on the transmission grid to move the wheeled electricity through the serving utility's transmission systems. To compensate for these losses, slightly more wheeled electricity than will actually be required will need to be ordered. A typical loss factor for a serving utility might be one half of 1% (.005) of the total volume usage. To compensate for this reduction, divide the amount needed by .995 to arrive at what would be required to flow into the serving utility's transmission grid.

```
NEEDED QUANTITY –
      1,000 kVA          600,000 kWh

ORDERED QUANTITY WITH LOSS INCLUDED –
      1,000 kVA      X    1.005   =    1,005 kVA
                              and
      600,000 kWh    X    1.005   =    603,000 kWh
```

This loss will have to be calculated if the serving utility requires nominations based upon the amount of wheeled electricity received from the transmission grid. If the serving utility will allow the nomination to be made for the amount of wheeled electricity delivered to the retail customer, then the retainage calculation will not be required.

C. **Billing periods.**

It will be necessary to know the serving utility's cycle for the nomination periods (normally on a calendar month basis), since most wheeled electricity suppliers and transmission grids will probably take nominations on a calendar month basis, from the first to the last day of each month. If the serving utility does not do their billings on the same cycle as the transmission grid and wheeled electricity supplier, then to be completely accurate, the customer's meters will have to be individually read as the serving utility's bill will not be in cycle with the other bills.

4. **THE POLICIES OF THE RETAIL WHEELING TRANSMISSION GRID –**

In general, the same areas as were outlined in "The Policies of the Serving Utility" (3.) will have to be investigated in the same manner as previously described.

# *HOW TO DOCUMENT AND FOLLOW-UP ON RETAIL WHEELED ELECTRICITY*

**Figure 6.3**   Retail Wheeled Electricity Nomination Work Sheet

---

### RETAIL WHEELED ELECTRICITY NOMINATION WORK SHEET

1. *Today's Date_____ Date Nomination Due_____*

2. *Nomination Month_____*

3. *Days in Nomination Month_____*

4. *Nominated Quantity_____ kVA/kW_____ kWh*

5. *Allowed Imbalance_____ kVA/kW _____kWh*

6. *Current Imbalance_____ kVA/kW _____kWh*

---

7. *Amount of electricity needed for the month:*
   *Amount in [4] plus the difference between amount in [5] and amount in [6].*
   *[5] (_____ kVA/kW _____ kWh – [6]_____ kVA/kW _____ kWh) +*
   *[4] (_____ kVA/kW_____ kWh) = _____ kVA/kW_____ kWh*

8. *Amount of electricity needed daily:*
   *Amount in [7] divided by amount in [3].*
   *[7] (_____ kVA/kW _____ kWh ÷ [3] _____ ) =*
   *Amount of electricity needed daily in the facility –*
   *_____ kVA/kW _____ kWh*

9. *Serving utility loss factor (_____).*
   *Multiply amount in [8] by loss factor:*
   *[8] (_____ kVA/kW _____ kWh X_____ loss factor) =*
   *_____ kVA/kW _____ kWh.*
   *Add this amount to the amount in [8]:*
   *(_____ kVA/kW _____ kWh + [8] _____ kVA/kW_____ kWh,*
   *to obtain the amount delivered into the serving utility's system –*
   *_____ kVA/kW _____ kWh.*

10. *Transmission grid loss factor (_____).*
    *Multiply amount in [9] by loss factor:*
    *[9] (_____ kVA/kW _____ kWh X_____loss factor) =*
    *_____ kVA/kW _____ kWh.*
    *Add this amount to the amount in [9] –*
    *(_____ kVA/kW _____ kWh + [9] _____ kVA/kW _____ kWh.)*
    *To obtain wheeled electricity delivered into transmission grid –*
    *_____ kVA/kW _____kWh.*

11. *Amount of electricity needed for the entire nomination delivered into the interstate*
    *transmission grid. Multiply amount in [10] by days in nomination month [3] –*
    *[10] (_____ kVA/kW _____ kWh X_____ days) = _____ kVA/kW_____ kWh*
    *for the nomination month delivered into the transmission grid.*

## EXPLANATION OF FIGURE 6.3
## RETAIL WHEELED ELECTRICITY NOMINATION WORK SHEET

1. **TODAY'S DATE, DATE NOMINATION DUE –**

   These entries simply document the date this work sheet will be filled out together with the date the wheeled electricity nomination is due. Normally, the nomination will probably be due somewhere between the 15th and 30th of the month prior to the month of actual wheeled electricity usage.

2. **NOMINATION MONTH –**

   This is the month in which wheeled electricity will actually be delivered.

3. **DAYS IN NOMINATION MONTH –**

   Most wheeled electricity generators and interstate transmission grids will probably calculate monthly the wheeled electricity requirements on an average daily usage rate. This, however, does not mean that a buyer has to utilize the wheeled electricity on an even daily usage basis.

4. **NOMINATED QUANTITY –**

   This entry indicates the quantity of wheeled electricity that will be used for the entire nomination month at the customer's meter point. Generally the nominated quantity and actual usage quantity probably will not be the same but will be close. If drastic or major differences in actual as opposed to nominated quantities appear to be occurring, renominations will probably be able to be submitted as frequently as every day of the month, if required. However, since electricity will probably be used uniformly on a daily basis, a large quantity of wheeled electricity will probably not be able to be added or taken away on the last several days of the nomination month since average daily usage rates will effect what has already taken place. If renomination is required, it will have to be done on an as-needed basis and not on an accumulative basis at month's end.

5.  **ALLOWED IMBALANCE –**

    This quantity indicates the wheeled electricity imbalance that will
    be allowed on the serving utility's transmission grid. The serving
    utility will probably determine imbalance thresholds based upon
    their particular requirements. Probably an imbalance limit will be
    established for retail wheeling customers, which if exceeded, will
    result in penalties.

6.  **CURRENT IMBALANCE –**

    This quantity includes the current imbalance status at the end of the
    billing period immediately prior to the month for which the nomina-
    tion is being processed. There is always a so-called "float" month
    between the imbalance status month and the nomination month.
    This "float" month generally is not a problem if monthly nomina-
    tions are processed as outlined in this work sheet.

7.  **AMOUNT OF WHEELED ELECTRICITY NEEDED FOR
    THE MONTH –**

    This amount includes the expected usage during the nomination
    month as indicated in [#4], plus or minus the difference between the
    Current Imbalance in [#6], and the Allowed Imbalance in [#5]. This
    total will include any adjustment required due to actual imbalance
    at the end of the month immediately prior to the month the nomina-
    tion is being processed. Since the nomination will probably be
    processed before the receipt of the wheeled electricity billing for the
    prior month, contact with the serving utility will probably have to
    take place. This will involve establishing contact with a person at
    the serving utility who can provide imbalance details prior to the
    actual receipt of the billing.

8.  **AMOUNT OF WHEELED ELECTRICITY NEEDED DAILY –**

    This quantity is determined by dividing the Monthly Quantity in
    [#7] by the days in the Nomination Month in [#3] to arrive at an
    average daily quantity of wheeled electricity to be delivered to the
    buyer's meter point.

9. **SERVING UTILITY LOSS FACTOR –**

This factor will be established by the serving utility and represents its electricity losses through its transmission grid. Since this loss represents electricity that the buyer will not receive, compensation will have to be made to recover the lost electricity quantities. This loss factor calculation will increase the generation point quantity of electricity that will have to be purchased by the buyer to offset the serving utility transmission losses. These loss values will be approved by the State Utility Regulatory body and will require a rate case application to change, so they should generally remain consistent for extended periods of time.

10. **TRANSMISSION GRID LOSS FACTOR –**

This factor will be established by the transmission grid and will represent its electricity losses through its transmission grid. Since this loss will represent the electricity that the buyer does not receive, compensation will have to be made to recover the lost wheeled electricity quantities. This loss factor will increase the generation point quantities of wheeled electricity that will have to be purchased by the buyer to offset the transmission grid losses. These loss values will be approved by FERC and will require a rate case application to change so they should remain constant for extended periods of time.

11. **AMOUNT OF WHEELED ELECTRICITY NEED FOR THE ENTIRE NOMINATION MONTH DELIVERED INTO THE INTERSTATE TRANSMISSION GRID –**

This amount will represent the total quantity of wheeled electricity that the buyer will have to purchase from the generation point to be assured that the required buyer's meter point quantities will be available. All intrastate and interstate transmission grid losses will be included in this figure.

To help understand the information required on the nomination sheet shown in Figure 6.3, a filled out sheet is shown in Figure 6.4 that is based upon the following data:

1. Days in nomination month – 30
2. Nominated quantity – 1,500 kVA, 1,700,000 kWh
3. Allowed imbalance – (+.005) (-0%)
4. Current imbalance – + .005
5. Serving utility loss factor – .005
6. Transmission grid loss factor – .010

**Figure 6.4**  Filled Out Sample of Retail Wheeled Electricity Nomination Work Sheet

## RETAIL WHEELED ELECTRICITY NOMINATION WORK SHEET

1.  Today's Date____07-13_____  Date Nomination Due __07-21_____

2.  Nomination Month_____July_____

3.  Days in Nomination Month _____30_____

4.  Nominated Quantity_____1,500_____ kVA/kW_____1,700,000_____ kWh

5.  Allowed Imbalance_____7.5_____ kVA/kW_____8,500_____kWh

6.  Current Imbalance_____7.5_____ kVA/kW_____8,500_____kWh

7.  Amount of electricity needed for the month:
    Amount in [4] plus the difference between amount in [5] and amount in [6].
    [5] ( 7.5____ kVA/kW _8,500___ kWh – [6] 7.5____ kVA/kW _8,500___ kWh) +
    [4] ( 1,500__ kVA/kW 1,700,000_ kWh) = _1,500___ kVA/kW 1,700,000__ kWh

8.  Amount of electricity needed daily:
    Amount in [7] divided by amount in [3].
    [7] ( _1,500____ kVA/kW 1,700,000__ kWh ÷ [3] __30_____ ) =
    Amount of electricity needed daily in the facility –
    _____1,500_____ kVA/kW _56,667_____ kWh

9.  Serving utility loss factor (___.005____).
    Multiply amount in [8] by loss factor:
    [8] ( 1,500_____ kVA/kW ____56,667_ kWh X ___.005___ loss factor) =
    _7.5_____ kVA/kW _284_____ kWh.
    Add this amount to the amount in [8]:
    ( __7.5___ kVA/kW_ 284_____ kWh + [8] __1,500__ kVA/kW ____56,667___ kWh,
    to obtain the amount delivered into the serving utility's system –
    __1,507.5_____ kVA/kW _____56,951_____ kWh.

10. Transmission grid loss factor (___.010_____).
    Multiply amount in [9] by loss factor:
    [9] (1,507.5____ kVA/kW ____56,951___ kWh X____.010_____loss factor) =
    _____15.08_____ kVA/kW ____56,951_____ kWh.
    Add this amount to the amount in [9] –
    ( 1,507.05__ kVA/kW_ 56,951___ kWh + [9] 15.08__ kVA/kW ____570___ kWh.)
    To obtain wheeled electricity delivered into transmission grid –
    __1,522.6___ kVA/kW___ 57,521_____kWh.

11. Amount of electricity needed for the entire nomination delivered into the interstate
    transmission grid. Multiply amount in [10] by days in nomination month [3] –
    [10] (1,523__ kVA/kW_57,521_ kWh X 30_ days) = 1,523_ kVA/kW 1,725,630__ kWh
    for the nomination month delivered into the transmission grid.

## THE MONTHLY FOLLOW-UP

Once retail wheeled electricity is flowing, a monthly follow-up on the actual dollar savings on both a monthly as well as an accumulative basis should be completed. The follow-up work sheet shown in Figure 6.5 on the following page will be simple and will not require a great amount of time to complete. The best time to work on it will be in conjunction with the nomination process. This work sheet will also provide the documentation to satisfy most accounting or cost control requirements in an organization.

**Figure 6.5**   Retail Wheeled Electricity Follow-up Work Sheet

---

### RETAIL WHEELED ELECTRICITY FOLLOW-UP WORK SHEET

1. Today's Date_____ 2. Month Being Documented _____ 3. Days in Follow-up Month_____

4. Cost of electricity if purchased through the serving utility:
   $ _____ kVA/kW $ _____ kWh.

5. Quantity of wheeled electricity nominated for the entire follow-up month: (Figure shown in Item [7] on the Nomination Work Sheet) _____ kVA/kW_____ kWh.

6. Quantity of wheeled electricity purchased for the entire follow-up month: (Figure shown in Item [11] on the Nomination Work Sheet) _____ kVA/kW_____ kWh.

7. Electricity cost at point of generation: $_____ kVA/kW $_____ kWh.

8. Agent fee: $_____ kVA/kW $_____ kWh.

9. Interstate transmission grid cost: $ _____ kVA/kW $ _____ kWh.

10. Intrastate transmission grid cost: $ _____ kVA/kW $ _____ kWh.

11. Miscellaneous Costs:
    A. _____   $ _____ kVA/kW $_____ kWh.
    B. _____   $ _____ kVA/kW $_____ kWh.
    C. _____   $ _____ kVA/kW $_____ kWh.
    D. _____   $ _____ kVA/kW $_____ kWh.

12. Miscellaneous Monthly Costs:
    A. _____   _____ .
    B. _____   _____ .
    C. _____   _____ .

13. Total cost of wheeled electricity: (Items [7], [8], [9], [10], [11], [12] totaled)
    $ _____ kVA/kW $ _____ kWh $ _____ Monthly Charge.

14. Total cost of wheeled electricity for entire month: Amount on line [13] ($_____ kVA/kW
    $_____ kWh) X Amount on line [6] (_____ kVA/kW _____kWh) =
    $_____ kVA/kW $ _____ kWh + ($ _____ Monthly Charge) =
    $_____ Total Cost.

15. Total cost if serving utility used for the follow-up month: Amount on line [4]
    ($_____ kVA/kW $ _____ kWh) X Amount on line [5]
    ($_____ KVA/kW $_____ kWh) = $ _____ kVA/kW
    $_____ kWh = ($ _____ Monthly Charge) = $_____ Total Cost.

16. Follow-up month savings using buyer wheeled electricity: Amount on line [15]
    ($_____ Total Cost)  – Amount on line [14] ($ _____ Total Cost) =
    $_____ Total Monthly Savings.

17. Accumulative total savings: Amount from line [17] ($ _____ ) on previous month's
    follow-up sheet  + Amount on line [16] from this follow-up sheet ($ _____ ) =
    $_____ Accumulated Savings To Date.

## EXPLANATION OF FIGURE 6.5
## THE RETAIL WHEELED ELECTRICITY FOLLOW-UP WORK SHEET

1. **Today's Date** –

   The date this work sheet is being completed. This date will be after the receipt of the wheeled electricity billings from the seller and serving utilities for the month being documented.

2. **Month Being Documented** –

   The month the follow-up is detailing.

3. **Days in Follow-up Month** –

   The actual number of days in the month being analyzed.

4. **Cost of Electricity if Purchased Through the Serving Utility** –

   This is the customer meter point cost of electricity if it were to be purchased from the serving utility. This figure is obtained by contacting the serving utility and determining their electricity cost for the class of service required for the buyer. Once this cost is determined, it remains rather consistent month to month with the exception, perhaps, of periodic fuel cost adjustments. If these adjustments are present, they can be updated as required by contacting the serving utility. This cost is divided into two components kVA and kWh.

5. **Quantity of Wheeled Electricity Nominated for the Entire Month** –

   This quantity is obtained from the Nomination Work Sheet, Item [#7]. This quantity represents the total amount of wheeled electricity that was nominated for the month being analyzed at the customer's meter point.

6. **Quantity of Wheeled Electricity Purchased for the Entire Follow-Up Month** –

   This quantity is obtained from the Nomination Work Sheet, Item [#11]. This quantity represents the total wheeled electricity required to provide the nominated quantity of wheeled electricity at the customer's meter point for the month being analyzed. Included in this quantity are all loss factors that are applicable.

7. **Electricity Cost at Point of Generation –**

This figure represents the wheeled electricity cost at the point of generation. It is determined by the contractual agreement between the buyer and seller. It typically will be determined by spot market or fixed pricing procedures. This cost will be obtained from the seller's billing for the month being analyzed.

8. **Agent Fee –**

This figure represents the seller's fee to the buyer for their services. This cost would be obtained from the seller's billing for the month being analyzed.

9. **Interstate Transmission Grid –**

This figure represents the actual interstate transmission grid trans- portation cost between the point of generation and the serving utili- ty receipt point. This cost will be obtained from the seller's billing for the month being analyzed.

10. **Intrastate Transmission Grid Transportation Cost –**

This figure represents the actual serving utility transmission grid transportation cost between the serving utility receipt point and the buyer's meter point. This cost will be obtained from the serving utility's billing for the month being analyzed.

11. **Miscellaneous Costs –**

These costs, if they occur, will be related to special or unusual costs and can occur anywhere between the wheeled electricity point of generation and the customer's meter point. Depending upon where these costs occur, they will be obtained either from the seller's or serving utility's billings for the month being analyzed.

12. **Miscellaneous Monthly Costs –**

These items generally will not be calculated on kVA or kWh used, but rather upon a flat monthly basis. These items could include cus- tomer charges, equipment rental/least costs, etc.

13. **Total Cost of Wheeled Electricity –**

This is a total of the individual costs listed in Items [7] through [12]. This cost represents the total wheeled electricity cost from the point of generation through the customer's meter point. Interstate or serving utility transmission losses are included in Item [6] which, was carried over from the electricity nomination sheet for the month involved.

14. **Total Cost of Wheeled Electricity for the Entire Month –**

This cost would be the total wheeled electricity cost including all electricity costs, seller fees, interstate and serving utility transmission grid transportation costs, interstate and serving utility loss costs and any miscellaneous costs and/or fees that might be present. The cost in this item represents the total wheeled electricity cost to the buyer for the entire month being analyzed.

15. **Total Cost if Serving Utility Electricity Used for the Follow-up Month –**

This cost is what electricity would have cost the buyer if they would have utilized serving utility electricity supplies. It represents what the total electricity cost to the buyer would have been for the entire month being analyzed if electricity was purchased directly from the serving utility.

16. **Follow-up Month Savings Using Wheeled Electricity –**

This savings figure shows the total electricity cost savings for the month being analyzed by utilizing wheeled electricity as opposed to serving utility supplied electricity.

17. **Accumulative Total Savings –**

This accumulative total shows the savings to date by utilizing wheeled electricity.

To help understand the information required on the follow-up work sheet shown in Figure 6.5, a filled out work sheet is shown in Figure 6.6 that is based upon the following data:

1. Today's date – 08-27

2. Month being documented – July

3. Days in follow-up month – 30

4. Cost of electricity if purchased through serving utility –
   A. kVA – $5.50
   B. kWh – $0.0300

5. Quantity of electricity nominated for the entire month –
   A. kVA – 1,500
   B. kWh – 1,700,000

6. Quantity of electricity purchased for entire month –
   A. kVA – 1,523
   B. kWh – 1,725,630

7. Electricity cost at point of generation –
   A. kVA – $4.50
   B. kWh – $0.0111

8. Agent fee –
   A. kVA – $0.0000
   B. kWh – $0.0010

9. Interstate transmission grid cost –
   A. kVA – $0.1000
   B. kWh – $0.0030

10. Intrastate transmission grid cost –
    A. kVA – $0.2500
    B. kWh – $0.0030

11. Miscellaneous costs –
    A. FERC fees – $0.0001/kWh
    B. Access charges – $0.0020/kWh
    C. State regulatory fees – $0.0001/kWh
    D. Stranded investment cost – $0.0020/kWh

12. Miscellaneous monthly costs –
    A. Intrastate utility equipment charges– $200.
    B. Customer charge – $100.

**Figure 6.6**  Filled Out Sample of Retail Wheeled Electricity Follow-up Work Sheet

---

### RETAIL WHEELED ELECTRICITY FOLLOW-UP WORK SHEET

1. Today's Date __08-27__ 2. Month Being Documented __July__ 3. Days in Follow-up Month __30__

4. Cost of electricity if purchased through the serving utility:
   $_____5.50_____ kVA/kW $____.0300_____ kWh.

5. Quantity of wheeled electricity nominated for the entire month: (Figure shown in Item [7] on the Nomination Work Sheet) _____1,500_____ kVA/kW _____1,700,000_____ kWh.

6. Quantity of wheeled electricity purchased for the entire follow-up month: (Figure shown in Item [11] on the Nomination Work Sheet) ____1,523____ kVA/kW ____1,725,630____ kWh.

7. Electricity cost at point of generation: $_____4.50_____ kVA/kW $____.0111____ kWh.

8. Agent fee: $_____-0-_____ kVA/kW $_____.0010_____ kWh.

9. Interstate transmission grid cost: $____.1000____ kVA/kW $____.0030____ kWh.

10. Intrastate transmission grid cost: $____.2500____ kVA/kW $____.0030____ kWh.

11. Miscellaneous Costs:
    A. **FERC fees** _____ $_____0_____ kVA/kW $__.0001__ kWh.
    B. **Access charge** _____ $_____0_____ kVA/kW $__.0020__ kWh.
    C. **State Regulatory fees** _____ $_____0_____ kVA/kW $__.0001__ kWh.
    D. **Stranded Investment charge** $_____0_____ kVA/kW $__.0020__ kWh.

12. Miscellaneous Monthly Costs:
    A. **Equipment charges** _____ 200. _____ .
    B. **Customer charge** _____ 100. _____ .
    C. _____ _____ .

13. Total cost of wheeled electricity: (Items [7], [8], [9], [10], [11], [12] totaled)
    $_____4.85_____ kVA/kW $____.0213____ kWh $____300.____ Monthly Charge.

14. Total cost of wheeled electricity for entire month: Amount on line [13] ($_____4.85_____ kVA/kW
    $_____.0213_____ kWh) X Amount on line [6] (_____1,523_____ kVA/kW ____1,725,630____ kWh) =
    $_____7,387._____ kVA/kW $____36,756.____ kWh + ($_____300._____ Monthly Charge) =
    $_____44,443._____ Total Cost.

15. Total cost if serving utility used for the follow-up month: Amount on line [4]
    ($_____5.50_____ kVA/kW $_____.0300_____ kWh) X Amount on line [5]
    ($_____1,500._____ kVA/kW $_____1,700,000_____ kWh) = $_____8,250._____ kVA/kW
    $_____51,000._____ kWh = ($_____300._____ Monthly Charge) = $____59,550.____ Total Cost.

16. Follow-up month savings using buyer wheeled electricity: Amount on line [15]
    ($_____59,550._____ Total Cost) – Amount on line [14] ($_____44,443._____ Total Cost) =
    $_____15,107._____ Total Monthly Savings.

17. Accumulative total savings: Amount from line [17] ($_____14,915._____ ) on previous month's
    follow-up sheet + Amount on line [16] from this follow-up sheet ($_____15,107._____ ) =
    $_____30,022._____ Accumulated Savings To Date.

## SYNOPSIS OF RETAIL WHEELED ELECTRICITY

At this point, the basics required to understand the process of retail wheeling have been covered. The likelihood of being able to do this process is increasing daily as the deregulation process continues. Also, serving utilities are becoming more receptive to discussing electricity cost reduction with retail customers. The potential for savings will be great and the process for realizing these savings will not be that difficult if the procedure as outlined below is methodically followed.

1. Establish a working relationship with the serving utility representative. Many times a special program can be worked out with the serving utility that will save money and reduce electricity costs without the retail wheeling process.

2. If a program with the serving utility is not possible, find out what they think their retail wheeling requirements will be. They may require an onsite back-up generator source before they will allow retail wheeling of electricity. If they require this, calculate the cost of an onsite back-up generation source in relation to the savings that may be possible.

3. Make certain the selection of the wheeled electricity source is completed with much care, since the reliability of this source will be the key to continuing satisfaction and electricity cost savings. Use the guidelines in this section and do not neglect to ask questions and verify dependability of the selected wheeling sources.

4. When you are finally able to retail wheel electricity, take time each month to analyze and record the information on billings from the serving utility, transmission grid transportation company and the seller since this data will be needed to accurately complete the nomination for the next month. Also, record savings information on the monthly follow-up work sheet as outlined in this chapter. The time to analyze the monthly bills, prepare the nomination and record savings information should take no more than one to two hours for each facility or location that will retail wheel electricity. The time required to do this monthly record keeping will be a very small price to pay when compared to the savings which may be able to be realized.

5.  If these steps are followed, a satisfactory, less costly electricity pur-
    chase program can result. Remember, the savings realized in this
    process are all bottom line savings. For example, a $100,000 annual
    electricity cost savings in a company that earns 10% before tax
    profits would mean that $1,000,000 in new sales would have to be
    generated to provide the same $100,000 that was realized in the
    wheeled electricity program.

# SECTION III

## *Electricity Wheeling Alternatives*

### Chapter 7

# Chapter 7

# Electricity Retail Wheeling Alternatives

## WHERE DO WE GO FROM HERE?

Now that we have discussed retail wheeling of electricity, the question may well be – what opportunity for savings in electricity costs is available until retail wheeling becomes a reality in my electric utility service territory?

The answer to this question may surprise you since in a number of states, electricity rates are currently allowed to be negotiated between utilities and their retail customers. Actual competition, or the knowledge that it will be forthcoming, is already manifesting itself in reduced electricity rates in many states. Before a for-profit utility can deviate from a filed tariff schedule rate, the appropriate regulatory agency must approve the transaction. Following in Figure 7.1 is a listing of all 50 states and the District of Columbia showing their current status with relation to the following items:

1. Are negotiated electricity rates allowed in your jurisdictional area of oversight?

2. If negotiated electricity rates are allowed, are any in effect at this time?

3. Is retail wheeling of electricity currently allowed?

4.  Has your agency performed any studies/analyses concerning the impact of electricity retail wheeling in your jurisdictional area of oversight?

Each State Utility Regulatory Agency was contacted by telephone and the previous (4) questions were asked. Following is the response by state.

**Figure 7.1** Regulatory Status/Retail Wheeled Electricity

| STATE | Regulatory Agency Telephone No. | Are negotiated rates allowed? | Are there any negotiated rates in effect? | Is retail wheeling of electricity currently allowed? | Have you done any retail wheeling studies? |
|---|---|---|---|---|---|
| Alabama | (205) 242-5209 | Yes | Yes | No | No |
| Alaska | (907) 276-6222 | Yes | Yes | Only Wholesale | No |
| Arizona | (602) 542-4251 | Yes | Yes | No | No |
| Arkansas | (501) 682-2051 | Yes | Yes | No | No |
| California | (415) 703-1282 | Yes | Yes | No | Extensive Study |
| Colorado | (303) 894-2000 | Yes | Yes | No | No |
| Connecticut | (203) 827-1533 | Yes | Yes | No | Yes |
| Delaware | (302) 739-4247 | Filed – Not Yet Approved | Filed – Not Yet Approved | No | No |
| District of Columbia | (202) 626-5100 | No | No | No | No |
| Florida | (904) 488-3464 | Yes | Yes | No | No |
| Georgia | (404) 656-4501 | Yes | No | No | No |
| Hawaii | (808) 586-2020 | No | No | No | No |
| Idaho | (208) 334-0300 | Yes | Yes | No | No |
| Illinois | (217) 782-5793 | Yes | Yes | No | Yes |
| Indiana | (317) 232-2701 | Yes | Yes | No | No |
| Iowa | (515) 281-5974 | Yes | Yes | No | Yes |
| Kansas | (913) 271-3100 | Yes | Yes | No | No |
| Kentucky | (502) 564-3940 | Yes | Yes | No | No |
| Louisiana | (504) 342-4427 | Yes | Yes | No | No |
| Maine | (207) 287-3831 | Yes | Yes | No | No |
| Maryland | (410) 767-8066 | Yes | Yes | No | Yes |
| Massachusetts | (617) 727-3500 | Yes | Yes | No | No |
| Michigan | (517) 334-6445 | Yes | Yes | Yes – (Special Situations Only) | Yes |
| Minnesota | (612) 296-7124 | Yes | Yes | No | Yes |
| Mississippi | (601) 961-5400 | Yes | Yes | No | Informally |
| Missouri | (314) 751-3234 | Yes | Unknown | No | No |
| Montana | (406) 444-6199 | Yes | Yes | No | No |
| Nebraska | (402) 471-3101 | No Investor Owned Electric Utilities | N/A | N/A | N/A |
| Nevada | (702) 687-6007 | Yes | Unknown | Yes – (Special Situations Only) | Yes |
| New Hampshire | (603) 271-2431 | Yes | Yes | No | No |
| New Jersey | (201) 648-2026 | Yes | Yes | No | Yes |
| New Mexico | (505) 827-6940 | Yes | Yes | No | Yes |
| New York | (518) 474-7080 | Yes | Yes | Yes – (Special Situations Only) | Yes |

**Figure 7.1**  Regulatory Status/Retail Wheeled Electricity (Continued)

| STATE | Regulatory Agency Telephone No. | Are negotiated rates allowed? | Are there any negotiated rates in effect? | Is retail wheeling of electricity currently allowed? | Have you done any retail wheeling studies? |
|---|---|---|---|---|---|
| North Carolina | (919) 733-4249 | Yes | Yes | No | Yes |
| North Dakota | (701) 224-2400 | Yes | Yes | No | Yes |
| Ohio | (614) 466-3016 | Yes | Yes | No | Yes |
| Oklahoma | (405) 521-2261 | Yes | Yes | No | No |
| Oregon | (503) 378-6611 | Yes | Yes | No | No |
| Pennsylvania | (717) 783-1740 | Yes | Yes | No | Yes |
| Rhode Island | (401) 277-3500 | Yes | Yes | No | No |
| South Carolina | (803) 737-5100 | Yes | Yes | No | Yes |
| South Dakota | (605) 773-3201 | Yes | Yes | No | No |
| Tennessee | (615) 741-2904 | Yes | Yes | No | No |
| Texas | (512) 458-0100 | Yes | Yes | No | Yes |
| Utah | (801) 530-6716 | Yes | Yes | No | Yes |
| Vermont | (802) 828-3458 | Yes | Yes | No | Yes |
| Virginia | (804) 371-9611 | Yes | Yes | No | No |
| Washington | (206) 753-6423 | No | No | No | No |
| West Virginia | (304) 340-0300 | Yes | Yes | No | No |
| Wisconsin | (608) 266-2001 | No | No | No | Yes |
| Wyoming | (307) 777-7427 | Yes | Yes | No | No |

As the data in Figure 7.1 shows, there are many states that allow electricity rate negotiation (45), but only a minority of the states have evaluated retail wheeling (21). Even though the number of states investigating retail wheeling currently seems small, much progress is being made in defining and understanding how retail wheeling will evolve. It is also interesting to note the large number of states that allow electricity rate negotiation in one form or another. There are also some special arrangements that have recently been negotiated between electric utilities and large electricity users to insure that the customer remains a retail electric user for a relatively long period of time. All of these negotiation arrangements have happened due to the pressure of competition. To understand the changes that are taking place in the electric utility industry, Figure 7.2 is shown.

**Figure 7.2**  Current vs Future Utility Status

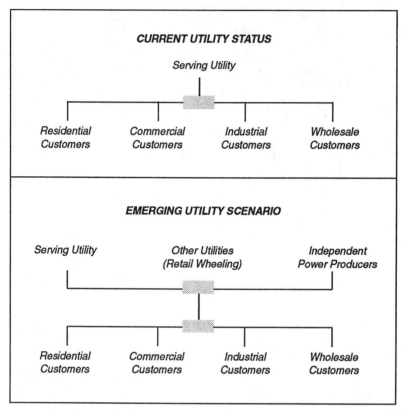

As Figure 7.2 shows, there are many changes in store for electric utilities. How individual utilities react to these changes will vary, but in general, it appears that most electric utilities recognize change is coming and the utilities are trying to work with the customers to assist them in reducing their electric utility costs.

## WHAT DO NEGOTIATED RATES LOOK LIKE?

Following, in Figure 7.3, are examples of (11) different negotiated rates actually in effect in various states. These rates have been approved by the appropriate regulatory agencies involved. As you will note, these rates have been developed because of a specific need; increased electricity usage, competitive load retention, load management, or self-generation deferral. There are literally hundreds of these types of rates available today. Shown in Figure 7.3 are (11) actual negotiated rates that are representative of what is currently available to retail customers that qualify. The (11) examples in Figure 7.3 represent (11) different states and illustrate their differing approaches to rate negotiation. Rates of this type are available for public examination upon request to the appropriate regulatory commission.

**Figure 7.3** Negotiated Rate Samples

No. 1

| | |
|---|---|
| ***RATE TYPE:*** | *Off-Tariff* |
| ***DESCRIPTION:*** | *Increase Electricity Usage – Rate applies to individual customers or to groups of customers qualifying for the Rate. In addition, all directly competing customers will be offered the Rate. Rate discounts will be provided on a case-by-case basis after performing a cost/benefit analysis. The ceiling for any rate provided will be the approved rate on file for the customer's rate class. The floor will be equal to the customer's energy cost plus any customer costs. The discount provided must be a major factor in the customer's decision to remain on the system, to increase consumption, or to locate within the utility's service area. A rate discount shall be offered for a period not to exceed 1 year, although a discount may be offered for a total of 36 consecutive months if annual cost/benefit analyses support continuation of the discount. The discount should not encourage deterioration of the customer's load characteristics. The utility is required to file semi-annual reports with the State Regulatory Commission detailing the results of the Rate.* |

**Figure 7.3** Negotiated Rate Samples (Continued)

No. 2

> **RATE TYPE:** *Off-Tariff*
>
> **PURPOSE:** *Competitive Load Retention – Residential Customers.*
>
> **DESCRIPTION:** *The rate will be in effect during the heating season and will be available to residential customers who use both wood and electricity for space heating. Eligible customers will receive a monthly credit for electricity consumed in excess of their weather-normalized period consumption in previous years. The rate is designed to induce residential customer to desist from burning wood for space heating purposes.*

No. 3

> **RATE TYPE:** *Off-Tariff*
>
> **PURPOSE:** *Load Management/Residential Customers*
>
> **DESCRIPTION:** *Interruptible – Dual-fuel rate under which the utility can shut-off power for space and water heating during peak periods. Customers then can switch to natural gas or oil.*

**Figure 7.3**  Negotiated Rate Samples (Continued)

No. 4

*RATE TYPE:*    Off-Tariff

*PURPOSE:*      Increase Electricity Usage

*DESCRIPTION:*  Available to new and existing industrial customers. A
10% discount applies to usage above a base year
level; a minimum bill of 95% of billing units recorded
in the same month of the base year also applies. For
new customers, the 10% discount applies to all usage
until the first full calendar year in operation is
established as the base year. Eligibility is restricted to
manufacturing customers with a minimum demand of
500 kW. The minimum increase in demand for an
existing customer is 100 kW.

No. 5

*RATE TYPE:*    Experimental

*PURPOSE:*      Increase Off-Peak Electricity Usage

*DESCRIPTION:*  Rate provides a 50% discount for all electricity used
from November to April in excess of consumption for
the corresponding month of the previous year.
Customer must pay a $50.00 monthly fee to be
entitled to the discount rate.

**Figure 7.3** Negotiated Rate Samples (Continued)

No. 6

---

*RATE TYPE:*     *Off-Tariff Special Customer Arrangement*

*PURPOSE:*       *Electricity Cost Reduction*

*DESCRIPTION:* *A special billing arrangement has been contracted with a seasonal customer who previously was served under 11 separate accounts. The arrangement provides the customer with an incentive to manage the entire load efficiently by combining the energy and demand from all meters. In addition, the arrangement allows the customer relief during summer months when many of the 11 accounts experience no activity.*

---

No. 7

---

*RATE TYPE:*     *Experimental*

*PURPOSE:*       *Load Shifting*

*DESCRIPTION:* *Off-peak tariff designed to provide an incentive for large customers to shift demand off-peak by reducing or eliminating demand charges for those customers who chose to shift demand to off-peak periods. The demand charge is based on the maximum metered demand during on-peak hours of 4 pm to 8 pm from June 20 through September 19. Previously, demand charges were calculated without regard to when demand occurred. The intent of the tariff is to improve system load factor.*

---

**Figure 7.3**  Negotiated Rate Samples (Continued)

No. 8

---

*RATE TYPE:*       *Experimental*

*PURPOSE:*         *Load Management*

*DESCRIPTION:*  *Voluntary load reduction program with industrial customers. The program offers users who cut demand by at least 500 kW a credit of $1/kW of curtailment and a bonus of $20/kW if curtailment occurs on the day of the system peak. Customers are required to telephone the utility for information relating to the utility's demand situation in the morning and judge whether they want to curtail demand during that day.*

---

No. 9

---

*RATE TYPE:*       *Experimental, Modified Real Time Pricing*

*PURPOSE:*         *Load Management/Peak Shaving*

*DESCRIPTION:*  *The State Regulatory Commission authorized the utility to allow interruptible customers to "buy-through" a potential service interruption by paying higher real-time prices for power. The buy-through could be granted if the utility was approaching a system peak but still had enough margin to keep interruptible customers operating. The price for energy during the buy-through would reflect real-time pricing and would equal the marginal fuel cost incurred to provide the power. An advantage to the utility under this arrangement is avoidance of lost revenue due to curtailment.*

---

**Figure 7.3**  Negotiated Rate Samples (Continued)

No. 10

---

*RATE TYPE:*      *Off-Tariff*

*PURPOSE:*        *Self-Generation Deferral*

*DESCRIPTION:* *The State Regulatory Commission has approved a contract between the utility and a customer that provides rate discounts of about 17.5% in exchange for the customer's deferral of a planned cogeneration plant for at least four years. Under the contract, the customer will pay a demand charge of $6.75/kW/ month with a 10,000 kW minimum demand and will pay a 2.5 cents/kWh energy charge. Both rates are subject to a 1% annual escalation. The agreement will reduce the customer's $4 million annual electricity bill by about $700,000. In addition, the utility has first option to build and operate the cogeneration plant should the customer decide to build it at the end of the deferral period*

---

No. 11

---

*RATE TYPE:*      *Off-Tariff*

*PURPOSE:*        *Self-Generation Deferral*

*DESCRIPTION:* *A rate for industrial customers considering cogeneration, most likely those in the 20 MW to 25 MW range who use 10,000 pounds/hr of steam and at least 10 MW peak demand/month. Rates are different for each customer, but the utility will try to match economics of a cogeneration facility (including installation investment costs). The cost of a cogeneration unit is reflected in rates rather than through an up-front payment to the utility.*

---

## HOW TO OBTAIN COPIES OF NEGOTIATED RATES

Normally, the state or local regulatory agency involved will be required to approve any nonstandard tariff negotiated rates. These rates, when approved, generally become a matter of public record and as such are available to the public. Following in Figure 7.4 is shown negotiated rate information that was obtained from (2) different state regulatory agencies. This information was obtained by telephoning the regulatory agency and requesting this information. The information shown represents the various negotiated rates that have been instituted together with the specific regulatory agency docket numbers that are applicable to each rate. For detailed specific negotiated rate information as shown in Figure 7.3, the applicable docket number would be referenced and a request by that docket number would be made to the proper regulatory agency. In the following examples, the state and customer identity have been removed. The information in Figure 7.4, Sample (1) represents all of the negotiated rates for the state shown. In Sample (2), the negotiated rates shown are for only (1) utility in the state selected. In Sample (1), there are (33) negotiated rates in the entire state. In Sample (2), there are (80) negotiated rates for only (1) utility. These samples illustrate the diversity of rate negotiation from state-to-state.

**Figure 7.4**  Negotiated Rates Listings

## Sample 1

| CUSTOMER | RATE CLASS | DATE FILED | AUTO-MATIC APPR. | COMMIS-SION ORDER | DOCKET # | ALLOW (Y/N) | CURRENTLY IN EFFECT (Y/N) | PEND-ING | CONTRACT SIZE MW | CONTRACT TERM (YRS) |
|---|---|---|---|---|---|---|---|---|---|---|
| Lumber Company | D-4 | 25-Aug-93 | A | 03-Sep-93 | 93-216 | Y | N | N | .07 | 1 |
| Lumber Company | D-4 | 23-Sep-94 | A | 07-Oct-94 | 94-337 | Y | Y | N | .07 | 2 |
| Miscellaneous Mfg. | D-4 & D-3 | 27-Dec-93 | | 11-Feb-94 | 93-355 | Y | Y | Y | 27.5 | 5 |
| Miscellaneous Mfg. | D-1 | 02-Jun-94 | A | 13-Jun-94 | 94-197 | Y | Y | N | 1.25 | 3 |
| Miscellaneous Mfg. | D-5 | 18-Feb-88 | | 26-May-88 | 88-048 | | N | | | |
| Miscellaneous Mfg. | D-5 | 29-Jan-93 | | 10-Mar-94 | 93-016 | Y | Y | N | 24 | 3 |
| Produce Company | D-1 | 07-Mar-94 | A | 16-Mar-94 | 94-008 | Y | Y | N | 2.2 | 3 |
| Shopping Plaza | D-1 | 04-Nov-93 | A | 09-Nov-93 | 93-290 | N | N | Y | Denied | 3 |
| Log Home Mfg. | D-1 | 25-Jan-94 | A | 03-Feb-94 | 94-031 | Y | Y | N | 1.3 | 1 |
| Miscellaneous Mfg. | D-4 | 05-Nov-93 | A | 03-Sep-93 | 93-302 | N | N | N | Denied | 3 |
| Miscellaneous Mfg. | D-4 | 16-May-94 | A | 25-May-94 | 94-175 | Y | Y | N | 0.5 | 3 |
| Chemical Mfg. | LGS-ST-TOU | 10-Dec-92 | | 25-Mar-94 | 92-331 | Y | Y | N | 27 | 8 |
| Wood Products Co. | LGS-T-TOU | 29-Jun-93 | | 29-Nov-93 | 91-007 | Y | Y | N | 6 | Indef. |
| Wood Products Co. | LGS-T-TOU | 03-Dec-93 | | 19-Jan-94 | 93-335 | Y | Y | Y | 12 | 1 |
| Paper Company | LGS-T-TOU | 10-Jan-91 | | 07-Feb-91 | 91-007 | Y | Y | N | 40 | Indef. |
| Paper Company | LGS-T-TOU | 06-Jan-93 | | 08-Jan-93 | 91-344 | Y | Y | N | 5 | 2 |
| Miscellaneous Mgf. | IGS-P-TOU | 08-Apr-94 | | 14-Jun-94 | 94-122 | Y | Y | Y | 1 | 5 |
| Paper Company | LGS-T-TOU | 10-Jan-91 | | 07-Feb-91 | 91-007 | Y | Y | N | 16 | Indef. |
| Fiber Mfg. | LGS-ST-TOU | 23-Nov-93 | | 13-Dec-93 | 93-320 | Y | Y | N | 20 | 3 |
| Lumber Company | MGS-S | 10-May-94 | | Delib. 6/13/94 | 94-168 | Y | Y | N | 1 | 2 |
| Carpet Mfg. Co. | LGS-ST or P | 04-May-94 | | | 94-153 | | N | | | 8 |
| Miscellaneous Mfg. | IGS-O-TOU | 13-Sep-93 | | 25-Oct-93 | 93-238 | Y | N | N | 0.8 | 1 |
| Forest Products | varies | 21-Sep-94 | | 26-Sep-94 | 94-276 | Y | Y | N | 23 | 3 |
| Ski Area | varies | 15-Apr-94 | | Delib. 6/13/94 | 94-134 | Y | Y | N | 15.5 | Indef. |
| Paper Company | LGS-ST-TOU | 02-Jun-94 | | 14-Jun-94 | 94-202 | Y | Y | N | 8 | 5 |
| Ski Area | LGS-ST-TOU | 13-Sep-93 | | 25-Oct-93 | 93-239 | Y | N | N | 9.4 | 1 |
| Ski Area | | 14-Dec-89 | | 08-Feb-90 | 89-426 | | N | | | |
| Ski Area | | 16-Nov-92 | | 08-Jan-93 | 92-313 | Y | N | N | | |
| Forest Products | E-S | 15-Mar-94 | A | 29-Mar-94 | 94-078 | Y | Y | N | 0.75 | 1 |
| Forest Products | E-S | 20-Apr-94 | A | 27-Apr-94 | 94-135 | Y | Y | N | 0.4 | 1 |
| Miscellaneous Mfg. | E-S | 18-Jan-94 | A | 27-Jan-94 | 93-236 | Y | Y | N | 0.23 | 1 |
| Lumber Company | E-S | 12-Apr-94 | A | 21-Apr-94 | 94-127 | Y | Y | N | 0.1 | 1 |

**Figure 7.4**  Negotiated Rates Listings (Continued)

## Sample 2

| | CUSTOMER TYPE | CASE NO. | | | CUSTOMER TYPE | CASE NO. |
|---|---|---|---|---|---|---|
| | COMPETITION CUSTOMERS | | | 46 | Metal Processing | 93-1212 |
| | | | | 47 | Miscellaneous Manufacturing | 92-1372 |
| 01 | Miscellaneous Manufacturing | 91-2108 | | 48 | Miscellaneous Company | 89-865 |
| 02 | Metal Fabricating Company | 93-745 | | 49 | College | 93-1381 |
| 03 | Metal Fabricating Company | 93-1021 | | 50 | Metal Processing Company | 92-1252 |
| 04 | Chemical Company | 93-724 | | 51 | Miscellaneous Company | 92-1942 |
| 05 | Metal Fabricating Company | 91-1650 | | 52 | Miscellaneous Manufacturing | 91-2289 |
| 06 | College | 89-1405 | | 53 | Miscellaneous Company | 91-777 |
| 07 | Food Products Company | 90-493 | | 54 | Miscellaneous Company | 90-858 |
| 08 | Miscellaneous Manufacturing | 91-1561 | | 55 | Miscellaneous Company | 90-1377 |
| 09 | Hospital | 89-1912 | | 56 | Miscellaneous Company | 89-868 |
| 10 | Miscellaneous Manufacturing | 93-12-2 | | 57 | Miscellaneous Manufacturing | 92-1365 |
| 11 | Food Processors | 92-309 | | 58 | Miscellaneous Manufacturing | 93-324 |
| 12 | Metal Fabrication Company | 92-2196 | | 59 | Miscellaneous Manufacturing | 89-1161 |
| 13 | Hospital | 90-1778 | | 60 | Miscellaneous Company | 89-868 |
| 14 | Metal Products Company | 92-801 | | 61 | Miscellaneous Manufacturing | 89-148 |
| 15 | Miscellaneous Manufacturing | 92-2360 | | 62 | Miscellaneous Company | 89-865 |
| 16 | Metal Fabrication | 92-1187 | | 63 | Property Management Company | 91-955 |
| 17 | Metal Fabrication | 93-531 | | 64 | Property Management Company | 91-954 |
| 18 | Tool Company | 92-1353 | | 65 | Hospital | 93-87 |
| 19 | Metal Processing Company | 92-1492 | | 66 | Miscellaneous Manufacturing | 92-2197 |
| 20 | Miscellaneous Manufacturing | 92-2297 | | 67 | Miscellaneous Company | 92-1331 |
| 21 | Miscellaneous Manufacturing | 92-2297 | | 68 | Miscellaneous Manufacturing | 92-1836 |
| 22 | Metal Fabrication Company | 91-2190 | | 69 | Miscellaneous Manufacturing | 91-1692 |
| 23 | Food Processing | 93-768 | | 70 | Miscellaneous Manufacturing | 92-35 |
| 24 | Property Management Company | 89-1777 | | 71 | Miscellaneous Manufacturing | 92-1099 |
| 25 | Automotive Company | 93-723 | | 72 | Miscellaneous Manufacturing | 92-848 |
| 26 | Automotive Company | 92-799 | | | | |
| 27 | Metal Processing Company | 89-1312 | | | | |
| 28 | Park District | 91-295 | | | | |
| 29 | Metal Processing Company | 91-778 | | | COGEN CUSTOMERS | |
| 30 | Miscellaneous Manufacturing | 91-51 | | | | |
| 31 | Automotive Company | 92-597 | | 73 | Miscellaneous Company | 93-1445 |
| 32 | Automotive Company | 92-952 | | | | |
| 33 | Metal Manufacturing | 92-1311 | | | | |
| 34 | Miscellaneous Manufacturing | 92-2057 | | | | |
| 35 | Steel Processing Company | 92-1581 | | | | |
| 36 | Miscellaneous Company | 88-1573 | | | | |
| 37 | Miscellaneous Manufacturing | 92-334 | | | ECONOMIC DEVELOPMENT CUSTOMERS | |
| 38 | Miscellaneous Company | 90-1376 | | | | |
| 39 | Metal Manufacturing Company | 92-1695 | | 74 | Metal Processing Company | 92-1649 |
| 40 | Miscellaneous Manufacturing | 91-237 | | 75 | Miscellaneous Company | 89-357 |
| 41 | Miscellaneous Company | 92-1116 | | 76 | Miscellaneous Company | 90-86 |
| 42 | Hospital | 90-859 | | 77 | Miscellaneous Manufacturing | 92-854 |
| 43 | Hospital | 93-1747 | | 78 | Metal Processing Company | 92-100 |
| 44 | Food Processing | 90-87 | | 79 | Miscellaneous Company | 87-1790 |
| 45 | Hospital | 89-1452 | | 80 | Miscellaneous Manufacturing | 93-679 |

## WHAT WILL HAPPEN WHEN ELECTRICITY COMPETITION BECOMES A REALITY?

In Figure 7.5 is shown an actual advertising brochure that is currently being utilized in an electricity service area that has (2) serving utilities from which a customer can choose. Although this type of competition is not now widespread, it does represent what will probably happen when electricity competition becomes available. The brochure shown is circulated by a municipal electric utility in a service territory that also includes a for-profit electric utility. In this particular state, a municipal utility can compete with the for-profit utility for customers. Notice how this brochure is worded and the example that is given showing a commercial bill comparison. If this type of competition was available in your particular electricity service area, do you think it might tend to reduce your electricity costs? The specific state, utility and customer identification have been removed, but all other data is as presented in the brochure.

**Figure 7.5** Advertising Brochure Sample

---

# THE ALTERNATIVE POWER SOURCE

---

_____ ranks first in the sate of _____ of 84 municipal power companies, and 38th nationally out of 2,000 municipal power companies. Offering Commercial customers an average savings of 25 percent per month, investor-owned utilities now recognize that _____ Power is a reliable, growing municipal energy source.

While _____ competitor, _____ attempts to fight off its bond rating being lowered to a "junk bond level" or below investment grade _____ Standard & Poor's bond rating group has rated _____ during the Phase I expansion.

### ...The Advantage

Now, entering into Phase II, _____ aggressive goal remains...delivering low cost, reliable power to the _____ consumer. And, _____ expansion has gone forward without a rate increase. In fact, _____ has held rates steady for over a decade...a trend _____ intends to continue.

### COMMERCIAL BILL COMPARISON
**100 KW Demand Using 30,000 Kilowatt Hours Per Month**

| MONTH | POWER | ELECTRIC COMPANY | SAVINGS |
|---|---|---|---|
| January 1993 | $2,428.66 | $3,448.10 | $1,019.44 (29.57%) |
| February 1993 | 2,424.25 | 3,448.10 | 1,023.85 (29.69%) |
| March 1993 | 2,364.79 | 3,386.06 | 1,021.27 (30.16%) |
| April 1993 | 2,412.70 | 3,386.06 | 973.36 (28.75%) |
| May 1993 | 2,386.36 | 3,386.06 | 999.70 (29.52%) |
| June 1993 | 2,601.75 | 3,696.56 | 1,094.81 (29.62%) |
| July 1993 | 2,557.50 | 3,696.56 | 1,139.06 (29.87%) |
| August 1993 | 2,568.69 | 3,696.56 | 1,127.87 (30.15%) |
| September 1993 | 2,546.52 | 3,645.83 | 1,099.31 (30.15%) |
| October 1993 | 2,551.35 | 3,335.33 | 783.98 (23.51%) |
| November 1993 | 2,402.59 | 3,335.33 | 932.74 (27.97%) |
| December 1993 | 2,375.08 | 3,335.33 | 960.25 (28.79%) |
| **TOTAL** | **$29,620.24** | **$41,795.88** | $12,175.64 (29.13%) |
| **AVERAGE BILL** | **$2,467.04** | **$3,521.20** | $1,054.16 |

---

### More than reliable low cost energy

_____ is also working to assure the continued prosperity of the City of _____ and her people; because building a solid economic base is vital to _____ future, and your company. _____ is helping businesses develop, expand and relocate through joint efforts with the City of _____ Departments of Community and Economic Development.

## LAST MINUTE INFORMATION

As the writing of this publication was being completed, five items of information were obtained as follows:

1. **Electricity Futures Contracts –**

The New York Mercantile Exchange approved the preliminary terms and conditions for two electricity futures contracts. This exchange anticipates that these contracts will begin trading before the end of 1995. The contracts will be for 736 MWh of electricity. The price will be quoted in dollars per MWh. One contract will be for delivery at the border of California and Oregon, the other contract will be for delivery at the Palo Verde generating station in Arizona. These futures contracts are being created because of the anticipated needs of the electric industry. These contracts will be utilized as a hedge against electricity price variations and availability. Initially, the delivery points of California, Oregon and Arizona will favor West coast utilities/customers. This strategy makes sense because this area appears to be further along in electricity retail wheeling than are most other parts of the country. If these initial electricity futures contracts prove successful, there probably will be other delivery points established as electricity retail wheeling spreads to other parts of the country. Once retail wheeling is recognized as a viable procedure, probably futures contracts for electricity will have delivery points, at least for each of the (9) NERC regions in the United States. (See Chapter 4 in this publication.) It is well to note that in general futures contracts have very low delivery rates since they are primarily used to hedge prices and not to actually take delivery of a commodity. Since this will probably be true of electricity futures, they will have little value unless wheeling of electricity evolves to the point that customers/marketers can utilize these contracts to hedge or lock in known cost factors. NYMEX would probably not institute these futures contracts unless they feel that there will be sufficient market volume to make their creation a profitable venture. Retail wheeling will be the only vehicle for this volume.

2.  **Alabama State Regulatory Commission Order –**

    In January of 1995, the Alabama Public Service Commission
    approved a petition filed by the Alabama Power Company. This
    petition requested approval of a contract with a retail customer for
    both firm and nonfirm electricity capacity for a period of (10) years.
    The contract was for sale of electricity at lower than prevailing tar-
    iff schedule rates (negotiated rate). In the Commission approval,
    they made the following statement:

    > *"We are of the opinion that approval of the contract is in
    > keeping with our policy of encouraging the expansion and
    > retention of industry in Alabama Power Company's ser-
    > vice territory, and that it would be in the public interest to
    > approve same."*

    This customer was able to negotiate with their utility because the
    Commission's position was that it was in the "public's interest"
    even though it would result in lower incremental revenue for the
    utility.

3.  **Boston Edison Discounted Rates –**

    The Massachusetts Regulatory Commission approved a Boston
    Edison rate request to reduce electricity rates by 20% for their large
    industrial users. These rate reductions were requested to retain
    Boston Edison's rate base. Some of the large industrial users were
    threatening to move their operations, install cogeneration, or to
    wheel in less expensive electricity. In order for companies to
    receive the discount, they must agree to continue purchasing Boston
    Edison power for (6) years at a 80% minimum level of the purchas-
    es made in the preceding 12 months. Only about 12 companies will
    be able to qualify for this discount initially. The discount will not
    effect other Boston Edison customers since any revenue losses will
    be compensated for by Boston Edison cost-cutting procedures.
    Although this rate reduction will not effect most of Boston Edison's
    customer base, it is a start. As time passes, probably more and more
    smaller industrial and commercial customers will demand similar

concessions. This initial rate reduction will only be the "tip of the iceberg" in ongoing rate concessions.

4. **Central Main Power Company –**

The Regulatory Commission in Maine approved a rate case request by Central Maine Power Company to reduce its rates to larger industrial users by 15%. As was the case with Boston Edison, this action was taken to preserve customer base load.

5. **Pacific Gas and Electric Company –**

In a letter to the California Public Utilities Commission, Pacific Gas and Electric Company proposed allowing its large customers the freedom to choose their own electricity suppliers starting in January of 1996. This proposal was received with something less than enthusiasm by the other competing utilities. Most of PG&E's competitors favor a more gradual phasing-in of deregulation. There is considerable debate over PG&E's proposal for larger customers as opposed to proposals that cover more customer classes. Although the outcome of this proposal is unknown, it is certain that it will ultimately benefit all customers, not only of PG&E, but also of PG&E's competitors. PG&E, the largest for-profit utility in the United States, seems to be at the forefront of realizing that deregulation is inevitable. It has reduced wholesale electric rates as well as cutting overhead costs by large reductions in its work force.

More and more rate concessions are being proposed as the realization that electricity is a commodity and it should be priced as such is becoming more widespread. Keep up to date on what is going on in your utility's service area as well as in your state with relation to the effect of even the potential for electricity retail wheeling. It may surprise you what can be done in conjunction with your serving electric utility to reduce your incremental electricity costs.

## SYNOPSIS OF ELECTRICITY RETAIL WHEELING

At this point, all of the basics required to investigate the possibility of electricity retail wheeling have been discussed. The likelihood of being successful in this effort is increasing daily as the deregulation process continues. Also, serving electric utilities are becoming more receptive to discussing electricity cost reduction with customers. The potential for savings is great and the process for realizing these savings is possible if the process as outlined below is methodically followed:

1. Establish a working relationship with the serving electric utility representative. Many times a special program can be worked out with them that will save money and reduce the effort required in getting a program instituted.

2. Utilize the information in this publication to investigate the potentials for electricity cost reductions through negotiation or retail wheeling. Investigate the following items:

   A. Has the serving electric utility ever negotiated a rate with a retail customer? If they have, what were the details? How does the usage characteristics of the negotiated rate compare to the one being analyzed?

   B. If the serving electric utility has not or will not negotiate an electric rate, will they assist in customer side of the meter point costs that might occur in renovation or expansion projects that are related to electricity usage?

   C. When undertaking new construction, always, prior to actual construction, consult with the serving electric utility to determine what cash/rate incentives they might offer to obtain your electricity load. Always consult with the utility prior to actually beginning construction since any leverage disappears if actual construction has started.

   D. If special electricity usage, efficiency, etc. studies are needed, consult with the electric utility to determine whether they will finance the cost of these studies. This type of assistance seems to be available on a relatively wide basis.

   E. If an electric upgrade is required, determine whether the electric utility will finance at a below-market rate or assist in the project through up-front cash assistance.

   F. Join local intervenor groups. (See Chapter 2 in this publication.) These groups assist in keeping a retail customer informed on

current retail wheeling developments as well as provide intervention services in utility rate cases.

G.  Study the material in this publication so that you are familiar
with the retail wheeling transaction, the terms used and the
alternates available.

3.  If these steps are followed, less costly electricity will result.
Remember, savings are almost always bottom line. For example, a
$50,000 annual electricity cost savings in a company that earns 10%
before tax profits means that $500,000 in new sales would have to
be generated to provide the same $50,000 that was realized in the
electricity cost reduction program.

This publication is not describing an in-place procedure, but rather
is forecasting the beginning of a new unbundled, competitive, commodity based electricity environment where retail wheeling will play an
important part in the change that will take place. Even before this publication is printed, changes will have occurred in the retail wheeling environment. However, the basics as addressed herein will not change.
Learn the basics and regardless of how retail wheeling evolves, you will
be prepared to take advantage of what it offers.

Most entities will never retail wheel electricity even when it
becomes available, but its impact will be felt by all. Learn to use its
potential to reduce your electricity costs now and in the future.

# SECTION IV

## Appendices

# Appendix A

# Listing of For-Profit Utility Regulatory Agencies

This listing includes United States Federal and State Regulatory agencies as well as other non-United States agencies. This information – courtesy of the National Association of Regulatory Utility Commissioners, 1102 Interstate Commerce Commission Building, P.O. Box 684, Washington, DC 20044-0684; Tel. (202) 898-2200.

## REGULATORY AGENCIES
### (Year of agency's or predecessor's establishment shown after name)

### US FEDERAL REGULATORY AGENCIES

**Federal Energy Regulatory Commission (FERC) (1930)**
825 North Capitol Street, NE, Washington DC 20426
Tel. (202) 208-1088, Fax 208-2106, Bulletin Board 208-8997

**Nuclear Regulatory Commission (NCR) (1946)**
Washington, DC 20555, Tel. (301) 492-7000, Fax 504-1672

**Rural Electrification Administration (REA) (1934),**
  **United States Department of Agriculture**
Independence Avenue & 14th Street, SW, Washington, DC 20250
Tel. (202) 720-1255, Fax 720-1725

**United States Department of Energy (DOE) (1977)**
1000 Independence Avenue, SW, Washington, DC 20585
Tel. (202) 586-5000, Fax 586-8134, 586-4403

## US STATE REGULATORY AGENCIES

**Alabama Public Service Commission (PSC) (1881)**
P.O. Box 991, Montgomery, AL 36101-0991
Tel. (205) 242-5209, Fax 240-3079

**Alaska Public Utilities Commission (PUC) (1959)**
1016 West Sixth Avenue, Suite 400, Anchorage, AK 99501
Tel. (907) 276-6222, Fax 276-0160

**Arizona Corporation Commission (PUC) (1959)**
1200 West Washington Street, Phoenix, AZ 85007
Tel. (602) 542-2931, Fax 542-5560

**Arkansas Public Service Commission (PSC) (1935)**
1000 Center Building, Little Rock, AR 72201
Tel. (501) 682-2051, Fax 682-5731

**California Public Utilities Commission (PUC) (1911)**
California State Building, 205 Van Ness Avenue,
San Francisco, CA 94102-3298
Tel. (415) 703-1282, Fax 703-1758

**Colorado Public Utilities Commission (PUC) (1885)**
Logan Tower, Office Level 2, 1580 Logan Street,
Denver, CO 80203
Tel. (303) 894-2000, Fax 894-2065

**Connecticut Dept. of Public Utility Control (DPUC) (1911)**
1 Central Park Plaza, New Britain, CT 06051
Tel. (203) 827-1553, Fax 827-2613

**Delaware Public Service Commission (PSC) (1949)**
1560 South DuPont Highway, P.O. Box 457,
Dover, DE 19903-0457
Tel. (302) 739-4247, Fax 729-4849

**District of Columbia Public Service Commission (PSC) (1913)**
450 Fifth Street, NW, Washington, DC 20001
Tel. (202) 626-5100, Fax 638-1785

**Florida Public Service Commission (PSC) (1887)**
101 East Gaines Street, Fletcher Building,
Tallahassee, FL 32399-0850
Tel. (904) 488-3464, Fax 487-0509

**Georgia Public Service Commission (PSC) (1879)**
244 Washington Street, SW,
Atlanta, GA 30334-5701
Tel. (404) 656-4501, Fax 656-2341

**Hawaii Public Utilities Commission (PUC) (1913)**
465 South King Street, Kekuanao's Building, #103
Honolulu, HI 96813
Tel. (808) 586-2020, Fax 586-2066

**Idaho Public Utilities Commission**
P.O. Box 83720, Boise, ID 83720-0074
Tel. (208) 334-0300, Fax 334-3762

**Illinois Commerce Commission (CC) (1871)**
Leland Building, 527 East Capitol Avenue,
P.O. Box 19280, Springfield, IL 62794-9280
Tel. (217) 782-7295, Fax 782-1042

**Indiana Utility Regulatory Commission (URC) (1913)**
Suite E306, Indiana Government Center South,
302 West Washington Street, Indianapolis, IN 46204
Tel. (317) 232-2701, Fax 232-6758

**Iowa Utilities Board (UB) (1878)**
Lucas State Office Building, Des Moines, IA 50319
Tel. (515) 281-5979, Fax 281-8821

**Kansas State Corporation Commission (SCC) (1883)**
1500 SW Arrowhead Road, Topeka, KS 66604-4027
Tel. (502) 564-3940, Fax 271-3354

**Kentucky Public Service Commission (PSC) (1934)**
730 Schenkel Lane, P.O. Box 615, Frankfort, KY 40602
Tel. (502) 564-3940, Fax 564-7279

**Louisiana Public Service Commission (PSC) (1899)**
P.O. Box 91154, Baton Rouge, LA 70821-9154
Tel. (504) 342-4427, Fax 342-4087

**Maine Public Utilities Commission (PUC) (1914)**
242 State Street, State House Station 18,
Augusta, ME 04333
Tel. (207) 287-3831, Fax 287-1039

**Massachusetts Department of Public Utilities (DPU) (1919)**
100 Cambridge Street, Boston, MA 02202
Tel. (617) 727-3500, Fax 723-8812

**Michigan Public Service Commission (PSC) (1873)**
Mercantile Building, 6545 Mercantile Way,
P.O. Box 30221, Lansing, MI 48909-7721
Tel. (517) 334-6445, Fax 882-5170

**Minnesota Public Utilities Commission (PUC) (1871)**
121 East 7th Place, Suite 350, St. Paul, MN 55101-2147
Tel. (612) 296-7124, Fax 297-7073

**Mississippi Public Service Commission (PSC) (1884)**
19th Floor, Walter Sillers State Office Building,
P.O. Box 1174, Jackson, MS 39215-1174
Tel. (601) 961-5400, Fax 961-5469

**Missouri Public Service Commission (PSC) (1913)**
P.O. Box 360, Truman State Office Building,
Jefferson City, MO 65102
Tel. (314) 751-3234, Fax 751-1847

**Montana Public Service Commission (PSC) (1907)**
1701 Prospect Avenue, P.O. Box 202601,
Helena, MT 59620-2601
Tel. (406) 444-6199, Fax 444-7618

**Nebraska Public Service Commission (PSC) (1906)**
300 The Atrium, 1200 N Street, P.O. Box 94927,
Lincoln, NE 68509-4927
Tel. (402) 471-3101, Fax 471-0254

**Nevada Public Service Commission (PSC) (1911)**
727 Fairview Drive., Carson City, NV 89710
Tel. (702) 687-6001, Fax 687-6110

**New Hampshire Public Utilities Commission (PUC) (1911)**
8 Old Suncook Road, Building No 1,Concord, NH 03301-5185
Tel. (603) 271-2431, Fax 271-3878

**New Jersey Board of Public Utilities (BPU) (1907)**
44 South Clinton Avenue, CN-350, Trenton, NJ 08625-0350
Tel. (609) 777-3300, Fax 777-3330

**New Mexico Public Utility Commission (PUC) (1941)**
Marian Hall, 224 East Palace Avenue,Santa Fe, NM 87501-2013
Tel. (505) 827-6940, Fax 827-6973

**New York Public Service Commission (PSC) (1855)**
Three Empire State Plaza, Albany, NY 12223
Tel. (518) 474-7080, Fax 290-4435

**North Carolina Utilities Commission (UC) (1891)**
430 North Salisbury Street, Dobbs Building,
Raleigh, NC 27611
Tel. (919) 733-4249, Fax 733-7300

**North Dakota Public Service Commission (PSC) (1889)**
State Capitol, Bismarck, ND 58505
Tel. (701) 328-2400, Fax 224-2410

**Ohio Public Utilities Commission (PUC) (1867)**
180 East Broad Street, Columbus, OH 43215-3793
Tel. (614) 466-3016, Fax 466-7366

**Oklahoma Corporation Commission (CC) (1907)**
Jim Thorpe Office Building, P.O. Box 52000-2000,
Oklahoma City, OK 73152-2000
Tel. (401) 521-2211, Fax 521-6045

**Oregon Public Utility Commission (PUC) (1887)**
550 Capitol NE, Salem, OR 97310-1380
Tel. (503) 378-6611, Fax 378-5505

**Pennsylvania Public Utilities Commission (PUC) (1908)**
P.O. Box 3265, Harrisburg, PA 17105-3265
Tel. (717) 783-1840, Fax 787-4193

**Rhode Island Public Utilities Commission (PUC) (1839)**
100 Orange Street, Providence, RI 02903
Tel. (401) 277-3500, Fax 277-6805

**South Carolina Public Service Commission (PSC) (1879)**
P.O. Drawer 11649, Columbia, SC 292211
Tel. (803) 737-5100, Fax 737-5199

**South Dakota Public Utilities Commission (PUC) (1885)**
State Capitol, Pierre, SD 57501-5070
Tel. (605) 773-3201, Fax 773-3809

**Tennessee Public Service Commission (PSC) (1897)**
460 James Robertson Parkway, Nashville, TN 37243-0505
Tel. (615) 741-2904, Fax 741-2336

**Texas Public Utility Commission (PUC) (1975)**
7800 Shoal Creek Boulevard, Austin, TX 78757
Tel. (512) 458-0100, Fax 458-8340

**Texas Railroad Commission (RC)**
1701 North Congress Avenue, Room 12-100,
P.O. Box 12967, Austin, TX 78711-2967
Tel. (512) 463-7288, Fax 463-7161

**Utah Public Service Commission (PSC) (1917)**
160 East 300 South, P.O. Box 45585
Salt Lake City, UT 84145
Tel. (801) 530-6716

**Vermont Public Service Board (PSB) (1886)**
City Center Building, 89 Main Street, Drawer 20,
Montpelier, VT 05602-2701
Tel. (802) 828-2358, Fax 828-3351

**Virginia State Corporation Commission (SCC) (1902)**
Tyler Building, P.O. Box 1197, Richmond, VA 23209
Tel. (804) 371-9608, Fax 371-9376

**Washington Utilities and Transportation Commission (UTC) (1905)**
Chandler Plaza Building, P.O. Box 47250,
Olympia, WA 98504-7250
Tel. (206) 753-6423, Fax 586-1150

**West Virginia Public Service Commission (PSC) (1913)**
201 Brooks Street, P.O. Box 812, Charleston, WV 25323
Tel. (304) 340-0300, Fax 340-0325

**Wisconsin Public Service Commission (PSC) (1874)**
4802 Sheboygan Avenue, Madison, WI 53705
Tel. (608) 266-5481, Fax 266-3957

**Wyoming Public Service Commission (PSC) (1915)**
700 West 21st Street, Cheyenne, WY 82002
Tel. (307) 777-7427, Fax 777-5700

## CANADIAN PROVINCIAL REGULATORY AGENCIES

**Alberta Public Utilities Board (PUB) (1915)**
10055 - 106th Street, 11th Floor,
Edmonton, Alberta, T5J 2Y2
Tel. (403) 427-4901, Fax 427-6970

**British Columbia Utilities Commission (UC) (1939)**
Sixth Floor, 900 Howe Street, Vancouver,
British Columbia, V6Z 2N3
Tel. (604) 660-4700, Fax 660-1102

**New Brunswick Board of Commissioners of Public Utilities (BCPU)**
110 Charlotte Street, P.O. Box 5001,
Saint John, New Brunswick, E2L 4Y9
Tel. (506) 658-2504, Fax 633-0163

### Newfoundland and Labrador Board of Commissioners of Public Utilities (BCPU)
P.O. Box 21040, St. John's, Newfoundland A1A 5B1
Tel. (709) 726-6432, Fax 726-9604

### Nova Scotia Utility and Review Board (UARB) (1909)
Suite 300, 1601 Lower Water Street, Postal Unit M.,
P.O. Box 1692, Halifax, Nova Scotia B3J 3S3
Tel. (902) 424-4448, Fax 424-3919

### Ontario Energy Board (EB)
P.O. Box 2319, 2300 Yonge Street, 26th Floor,
Toronto, Ontario, M4P 1E4
Tel. (416) 481-1967, Fax 440-7656

### Ontario Hydro
700 University Avenue, Toronto, Ontario, M5G 1X6
Tel. (416) 592-9621

### Prince Edward Island Regulatory & Appeals Commission (RAC) (1946)
P.O. Box 577, Suite 501, 134 Kent Street,
Charlottetown, Prince Edward Island, C1A 7L1
Tel. (902) 892-3501, Fax 566-4076

### Quebec Natural Gas Board
Case postale 001, Tour de la Bourse, 800 Place Victoria,
2eme etage, bureau 255, Montreal, Quebec, H4Z 1A2
Tel. (514) 873-2452, Fax 873-2070

## OTHER REGULATORY AGENCIES

### Argentina Ente Nacional Regulador Del Gas
Av. Julio A. Roca 541, 2" Piso, (1322),
Buenos Aires, Republica Argentina
Tel. (541) 349-5333, Fax 334-5138

### Guam Public Utilities Commission
Suite 400, GCIC Building, P.O. Box 862, Agana, Guam 96910
Tel. (671) 477-9708, Fax 477-0783

**Israel Minister of Energy and Infrastructure**
Minister of Energy and Infrastructure, Government
of Israel, 234 Jafa Street, Jerusalem, Israel

**New Orleans City Council Utilities Regulatory Office (1954)**
Room 1E04A, City Hall, 1300 Perdido Street,
New Orleans, LA 70112
Tel. (504) 565-6355, Fax 565-6361

**New Orleans Department of Utilities (1912)**
1300 Perdido Street, Room 2W14, City Hall,
New Orleans, LA 70112
Tel. (504) 565-6260, Fax 565-6449

**New York Power Authority**
1633 Broadway, New York, NY 19919
Tel. (212) 468-6000, Fax 468-6478

**Puerto Rico Public Service Commission (1952)**
P.O. Box 870, Hato Rey Station, San Juan 00919-0870
Tel. (809) 756-1919, Fax 758-0630

**United Kingdom Office of Water Services**
Centre City Tower, 7 Hill Street,
Birmingham B5 4UA, UK
Tel. 021-625-1300, Fax 021-625-1400

**Virgin Islands Public Services Commission (1940)**
P.O. Box 40, Charlotte Amalie, St. Thomas 00804-0040
Tel. (809) 776-1291, Fax 774-4971

# Appendix B

# Listing of For-Profit Utilities

Listed in this section are the for-profit electric utilities by state. These electric utilities generate in excess of 75% of all electricity used in the United States.

## FOR-PROFIT UTILITIES

### Alabama

| | |
|---|---|
| Alabama Power Co. | (205) 250-1000 |

### Alaska

| | |
|---|---|
| Alaska Electric Light & Power Co. | (907) 586-2222 |
| Alaska Power & Telephone Co. | (206) 385-1733 |
| Bethel Utilities Corp., Inc. | (907) 562-2500 |
| Haines Light & Power Co., Inc. | (907) 766-2331 |
| McGrath Light & Power | (907) 524-3009 |
| Pelican Utility Co. | (907) 735-2204 |

### Arizona

| | |
|---|---|
| Arizona Public Service Co. | (602) 250-1000 |
| Citizens Utilities Co. | (203) 329-8800 |
| Tucson Electric Power Co. | (602) 622-6661 |

### Arkansas

| | |
|---|---|
| Arkansas Power & Light Co. | (501) 377-4000 |
| Entergy Power, Inc. | (504) 529-5262 |
| Southwestern Electric Power Co. | (318) 222-2141 |

## California

| | |
|---|---|
| Pacific Gas & Electric Co. | (415) 972-7000 |
| Pacific Power & Light Co. | (503) 464-5000 |
| San Diego Gas & Electric Co. | (619) 696-2000 |
| Sierra Pacific Power Co. | (702) 689-4011 |
| Southern California Edison Co. | (818) 302-1212 |

## Colorado

| | |
|---|---|
| Public Service Colorado | (303) 571-7511 |

## Connecticut

| | |
|---|---|
| Bozrah Light & Power Co. | (203) 889-7388 |
| Citizens Utilities Co. | (203) 329-8800 |
| Connecticut Light & Power | (203) 249-5711 |
| Fletcher Electric Light Co. | (413) 569-6158 |
| United Illuminating Co. | (203) 787-7200 |

## Delaware

| | |
|---|---|
| Delmarva Power & Light Co. | (302) 429-3011 |

## District of Columbia

| | |
|---|---|
| Potomac Electric Power Co. | (202) 872-2000 |

## Florida

| | |
|---|---|
| Florida Power & Light Co. | (305) 552-3552 |
| Florida Power Corp. | (813) 866-5151 |
| Florida Public Utilities Co. | (407) 832-2461 |
| Gulf Power Co. | (904) 444-6111 |
| Tampa Electric Co. | (813) 228-4111 |

## Georgia

| | |
|---|---|
| Georgia Power Co. | (404) 526-6526 |
| Savannah Electric & Power Co. | (912) 232-7171 |

## Hawaii

| | |
|---|---|
| Hawaiian Electric Co. | (808) 543-7771 |
| Maui Electric Co. | (808) 871-8961 |

## Idaho

| | |
|---|---|
| Idaho Power Co. | (208) 383-2200 |

## Illinois

| | |
|---|---|
| Central Illinois Public Service | (217) 523-3600 |
| Central Illinois Light Co. | (304) 672-5271 |
| Commonwealth Edison Co. | (312) 294-4321 |
| Illinois Power Co. | (217) 424-6600 |
| Interstate Power Co. | (319) 582-5421 |
| Iowa Illinois Gas & Electric Co. | (319) 326-7111 |
| Mt. Carmel Public Utility Co. | (618) 262-5151 |
| Union Electric Co. | (314) 621-3222 |

## Indiana

| | |
|---|---|
| Indiana Michigan Power Co. | (219) 425-2111 |
| Indianapolis Power & Light | (317) 261-8261 |
| Northern Indiana Public Service | (219) 853-5200 |
| PSI Energy, Inc. | (317) 839-9611 |
| Southern Indiana Gas & Electric | (812) 424-6411 |

## Iowa

| | |
|---|---|
| IES Utilities, Inc. | (319) 398-4411 |
| Interstate Power Co. | (319) 582-5421 |
| Iowa-Illinois Gas & Electric | (319) 326-7111 |
| Iowa Power, Inc. | (515) 281-2900 |
| Iowa Public Service, Co. | (712) 277-7500 |
| Midwest Power Systems | (712) 277-7500 |

## Kansas

| | |
|---|---|
| Centel Corp. | (312) 399-2500 |
| Empire District Electric Co. | (417) 623-4700 |
| Kansas City Power & Light Co. | (816) 556-2200 |
| Kansas Gas & Electric Co. | (316) 261-6611 |
| Southwestern Public Service Co. | (806) 378-2121 |
| Western Resources - KP&L | (913) 296-6300 |

## Kentucky

| | |
|---|---|
| Kentucky Power Co. | (606) 327-1111 |
| Kentucky Utilities Co. | (606) 255-2100 |
| Louisville Gas & Electric Co. | (502) 672-2000 |
| Union Light, Heat & Power | (513) 381-2000 |

## Louisiana

| | |
|---|---|
| Central Louisiana Electric Co. | (318) 484-7400 |
| Gulf States Utilities Co. | (409) 838-6631 |
| Louisiana Power & Light | (504) 366-2345 |
| New Orleans Public Service | (504) 595-3100 |
| Southwestern Electric Power Co. | (318) 222-2141 |

## Maine

| | |
|---|---|
| Bangor Hydro Electric Co. | (207) 945-5621 |
| Central Maine Power Co. | (207) 623-3521 |
| Maine Public Service Co. | (207) 768-5811 |
| Maine Yankee Atomic Power | (207) 622-4868 |

## Maryland

| | |
|---|---|
| Baltimore Gas & Electric Co. | (301) 234-5000 |
| Conowingo Power Co. | (301) 398-1400 |
| Delmarva Power & Light Co. | (302) 429-3011 |
| Potomac Edison Co. | (301) 790-3400 |

## Massachusetts

| | |
|---|---|
| Boston Edison Co. | (617) 424-2000 |
| Cambridge Electric Light Co. | (617) 225-4000 |
| Canal Electric Co. | (617) 291-0950 |
| Commonwealth Electric Co. | (617) 291-0950 |
| Eastern Edison Co. | (617) 580-1213 |
| Fitchburg Gas & Electric Co. | (508) 343-6931 |
| Great Bay Power Corp. | (617) 357-9590 |
| Holyoke Water Power Co. | (413) 536-5520 |
| Massachusetts Electric Co. | (508) 366-9011 |
| Montaup Electric Co. | (617) 678-5283 |
| Nantucket Electric Co. | (617) 228-1870 |
| New England Power Co. | (508) 366-9011 |
| Western Massachusetts Electric Co. | (413) 285-5871 |
| Yankee Atomic Electric Co. | (508) 779-6711 |

## Michigan

| | |
|---|---|
| Consumers Power Co. | (517) 788-0550 |
| Detroit Edison Co. | (313) 237-8000 |
| Edison Sault Electric Co. | (906) 632-2221 |
| Indiana Michigan Power Co. | (219) 425-2111 |
| Upper Peninsula Power Co. | (906) 487-5000 |
| Wisconsin Public Service Co. | (414) 433-1234 |

## Minnesota

| | |
|---|---|
| Interstate Power Co. | (319) 582-5421 |
| Minnesota Power & Light | (218) 722-2641 |
| Northern States Power, Minnesota | (612) 330-5500 |
| Otter Tail Power Co. | (218) 739-8200 |

## Mississippi

| | |
|---|---|
| Mississippi Power & Light | (601) 864-1211 |
| Mississippi Power Co. | (601) 969-2311 |
| System Energy Resources | (601) 984-9000 |

## Missouri

| | |
|---|---|
| Empire District Electric Co. | (417) 623-4700 |
| Kansas City Power & Light | (816) 556-2200 |
| St. Joseph Light & Power | (816) 233-8888 |
| Union Electric Co. | (314) 621-3222 |
| Utilicorp United, Inc. | (816) 421-6000 |

## Montana

| | |
|---|---|
| Black Hills Power & Light Co. | (605) 348-1700 |
| Montana-Dakota Utilities Co. | (701) 722-7900 |
| Montana Power Co. | (406) 723-5421 |

## Nebraska

None

## Nevada

| | |
|---|---|
| Nevada Power Co. | (702) 367-5000 |
| Sierra Pacific Power Co. | (701) 689-4011 |

## New Hampshire

| | |
|---|---|
| Connecticut Valley Electric | (603) 543-3188 |
| Exeter Hampton Electric Co. | (603) 772-5916 |
| Granite State Electric Co. | (603) 448-1290 |
| North Atlantic Energy | (603) 474-9521 |
| Public Service New Hampshire | (603) 669-4000 |
| Rockland Electric Co. | (201) 327-6900 |

## New Jersey

| | |
|---|---|
| Atlantic City Electric Co. | (609) 645-4100 |
| Jersey Central Power & Light | (201) 455-8200 |
| Public Service Electric & Gas | (201) 430-7000 |
| Rockland Electric Co. | (201) 327-6900 |

## New Mexico

| | |
|---|---|
| Public Service New Mexico | (505) 848-2700 |
| Southwestern Public Service Co. | (806) 378-2121 |

## New York

| | |
|---|---|
| Allegheny Generating Co. | (212) 752-2121 |
| Central Hudson Gas & Electric | (914) 452-2000 |
| Consolidated Edison Co. | (212) 460-4600 |
| Long Island Lighting Co. | (516) 933-4590 |
| New York State Electric & Gas | (607) 729-2551 |
| Niagara Mohawk Power Corp. | (315) 474-1511 |
| Orange & Rockland Utility | (914) 352-6000 |
| Pennsylvania Electric Co. | (817) 533-8111 |
| Pike County Light & Power | (914) 856-4422 |
| Rochester Gas & Electric Corp. | (716) 546-2700 |

## North Carolina

| | |
|---|---|
| Carolina Power & Light Co. | (919) 546-6111 |
| Duke Power Co. | (704) 373-4011 |
| Nantahala Power & Light Co. | (704) 524-2121 |
| Virginia Electric & Power Co. | (804) 771-3000 |

## North Dakota

| | |
|---|---|
| Montana-Dakota Utilities | (701) 222-7900 |
| Northern States Power Co. | (612) 330-5500 |
| Otter Tail Power Co. | (218) 739-8200 |

## Ohio

| | |
|---|---|
| Cincinnati Gas & Electric Co. | (513) 381-2000 |
| Cleveland Electric Illuminating Co. | (216) 622-9800 |
| Columbus Southern Power | (614) 464-7700 |
| Dayton Power & Light Co. | (513) 224-6000 |
| Indiana Kentucky Electric Corp. | (614) 289-2376 |
| Monongahela Power Co. | (304) 366-3000 |
| Ohio Edison Co. | (216) 384-5100 |
| Ohio Power Co. | (216) 456-8173 |
| Ohio Valley Electric Corp. | (614) 289-2376 |
| Toledo Edison Co. | (419) 249-5000 |

## Oklahoma

| | |
|---|---|
| Oklahoma Gas & Electric Co. | (405) 272-3000 |
| Public Service Oklahoma | (918) 599-2000 |
| Southwestern Public Service Co. | (806) 378-2121 |

## Oregon

| | |
|---|---|
| Pacificorp | (503) 464-5000 |
| Portland General Electric Co. | (503) 464-8000 |

## Pennsylvania

| | |
|---|---|
| Duquesne Light Co. | (412) 393-6000 |
| Metropolitan Edison Co. | (215) 929-3601 |
| Peco Energy Co. | (215) 841-4000 |
| Pennsylvania Electric Co. | (814) 533-8111 |
| Pennsylvania Power & Light | (215) 774-5151 |
| Pennsylvania Power Co. | (412) 652-5531 |
| Philadelphia Electric Co. | (215) 841-4000 |
| Pike County Light & Power Co. | (717) 296-7323 |
| UGI Utilities, Inc. | (717) 283-0611 |
| Wellsboro Electric Co. | (717) 724-3516 |
| West Penn Power Co. | (412) 837-3000 |
| York Haven Power Co. | (717) 266-3654 |

## Rhode Island

| | |
|---|---|
| Blackstone Valley Electric | (401) 333-1400 |
| Block Island Power Co. | (401) 466-5851 |
| Narragansett Electric Co. | (401) 941-1400 |
| Newport Electric Corp. | (401) 849-4455 |

## South Carolina

| | |
|---|---|
| Carolina Power & Light Co. | (919) 546-6111 |
| Duke Power Co. | (704) 373-4011 |
| Lockhart Power Co. | (803) 545-2211 |
| South Carolina Electric & Gas | (803) 748-3000 |

## South Dakota

| | |
|---|---|
| Black Hills Power & Light | (605) 348-1700 |
| Montana Dakota Utility Co. | (701) 222-7900 |
| Northern States Power Co. | (612) 330-5500 |
| Northwestern Public Service | (605) 352-8411 |
| Otter Tail Power Co. | (218) 739-8200 |

## Tennessee

| | |
|---|---|
| Arkansas Power & Light Co. | (501) 337-4000 |
| Kingsport Power Co. | (615) 378-5000 |

## Texas

| | |
|---|---|
| Central Power & Light Co. | (512) 881-5300 |
| El Paso Electric Co. | (915) 543-5711 |
| Gulf States Utilities | (409) 838-6631 |
| Houston Lighting & Power | (713) 228-9211 |
| Southwestern Electric Service Co. | (214) 741-3125 |
| Southwestern Public Service Co. | (806) 378-2121 |
| Texas Utilities Electric Co. | (214) 812-4600 |
| Texas-New Mexico Power Co. | (817) 731-0099 |
| West Texas Utility Co. | (915) 674-7000 |

## Utah

| | |
|---|---|
| Utah Power & Light Co. | (503) 464-5000 |

## Vermont

| | |
|---|---|
| Central Vermont Public Service | (802) 773-2711 |
| Citizens Utilities Co. | (203) 329-8800 |
| Franklin Electric Light Co. | (802) 285-2912 |
| Green Mountain Power Corp. | (802) 864-5731 |
| Rochester Electric Light & Power | (802) 773-9161 |
| Vermont Electric Co. | (802) 773-9161 |
| Vermont Yankee NUC Power | (802) 257-5271 |

## Virginia

| | |
|---|---|
| Appalachian Power Co. | (203) 329-8800 |
| Delmarva Power & Light Co. | (302) 429-3011 |
| Old Dominion Power Co. | (606) 255-2100 |
| Potomac Edison Co. | (301) 790-3400 |
| Virginia Electric & Power Co. | (804) 771-3000 |

## Washington

| | |
|---|---|
| Pacific Power & Light Co. | (503) 464-5000 |
| Puget Sound Power & Light | (206) 454-6363 |
| Washington Water Power Co. | (509) 489-0500 |

## West Virginia

| | |
|---|---|
| Appalachian Power Co. | (703) 985-2300 |
| Black Diamond Power Co. | (304) 342-2721 |
| Elk Power Co. | (304) 342-2721 |
| Elkhorn Public Service Co. | (304) 342-2721 |
| Kimball Light & Water Co. | (304) 342-2721 |
| Monongahela Power Co. | (304) 366-3000 |
| Potomac Edison Co. | (301) 790-3400 |
| Union Power Co. | (304) 342-2721 |
| United Light & Power Co. | (304) 342-2721 |
| War Light & Power Co. | (304) 342-2721 |
| Whaling Power Co. | (304) 234-3000 |

## Wisconsin

| | |
|---|---|
| Consolidated Water Power | (715) 422-3111 |
| Madison Gas & Electric Co. | (608) 252-7000 |
| Northern States Power Co. | (612) 330-5508 |
| Superior Water, Light & Power | (715) 394-5511 |
| Wisconsin Electric Power Co. | (414) 221-2345 |
| Wisconsin Power & Light | (608) 252-3311 |
| Wisconsin Public Service | (414) 433-1598 |

## Wyoming

| | |
|---|---|
| Black Hills Power & Light Co. | (605) 348-1700 |
| Cheyenne Light Fuel & Power Co. | (307) 638-3361 |
| Pacific Corp. | (503) 464-5000 |

# Appendix C

# Miscellaneous Utility Regulation Information

Listed herein is miscellaneous information relating to regulation of electric utilities. This information courtesy of National Association of Regulatory Utility Commissioners, 1102 Interstate Utility Commerce Commission Building, P.O. Box 684, Washington, DC 20044-0684; Phone (202) 898-2200.

TABLE 1    Agency Authority to Regulate Rates on Retail Sales to End-Users.

TABLE 2    Agency Authority to Regulate Standards for Meter Accuracy, Voltage Levels, Btu Content and Pressure of Natural Gas.

TABLE 3    Provisions for Service in Municipally-Annexed Areas.

TABLE 4    Number of Electric Utilities Subject to Agency Regulation.

TABLE 5    Bill Verification – Electric and Gas.

TABLE 6    Approved Rate Design Features for Electric Utility Customers Served With Demand Meters.

TABLE 7    Costing Methodology for Electric Utilities.

TABLE 8    Seasonal Peaking Electric Utilities, Demand Cost Allocation Methods Used.

**Table 1**   Agency Authority to Regulate Rates on Retail Sales To End-Users

| AGENCY | The Agency has authority to regulate or control rates on retail sales to - | | | | | | Industrial Customers of | |
| | Ultimate Consumers | | | | | | | |
| | ELECTRIC | | | GAS | | | | |
| | Private | Public | Co-op | Private | Public | TELEPHONE | Interstate pipeline companies | Natural gas producers |
|---|---|---|---|---|---|---|---|---|
| FCC | | | | | | X 10/ | | |
| FERC | | 1/ | | | | | 11/ | 11/ |
| ALABAMA PSC 6/ | X | X 6/ | | X | X 6/ | X | | |
| ALASKA PUC | X | X 2/ | X 27/ | X | X | X | | |
| ARIZONA CC | X | | | X | | X | | X |
| ARKANSAS PSC | X | | X | X | | X | | |
| CALIFORNIA PUC 6/ | X | X 6/ | | X | X 6/ | X | | |
| COLORADO PUC | X | | | X | | X | | |
| CONNECTICUT DPUC | X | | | X | | X | | 8/ |
| DELAWARE PSC 6/ | X | X 6/ | | X | X 6/ | X | | 8/ |
| D.C. PSC | X | X | X | X | X | X | | 8/ |
| FLORIDA PSC | X | X 17/ | X 17/ | X | | X | | |
| GEORGIA PSC | X | | | X | | X | | 8/ |
| HAWAII PUC 6/ | X | X 6/ | | X | X 6/ | X | | 8/ |
| IDAHO PUC 6/ | X | X 6/ | | X | X 6/ | X 36/ | | 8/ |
| ILLINOIS CC | X | | | X | | X | X | |
| INDIANA URC | X | X | X | X | X | X | | |
| IOWA UB 32/ | X | | X 23/ | X | | X 14/ | | |
| KANSAS SCC | X | X 4/ | X 37/ | X | X 4/ | X | X 19/ | X |
| KENTUCKY PSC 6/ | X | X 6/ | | X | X | X | | |
| LOUISIANA PSC | X | | | X 15/ | | X | | |
| MAINE PUC | X | X | X | X | X 8/ | X | | 8/ |
| MARYLAND PSC | X | X | X | X | X | X | | |
| MASSACHUSETTS DPU | X | X 5/ | | X | X 5/ | X | | 8/ |
| MICHIGAN PSC | X | | X | X | | X 35/ | X | |
| MINNESOTA PUC 6/ | X | X 6/ | X 23/ | X 28/ | 6/ | X 29/ | | 8/ |
| MISSISSIPPI PSC | X | X 4/ | | X | X 4/ | X | | |
| MISSOURI PSC 38/ | X | | | X | | X 40/ | | |
| MONTANA PSC | X | X | | X | X | X | | |
| NEBRASKA PSC 16/ | | | | X | | X | | |
| NEVADA PSC 6/ | X | X 6/ | 26/ | X | X 6/ | X | | |
| NEW HAMPSHIRE PUC | X | X 3/ | X | X | | X | | 8/ |
| NEW JERSEY BPU 41/ | X | 4/ | | X | | X | | |
| NEW MEXICO PUC | X | 22/ | X | X | | X | | X |
| NEW MEXICO SCC | | | | | | X | | |
| NEW YORK PSC | X 39/ | X 7/ | | X | X 7/ | X | | |
| NORTH CAROLINA UC | X | | | X | | X | X | 8/ |
| NORTH DAKOTA PSC | X | | | X | | X 31/ | | |
| OHIO PUC | X | | | X | | X | | |
| OKLAHOMA CC | X | | X | X | | X | | |
| OREGON PUC | X | | | X | X 8/ | X | | |
| PENNSYLVANIA PUC | X | X 4/ | | X | X 4/ | X | | |
| RHODE ISLAND PUC | X | X | X | X | X | X | | 8/ |
| SOUTH CAROLINA PSC | X | | | X | | X | | 8/ |
| SOUTH DAKOTA PUC | X | | | X | | X 24/ | | |
| TENNESSEE PSC | X | | | X | | X | X | |
| TEXAS PUC | X | X 18/ | X | | | X | | |
| TEXAS RC | | | | X | X 4/ | | | |
| UTAH PSC 6/ | X | X 6/ | | X | X 6/ | X 34/ | | |
| VERMONT PSB 41/ | X | X | X | X | X | X | | 8/ |
| VIRGINIA SCC 6/ | X | X 6/ | X | X | X 6/ | 34/ X 30/ | X | |
| WASHINGTON UTC | X | | | X | | | | |
| WEST VIRGINIA PSC | X | X 25/ | X | X | LTD | X | | |
| WISCONSIN PSC | X | X | 9/ | X | X | X 33/ | 8/ | 8/ |
| WYOMING PSC | X | X 4/ | X | X | X 8/ | | X 19/ | |
| PUERTO RICO PSC 41/ | | | | X | | X 13/ | | 8/ |
| VIRGIN ISLANDS PSC 41/ | | X | | | | X | | 8/ |
| CANADIAN RTC | | | | | | X | | |
| ALBERTA PUB | X | 21/ | | X | | X 22/ | | X 20/ |
| NOVA SCOTIA UARB | X | X | X | X 8/ | X 8/ | | | |
| ONTARIO EB 41/ | | | | X | | | | |
| ONTARIO TSC | | | | | | X | | |
| QUEBEC NGB | | | | X | | | | |
| QUEBEC TB | | | | | | X | | |

**Table 2**  Agency Authority to Regulate Standards for Meter Accuracy, Voltage Levels, BTU Content and Pressure of Gas

The Agency has authority to regulate standards by –

Left group — "Testing meters or by setting standards for the accuracy of meters by establishing standards for measuring voltage and/or cubic feet of gas." (ELECTRIC: Private, Public / GAS: Co-op, Private, Public)

Right group — "Establishing Standards for –" (Electric Voltage Levels: Private, Public, Co-op / BTU Content of Gas: Private, Public / Gas Pressure: Private, Public)

| AGENCY | ELEC Private | ELEC Public | GAS Co-op | GAS Private | GAS Public | Volt Private | Volt Public | Volt Co-op | BTU Private | BTU Public | Gas Pr. Private | Gas Pr. Public |
|---|---|---|---|---|---|---|---|---|---|---|---|---|
| FERC | | | | X | | | | | X 9/ | | X 9/ | |
| ALABAMA PSC | X | | | X | | X | | | X | | X | |
| ALASKA PUC | X | X 7/ | X 6/ | X | X 7/ | X | X 7/ | X 6/ | X | X 7/ | X | X 7/ |
| ARIZONA CC | X | | | X | | X | | X | X | | X | |
| ARKANSAS PSC | X | | | X | | X | | | X | | X | |
| CALIFORNIA PUC | X | | X | X | | X | | | X | | X | |
| COLORADO PUC  8/ | X | | X | X | | X | | X | X | | X | |
| CONNECTICUT DPUC | X | | | X | | X | | | X | | X | X |
| DELAWARE PSC | X | | X | X | | X | | X | X | | X | |
| DC PSC | X | | | X | | X | | | X | | X | |
| FLORIDA PSC | X | | | X | | X | | | X | | X | |
| GEORGIA PSC | X | | | X | | X | | | X | | X | |
| HAWAII PUC | X | | | X | | X | | | X | | X | |
| IDAHO PUC | X | | | X | | X | | | X | | X | |
| ILLINOIS CC | X | | | X | | X | | X | X | | X | X 11/ |
| INDIANA URC | X | | X | X | | X | | X | X | | X | |
| IOWA UB | X | X | X | X | X | X | X | X | X | X | X | X |
| KANSAS SCC | X | X 1/ | X | X | X 1/ | X | X | X 1/ | X | X 1/ | X | X 1/ |
| KENTUCKY PSC | X | X 2/ | X | X | X 2/ | X | X 2/ | X | X | X 2/ | X | X 2/ |
| LOUISIANA PSC | X | | | X | | X | | | X | | X | |
| MAINE PUC | X | X | | X | X | X | X | | X | X | X | X |
| MARYLAND PSC | X | X | X | X | X | X | X | X | X | X | X | X |
| MASSACHUSETTS DPU | X | X | | X | X | X | X | | X | X | X | X |
| MICHIGAN PSC | X | | X | X | 4/ | X | | X | X | 4/ | X | 4/ |
| MINNESOTA PUC | X | | X | X | | X | | X | X | | X | |
| MISSISSIPPI PSC | X | | X | X | | X | | X | X | X | X | X |
| MISSOURI PSC | X | | | X | | X | | | X | | X | |
| MONTANA PSC | X | X | | X | X | X | X | | X | X | X | X |
| NEBRASKA PSC | | | | | | | | | | | | |
| NEVADA PSC | X | | X | X | | X | | X | X | N/A | X | |
| NEW HAMPSHIRE PUC | X | X 2/ | X | X | X 12/ | X | X 2/ | X | X | X 12/ | X | X 12/ |
| NEW JERSEY BPU  14/ | X | X 2/ | | X | X 4/ | X | X 2/ | | X | X 4/ | X | X 4/ |
| NEW MEXICO PUC | X | | X | X | | X | | X | X | | X | |
| NEW MEXICO SCC | | | | | | | | | | | | |
| NEW YORK PSC | X | X 3/ | | X | X | X | X 3/ | | X | X | X | X |
| NORTH CAROLINA UC | X | | | X | | X | | X | X | | X | |
| NORTH DAKOTA PSC | X | X 13/ | X 13/ | X | X 13/ | X | | | X | X | X | |
| OHIO PUC | X | | | X | X | X | | | X | X | X | 5/ |
| OKLAHOMA CC | X | | X | X | | X | | X | X | | X | |
| OREGON PUC | X | | | X | 4/ | X | | | X | 4/ | X | 4/ |
| PENNSYLVANIA PUC | X | | | X | | X | | | X | | X | |
| RHODE ISLAND PUC | X | X | | X | X | X | | | X | | X | X |
| SOUTH CAROLINA PSC | X | | | X | | X | | | X | | X | X |
| SOUTH DAKOTA PUC | X | | | X | | X | | | X | | X | |
| TENNESSEE PSC | X | | | X | | X | | | X | | X | X |
| TEXAS PUC | X | | X | | | X | | X | | | | |
| TEXAS RC | | | | | | | | | | | | |
| UTAH PSC | X | X | X | X | | X | X | X | X | | X | |
| VERMONT PSB  14/ | X | X | X | X | X | X | X | X | X | X | X | |
| VIRGINIA SCC | X | | X | X | | X | | X | X | | X | |
| WASHINGTON UTC | X | | | X | | X | | | X | | X | |
| WEST VIRGINIA PSC | X | X | X | X | X | X | X | X | X | X | X | X |
| WISCONSIN PSC | X | X | | X | X | X | X | | X | X | X | X |
| WYOMING PSC | X | X 2/ | X | X | 4/ | X | X 2/ | X | X | 4/ | X | 4/ |
| PUERTO RICO PSC  14/ | X | | | X | | | | | X | | X | |
| VIRGIN ISLANDS PSC 14/ | | X | | X | | | | | | | | |
| CANADIAN RTC | | | | | | | | | | | | |
| NATL ENERGY BOARD | | | | | | X 11/ | X 11/ | | | | X 11/ | X 11/ |
| ALBERTA PUB  10/ | | | | | | | | | | | | |
| NOVA SCOTIA UARB  10/ | | | | | | | | | | | | |
| ONTARIO EB  14/ | | | | | | | | | | | | |
| QUEBEC NGB | | | | | | | | | X | | X | |

**Table 3**  Provisions for Service in Municipally-Annexed Areas

| AGENCY | Are There Provisions for Service in Areas Annexed by Municipality | Who Resolves Service Area Disputes in Annexed Areas? |
|---|---|---|
| ALABAMA PSC | Yes 37-14-3 and 37-14-32 basis of "closer to" facilities in place as of 1/1/84 | Courts--37-14-9 and 37-14-37 |
| ALASKA PUC | Yes §42.05.221(d) PUC may order exchange of customers and facilities. Also AS 29 | PUC--42.05.221(d) |
| ARIZONA CC | Yes court decision. Municipality may extend service in annexed area, is not required to purchase facilities of utility already serving | CC--40-281[B] |
| ARKANSAS PSC | Yes 23-18-331, exclusive service areas. | PSC or Circuit Court |
| CALIFORNIA PUC | Yes Gov. 37350.5 and Pub. U. 6262, city may purchase by exercise of eminent domain | Generally PUC Pub. U. 1001 |
| COLORADO PUC | Yes 31-15-77 or 40-9.5-203 muni has right to "purchase or condemn" IOU or co-op system | Court |
| CONNECTICUT DPUC | No | Not addressed |
| DELAWARE PSC | Exclusive service areas assigned by PSC/courts | Generally Delaware Supreme Court |
| DC PSC | N/A. No municipal utilities. | |
| FLORIDA PSC | PSC assigns exclusive service areas 366.04[2] | PSC--all service area disputes, 366.04[2e] |
| GEORGIA PSC | Annexation does not change right to serve for IOUs/co-ops/munis already serving 46-3-7 & 9 | PSC--all service area disputes 46-3-13 and 46-3-8[c] and [d] |
| HAWAII PUC | §§49-1 et seq--muni serves annexed area | Not addressed (one electric utility) |
| IDAHO PUC | Yes §61-332B & C--muni required to purchase IOU/co-op facilities previously serving area | District Court--61-334B |
| ILLINOIS CC | Yes 220 ILCS §414 (1993)--previously serving supplier may continue to serve. | CC--220 ILCS §411 (1993) CC approves service territory agreements between muni/co-op |
| INDIANA URC | Yes 8-1-2.3-3 assigns exclusive service area. 8-1-2.3-6 governs change in service area. Muni may apply to service annexed area. | URC (appeal to Court of Appeals) |
| IOWA UB | Annexation does not change right of current utility to serve §476.26. Exclusive service territory under §476.25. | |
| KANSAS SCC | Yes §66-1, 176--muni may terminate IOU/co-op service 180 days after annexation, ir required to purchase IOU/co-op facilities in order to serve annexed area. | SCC--all service area disputes 66-1, 174 |
| KENTUCKY PSC | Yes §96.538--certified supplier has dominant right to continue service. | PSC--all service area disputes |
| LOUISIANA PSC | Yes Court decisions--muni may refuse franchise to IOU/co-op, which may not extend service, but may continue service to existing customers | PSC for IOUs/co-ops, not for municipals |
| MAINE PUC | Yes T. 30, §4251.6--muni has right to purchase or acquire by eminent domain facilities of other suppliers. | PUC--all service area disputes Title 35 §2301 |
| MARYLAND PSC | Does not have exclusive service territories. MAC Article 78 §53--co-ops or IOUs. | Not addressed |
| MASSACHUSETTS DPU | No. | Not addressed (DPU elsewhere Ch. 164, §47) |
| MICHIGAN PSC | Yes §117.4f and 213.111--muni has right to purchase other suppliers facilities. | PSC for IOUs/co-ops, Court for municipals |
| MINNESOTA PUC | Yes §216B.41--Annexation does not affect right of current supplier to serve area. | PUC--all service area disputes 216B.39 |
| MISSISSIPPI PSC | Court can enjoin muni from extending service into newly annexed area already served by a regulated utility. | PSC for IOUs/co-ops, Court for municipals |
| MISSOURI PSC | Non-exclusive service areas; territorial agreements between power suppliers subject to PSC approval. §394.312 | Not specified, probably courts |
| MONTANA PSC | Yes §69-5-109--current supplier may continue to serve existing customers, but not expand. | District Court (69-5-110) for all service area disputes |
| NEBRASKA PSC | Power Review Board approves muni application. | Power Review Board--all service area disputes |
| NEVADA PSC | §§704.330 & 704.340 grant exclusive area. | PSC--all service area disputes 704.330 & .340 |
| NEW HAMPSHIRE PUC | PUC allocates exclusive area §374.22 Ch. 38 governs muni acquisition of utility | PUC--all service area disputes 374:22 |
| NEW JERSEY BPU | Munis may extend without BRC approval 40:62-22 | BRC--all service area disputes 48:7-5 |
| NEW MEXICO PUC | Franchises are non-exclusive; if city and annexed area served by 2 different regulated utilities, PUC decides who serves annexed area | PUC--disputes between public utilities; presumably courts for municipals |
| NEW YORK PSC | Non-exclusive service areas; muni has right, subject to local law and referendum, to construct, purchase or condemn facilities. Gen. Mun. Law Article 14A, §360(6). | Not addressed |
| NORTH CAROLINA UC | Co-ops/IOUs have exclusive right to serve premises wholly within 300 feet of their lines in existence as of annexation date if premises are wholly more than 300 feet from muni lines. | UC for IOUs/co-ops, courts for municipals |

**Table 3** Provisions for Service in Municipally-Annexed Areas (Continued)

| AGENCY | Are There Provisions for Service in Areas Annexed by Municipality | Who Resolves Service Area Disputes in Annexed Areas? |
|---|---|---|
| NORTH DAKOTA PSC | Yes §40-33-01 for municipalities; utility lawfully serving municipality may expand with certificate §49-03-01 | PSC--all service area disputes 49-03-01.4 |
| OHIO PUC | Munis have constitutional authority to appropriate needed facilities, but no obligation. | PUC for IOUs/co-ops, not for municipals |
| OKLAHOMA CC | IOUs/co-ops serving pre-annexation may continue to serve. 17 OS 1981, §158.21 | Not addressed--CC elsewhere 17 OS 1981 158.24 |
| OREGON PUC | City has right to condemn private property for its use in providing power service. 223.005(3) | PUC--758.400 et seq |
| PENNSYLVANIA PUC | Munis have no right to serve; co-op/IOU which had closest distribution line in 1975 has exclusive right to serve. Tit. 15, §3277 et seq | PUC (appeal to Commonwealth Court) T 15 §3281 |
| RHODE ISLAND PUC | No, other than cities/towns have power to grant franchises; non-exclusive service area. | Not addressed |
| SOUTH CAROLINA PSC | Muni may serve in adjacent territory if granted certificate §58-27-1230; existing supplier retains all current customers and those within 300 feet of lines §58-27-620. | PSC or courts for all service area disputes §58-27-650[B] |
| SOUTH DAKOTA PUC | Annexing municipality which owns its system may purchase other suppliers' facilities in area annexed. §49-34A-49 | PUC for all service area disputes §49-34A-43 |
| TENNESSEE PSC | Munis have power of eminent domain. §7-34-104[1]. §54-34-105 authorizes munis and co-ops to acquire service areas and equipment of non-consumer owned electric companies. | PSC 65-4-201 et seq; courts for municipals and co-ops (exempt from PSC authority) |
| TEXAS PUC | Muni has no right to serve or purchase without certificate of convenience and necessity, Tit. 32, Ch. 10, Art. 1446c, §50[2] and 55, unless there is no other service provider. | PUC or courts for all service area disputes Tit. 32, Ch. 10, Art. 1446c, art. VII |
| UTAH PSC | Munis have primary right to serve area; must pay fair market compensation to co-op/IOU for dedicated facilities. 10-8-14, -20, -21, and 10-2-401[4]. | Courts for dispute involving municipality; courts/PSC for dispute between city/co-op/IOU PSC for dispute between co-op/IOU/non-muni. |
| VERMONT PSB | Munis serve annexed areas. Tit. 30, §2902 | PSB--all service area disputes T 30, §249 |
| VIRGINIA SCC | Existing supplier may continue to serve in certified area until municipality exercises purchase option. 56-265.4:2 and court decision | SCC--all service area disputes §56.265.3 |
| WASHINGTON UTC | Exclusive service area franchise not permitted Munis may purchase other suppliers' facilities in certain instances. 35.92.054 and 35.84.020 | UTC has authority to authorize service area agreements between public and private utilities. |
| WEST VIRGINIA PSC | Munis may exercise eminent domain Code 8-19-3 | PSC--all service area disputes Code 24-2-1 |
| WISCONSIN PSC | Muni may not extend service area without consent of existing utility or determination by PSC that existing service is inadequate. 196.495 and 196.50. Special rule for co-ops. | PSC--all service area disputes §196.50 and 196.495[1][b] |
| WYOMING PSC | Municipality may exercise right of condemnation. §1-26-804 and 1-26-808; court decisions | Courts or PSC |

**Table 4**   Number of Electric Utilities Subject to Agency Regulation

| AGENCY | Private | Citation of Jurisdictional Authority | Public | Citation of Jurisdictional Authority | Co-op | Citation of Jurisdictional Authority |
|---|---|---|---|---|---|---|
| | | | | Electric | | |
| | | | | Power Marketing Agencies | | |
| FERC | 179 | 16 USC 791 et seq        5/ | 5 | 16 USC 791 et. seq.      5/ | 3 | 16 USC 791 et seq |
| ALABAMA PSC | 1 | §37, Code AL 1975 | 0 | No jurisdiction §37-1-34 | 0 | No jurisdiction §37-6-27 |
| ALASKA PUC | 22 | §6, Ch 113 SLA 1970 | 2 | §6, Ch 113 SLA 1970 | 11 | §6, Ch 113 SLA 1970 |
| ARIZONA CC | 5 | Art XV, AZ Constitution | 0 | No jurisdiction | 11 | Art XV, AZ Constitution |
| ARKANSAS PSC | 4 | A.C.A. 23-4-201 | 15 | Safety only | 18 | A.C.A. 23-18-308 |
| CALIFORNIA PUC | 3 | CA PU Code §701 | 0 | CA PU Code §8029.5-8057 Limited jurisdiction | 4 | PU Code 216, 217, 218, 2777 |
| COLORADO PUC | 2 | § 40-1-103 CRS 1993 | 16 | § 40-1-103 CRS 1993 | 28 | § 40-1-103 CRS 1993        9/ |
| CONNECTICUT DPUC | 3 | Title 16, CT Gen. Stat. | 0 | No jurisdiction | 0 | None in category |
| DELAWARE PSC | 1 | Delaware Code, Title 26 | 0 | No jurisdiction | 1 | DE Code, Title 26 |
| DC PSC | 1 | DC Code, Title 43 et seq | 0 | None in category | 0 | None in category |
| FLORIDA PSC | 5 | Ch. 366 | 33 | Ch. 366 (rate structure and territory) | 17 | Ch. 366 (rate structure and territory) |
| GEORGIA PSC | 2 | Title 46 | 52 | Title 46 §3-13 & 3-8[c] & [d] territory only | 42 | Title 46 Territory and Finance only |
| HAWAII PUC | 5 | Ch. 269, HI Rev. Stats. | 0 | None in category | 0 | None in category |
| IDAHO PUC | 5 | Title 61, Idaho Code | 0 | No jurisdiction | 0 | No jurisdiction |
| ILLINOIS CC | 10 | 220 ILCS 5 | 0 | §11-117-1.1 (1993)--service territory only | 0 | §11-117-1.1 (1993)--service territory only |
| INDIANA URC | 5 | IC 8-1-2-1 et seq. | 42 | IC 8-1-2-1 et seq. (Rates and territory) | 46 | IC 8-1-13-18, 8-1-2-1 |
| IOWA UB | 2 | IA Code Ch 476 & 478 | 110 | IA Code Ch 476 & 478 but not rates | 54 | IA Code Ch 476 & 478 |
| KANSAS SCC | 9 | Ch 66, KS Stat. Ann. | 14 | Ch 66, KS Stat. Ann. | 25 | Ch 66, KS Stat. Ann.    12/ |
| KENTUCKY PSC | 5 | Ch 278, KY Rev. Stats. | 0 | No jurisdiction - rates | 24 | Ch 278, KY Rev. Stats. |
| LOUISIANA PSC | 4 | State Constitution | 0 | Revised Statutes | 15 | RS 12:409(g)417.1, Const. |
| MAINE PUC | 6 | 35-A MRSA | 6 | 35-A MRSA (Rates outside corp. limits, territory) | 5 | 35-A MRSA |
| MARYLAND PSC | 5 | Ann. Code MD, Article 78 | 4 | Ann. Code MD, Article 78 | 4 | Ann. Code MD, Article 78 |
| MASSACHUSETTS DPU | 8 | Chapter 164 | 40 | Chapter 164 (limited) 1/ | 0 | No jurisdiction |
| MICHIGAN PSC | 9 | Act 106, PA 1909, Amen. | 0 | No jurisdiction | 14 | Act 106, PA 1909, Amended |
| MINNESOTA PSC | 2 | Ch. 216B (1974)        6/ | 126 | Ch. 216B (1974)        6/ (Territory/complaints) | 54 | Ch. 216B (1974)        6/ |
| MISSISSIPPI PSC | 2 | PU Act 1956 (Amended) PU Act 1983 | 21 | PU Act 1956 (Amended), PU Act 1983 | 28 | PU Act 1956 (Amended), PU Act 1983 |
| MISSOURI PSC | 6 | §386.250 RSMO supp. 1992 | 0 | No jurisdiction | 46 | Safety only-394.160 RsMO |
| MONTANA PSC | 5 | Title 69, MCA | 1 | Title 69, Ch. 7, MCA (Certain increases only) | 0 | No jurisdiction |
| NEBRASKA PSC | 0 | None in category | 0 | No jurisdiction | 0 | No jurisdiction |
| NEVADA PSC | 3 | NRS 704.020 | 0 | No jurisdiction - rates | 11 | NRS 704.673-704.677 |
| NEW HAMPSHIRE PUC | 11 | RSA 362:2 | 3 | RSA 362:2 Outside municipal limits only    10/ | 1 | RSA 362:2 |
| NEW JERSEY BPU 13/ | 4 | NJSA 48:2-13, et.seq. | 1 | Outside corporate limits | 1 | NJSA 48:2-13, et.seq. |
| NEW MEXICO PUC | 4 | NMSA 1978, §62-3-1, 62-31.1 | 0 | NMSA 1978, §62-6-5 (can petition for regulation) | 20 | NMSA 1978, §62-8-7 |
| NEW YORK PSC | 2 4/ | Pub. Serv. Law §2(12) (13), 5(1)(b) and Art 4 | 3 2/ | Pub. Service Law, §2 (16), 5(1)(b) and Art 4 | 5 | Rural Elec. Co-op Law §67 |
| NORTH CAROLINA UC | 7 | NCGS Ch 62, 3(23)a.1 | 0 | No jurisdiction | 0 | NC GS Ch 62, 110.2 et seq |
| NORTH DAKOTA PSC | 3 | 49-02-01 NDCC | 0 | No jurisdiction | 0 | No jurisdiction |
| OHIO PUC | 9 | Title 49, Ohio Rev. Code | 0 | No jurisdiction | 0 | No jurisdiction |
| OKLAHOMA CC | 4 | Title 17, §151 et seq | 0 | No jurisdiction | 31 | Title 17, §158.21        11/ |
| OREGON PUC | 3 | OR Rev. Stats, Ch 756, 757 | 0 | None, except safety, territory, curtailment | 19 | Safety, territory, curtailment |
| PENNSYLVANIA PUC | 12 | Tit. 15, §3277 et seq | 4 | Outside corporate limits | 0 | No jurisdiction |
| RHODE ISLAND PUC | 4 | Title 39, Chapter 2 | 1 | Title 39, Chapter 2 | 0 | None in category |
| SOUTH CAROLINA PSC | 4 | 58-27-140 | | Territory 58-27-610 | | Territory 58-27-610 |
| SOUTH DAKOTA PUC | 6 | SDCL 49-34A and 49-41B | 34 | 49-34A and 49-41B Territory & siting only | 35 | 49-34A and 49-41B Territory & siting only |
| TENNESSEE PSC | 5 | 65-4-101 | 0 | No jurisdiction | 26 | 67-901 for Ad Valorem assessment only |
| TEXAS PUC | 10 | VTCS, Art 1446c | 71 | VTCS, Art 1446c        7/ Outside corporate limits | 87 | VTCS, Art 1446c |
| UTAH PSC | 2 | UT Code, §54-2-1(19) | 1 | UT Code, § 17-6-1.1 | 0 | UT Code, §54-2-1(19) |
| VERMONT PSB    13/ | 10 | 30 VSA | 15 | 30 VSA | 2 | 30 VSA |
| VIRGINIA SCC | 5 | VA Code, Title 56 | 0 | No jurisdiction - rates | 13 | VA Code, Title 56 |
| WASHINGTON UTC | 2 | Title 80, RCW | 0 | No jurisdiction | 0 | No jurisdiction |
| WEST VIRGINIA PSC | 10 | WV Code, Ch. 24 | 2 | Limited review authority | 3 | WV Code, Ch. 24 |
| WISCONSIN PSC | 7 | Chapter 196 | 82 | Chapter 196 | 0 | No jurisdiction |
| WYOMING PSC | 8 | §37-1-101 WY Stats 1977 | 17 | §37-1-101 Outside municipal limits only | 1 | §37-1-101 WY Stats 1977 |

**Table 4**  Number of Electric Utilities Subject to Agency Regulation (Continued)

| AGENCY | Pri-vate | Citation of Jurisdic-tional Authority | Public | Citation of Jurisdic-tional Authority | Co-op | Citation of Jurisdic-tional Authority |
|--------|------|------|--------|------|------|------|
| | | | | Electric | | |
| PUERTO RICO PSC | | None in jurisdiction | | No jurisdiction | 13/ | None in jurisdiction |
| VIRGIN ISLANDS PSC | | | | Title 30, VIC, §1 Amen. | 13/ | |
| CANADIAN AGENCIES | | | | | | |
| ALBERTA PUB | 3 | PUB Act, EEM Act | 9 3/ | §291 Mun. Govt. Act | 165 | Hydro & Elec Energy Act |
| NOVA SCOTIA UARB | 1 | PU Act RSNS 1989, C.380 | 7 | PU Act RSNS 1989, C.380 | 0 | |
| ONTARIO EB | 0 | No jurisdiction | 0 | No jurisdiction | 0 | Does not regulate elec. |

## FOOTNOTES – TABLE 4

1/  One small municipal electric plant on Cuttyhunk Island exempted from Department jurisdiction under 1936 Act of Legislature.

2/  Plus 41 under jurisdiction of NY Power Authority. §1014 of the Public Authorities Law exempts the Power Authority from regulation by the Commission except for siting transmission and generation facilities under Article 7 and 8 and §18(a) of the Public Service Law. Municipalities which buy power from the Power Authority are also exempt from regulation by the PSC under §1005(5)(g) of the Public Authorities Law.

3/  Under partial Board jurisdiction. One municipally owned utility also under Board jurisdiction pursuant to Electric Energy Marketing Act.

4/  Excludes companies regulated from safety standpoint only.

5/  FERC has no jurisdiction over municipal electric utilities; FERC hydro regulation under Part I of FPA includes 82 private utilities and 294 municipals.

6/  Gas and electric regulation established April 12, 1974; rate regulation effective January 1, 1975.

7/  Municipals may elect Commission regulation. Certification required of all retail public utilities, including municipalities and political subdivisions. Four state affiliated river authorities under PUC jurisdiction for rates.

8/  Includes two state owned electric utilities.

9/  The rates of only 1 of the co-ops are under Commission regulation; Colorado still regulates the certificates, service territories, safety and consumer complaints of all cooperatives. Effective 1983, co-ops were permitted to exempt themselves from state agency rate regulation upon a ballot procedure. State commission has jurisdiction over municipal utilities only outside corporate limits and then only if rates charged outside corporate limits differ from rates charged inside corporate limits.

10/  And only if rates charged outside municipal limits are different from those charged within municipal limits.

11/  New law (HB1406), signed in early 1993 allows rural electric co-ops with fewer than 17,000 meters to vote to opt out of state regulation; as of May 1994, two co-ops had done so.

12/  Statute enacted in 1992 allows rural electric co-ops with fewer than 17,000 meters to opt out of state regulation; as of May 1994, 18 co-ops had done so.

13/  Commission did not respond to requests for update information; this data may not be current.

## Table 5   Bill Verification – Electric and Gas

| AGENCY | Uniform practices for billing format? Electric | Gas | D15 - Checking the accuracy of billing. What resources are available to customers to check accuracy of their bills? SEE KEY BELOW | Bills must contain - a. All back-up data | b. Enough data so that a customer can calculate | D 16 Bills are itemized for - a. Regular Service Charges | b. Other Recurring Charges | c. Special Charges | D 17 Agency has analyzed utility billing procedures | Comment |
|---|---|---|---|---|---|---|---|---|---|---|
| ALABAMA PSC | | | A, B | YES | NO | YES | NO | --- | YES | |
| ALASKA PUC | NO | NO | A, B | YES | Usually | Some | Some | Varies | NO | |
| ARIZONA CC | | | A, B | YES | NO | YES | YES | YES | NO | |
| ARKANSAS PSC | NO | NO | A, B, D | NO | Usually | YES | YES | varies | NO | |
| CALIFORNIA PUC | | | A, B, C, D | YES | YES | YES | YES | YES | YES | |
| COLORADO PUC | | | A, B | YES | YES | YES | YES | YES | YES | |
| CONNECTICUT DPUC 17/ | NO | NO | A, B, C, D | YES | YES | YES | YES | YES | YES | |
| DELAWARE PSC | NO | NO | A, B | YES | NO | YES | YES | YES | YES 12/ | |
| DC PSC | YES | YES | A, B | YES | YES-GAS | YES | YES | YES | YES | |
| FLORIDA PSC | YES | YES | A, B, C, D | YES | YES | YES | YES | YES | YES | |
| GEORGIA PSC | NO | | A, B | YES | NO | YES | NO 1/ | --- | YES | |
| HAWAII PUC | NO | YES | A, B, D | YES | YES | YES | YES | YES | YES 12/ | |
| IDAHO PUC | NO | NO | A, B, C, D | YES | YES | YES | YES | YES | YES | 2/ |
| ILLINOIS CC | YES | YES | A, B, C, D | YES | NO 4/ | Varies | Varies | Varies | YES | |
| INDIANA URC | NO | NO | A, B, D | YES | NO | YES | YES | NO | NO | |
| IOWA UB | NO | NO | A, B | YES | NO | NO | YES | YES | NO | |
| KANSAS SCC | NO | NO | A, B | YES | YES | YES | YES | YES | NO | |
| KENTUCKY PSC | NO | NO | A, B | NO | Varies | Varies | Varies | Varies | YES | 5/ |
| LOUISIANA PSC | | | A, B, C, D | NO | --- | YES | YES | NO | NO | 6/ |
| MAINE PUC | NO | NO | A, B, D | YES | YES | Varies | Varies | Varies | YES | |
| MARYLAND PSC | | | A, B, C, D 15/ | YES | YES | YES | YES | YES | YES 12/ | |
| MASSACHUSETTS DPU | NO | NO | A, B, D | NO | YES | YES | YES | YES | YES | 2/ |
| MICHIGAN PSC | NO | NO | A, B, C | YES | YES | YES | YES | YES | YES | 7/ |
| MINNESOTA PUC | | | A, B | YES | YES | YES | YES | YES | YES | |
| MISSISSIPPI PSC | | | A, B | YES | NO | YES | YES | YES | YES | 8/ |
| MISSOURI PSC | NO | NO | A, B, D | NO | NO 13/ | YES | NO | YES | NO | |
| MONTANA PSC | NO | NO | A, B, C, D | YES | YES | YES | YES | YES | NO | |
| NEBRASKA PSC | N/A | N/A | Does not regulate electric or gas | | | | | | | |
| NEVADA PSC 16/ | YES | YES | A, B | YES | YES | YES | YES | YES | YES | |
| NEW HAMPSHIRE PUC | NO | NO | A, B | YES | YES | YES | YES | YES | YES | 7/ |
| NEW JERSEY BPU 20/ | | | A, B, D | YES | YES | YES | YES | YES | NO | |
| NEW MEXICO PUC | | | A, B, C, D | YES | YES | YES | YES | YES | NO | |
| NEW YORK PSC | | | A, B | YES | YES 3/ | YES | YES | YES | YES | |
| NORTH CAROLINA UC | NO | NO | A, B, C, D | YES | NO | YES | NO | 10/ | YES | |
| NORTH DAKOTA PSC | NO | NO | A, B, C, D | YES | YES | YES | YES | YES | YES | |
| OHIO PUC | YES | YES | A, B, C, D | YES | YES | YES | YES | YES | YES | |
| OKLAHOMA CC | | | A, B | YES | NO | NO | NO | YES | YES | |
| OREGON PUC | NO | NO | A, B, C, D | YES | YES | YES | YES | Varies | NO | |
| PENNSYLVANIA PUC 18/ | NO | NO | A, B, C, D | NO | YES | YES | YES | YES | YES | |
| RHODE ISLAND PUC | | | A, B, C, D | YES | NO | YES | YES | NO | YES | |
| SOUTH CAROLINA PSC | NO | NO | A, B, C, D | YES | NO | YES | NO | YES | YES | |
| SOUTH DAKOTA PUC | NO | NO | A, B, C, D | YES | Varies | YES | YES | YES | YES | |
| TENNESSEE PSC | YES | NO | A, B, C, D | YES | NO | YES | YES | NO | NO | |
| TEXAS PUC 19/ | NO | N/A | A, B, C, D | YES | YES | YES | YES | Varies | NO | |
| TEXAS RC | N/A | YES | A, B, C, D | NO | NO | YES | YES | Varies | YES | |
| UTAH PSC | NO | NO | A, B, C, D | YES | NO | YES | YES | YES | YES | |
| VERMONT PSB 20/ | | | A, B | YES | NO | YES | YES | YES | YES | |
| VIRGINIA SCC | NO | NO | A, B, C, D | YES | NO | YES | YES | YES | NO | |
| WASHINGTON UTC | NO | NO | A, B | YES | YES | YES | YES | YES | YES | 14/ |
| WEST VIRGINIA PSC | | | A, B, C, D | YES | YES | YES | YES | YES | YES | |
| WISCONSIN PSC | | | A, B, C, D | YES | YES | YES | YES | YES | YES | 9/ |
| WYOMING PSC | | | A, B, D | YES | YES | YES | YES | YES | NO | |
| VIRGIN ISLANDS PSC 20/ | YES | N/A | A, B | YES | YES | YES | YES | YES | NO | |
| ALBERTA PUB | | | A, B | YES | NO | YES | YES | YES | NO | |
| BRITISH COLUMBIA UC | NO | NO | A, B, C, D | YES | NO | YES | YES | YES | YES | |
| NOVA SCOTIA UARB | NO | N/A | A, B | YES | YES | YES | YES | YES | YES | |
| ONTARIO EB 20/ | | | A, B, C | YES | | YES | YES | YES | NO | 11/ |
| QUEBEC NGB | N/A | YES | Rate Structure on invoice | YES | YES | YES | YES | YES | YES | |

A = Utility will assist customer
B = Agency will assist customer
C = Utility will provide copy of rate sheet(s) or tariff on request.
D = Utility will test meter on request
E = Other (specify)

**Table 5**   Bill Verification – Electric and  (Continued)

## FOOTNOTES – TABLE 5

1/     For instance, Atlanta Gas Light shows PGA and franchise tax separately on bill, but Georgia Power does not show fuel cost recovery and franchise taxes separately.

2/     Billing procedures reviewed by Consumer Assistance division staff for testimony in general rate cases.

3/     Commission in FAll 1985 directed utilities to provide plain language bills.

4/     Some utilities periodically send rate brochures to customers from which they can calculate bills.

5/     In connection with rate cases or complaints on a case-by-case basis.

6/     Tariffs constantly under review and policies revised as needed.

7/     Audits of utility company practices as they relate to Commission Billing Rules.

8/     Recently revised rules for utility service and maintain ongoing analysis for individuals at their request.

9/     Has expanded number of itemized billing components and provided energy conservation information.

10/     Generally stated separately but not specifically described.

11/     Guidelines for retail credit, collection and cut-off practices of public utility suppliers issued by Ministry of Energy. Compliance is not legally required but used as benchmark for accepted practices.

12/     Commission reviews billing procedures annually.

13/     Commission rules do not require companies to provide rate structures on bills, but some do.

14/     Utilities required to send all customers a reference guide explaining billing methods annually.

16/     Commission adopted Consumer Bill of Rights to standardize billing practices.

17/     Agency has established rules requiring certain information; the format varies from company to company.

18/     1992 policy statement directed companies to provide plain language bills; regulations outline information to be included on bill but do not prescribe a format.

19/     In 1995, PUC is considering foreign language rules for billing non-English-speaking customers.

20/     Commission did not respond to request for update information; this data may not be current.

**Table 6**   Approved Rate Design Features for Electric Utility Customers
Served with Demand Meters

| AGENCY | Demand Ratchets | Declining-Block Energy Rates | Declining-Block Demand Rates | Flat Energy Rates | Flat Demand Rates | Inverted Energy Rates | Inverted Demand Rates | Seasonal Rates | Power Factor Corrections |
|---|---|---|---|---|---|---|---|---|---|
| ALABAMA PSC | C,I | C,I | | C,I | C,I | | | C,I | C,I |
| ALASKA PUC | C,I | | | C,I | C,I | | | C,I | C,I |
| ARIZONA CC | I | C,I | | C,I | C,I | | | C,I | C,I |
| ARKANSAS PSC | C,I | C,I | | C,I | C,I | | | C,I | C,I |
| CALIFORNIA PUC | I | | | C,I | C,I | | | C,I | C,I |
| COLORADO PUC | C,I | | | C,I | C,I | | | C,I | C,I |
| CONNECTICUT DPUC | C,I | 3/ | | | C,I | | | C,I | C,I |
| DELAWARE PSC | C,I | | | C,I | C,I | | | C,I | C,I |
| DC PSC 1/ | C,I | | | | C | | | C | C |
| FLORIDA PSC | | | | C,I | C,I | | | | C,I |
| GEORGIA PSC | C,I | C,I | | | | | | C,I | C,I |
| HAWAII PUC | C,I | C,I | | C | C | | | | C,I |
| IDAHO PUC | | | | C,I | C,I | | | C | C,I |
| ILLINOIS CC | C | C,I | C,I | C,I | C,I | | | C,I | C,I |
| INDIANA URC | C,I | C,I | C,I | C,I | C,I | | | | C,I |
| IOWA UB | C,I | C,I | C,I | C,I | C,I | | | C,I | C,I |
| KANSAS SCC | C,I | C,I | C,I | C,I | C,I | | | C,I | C,I |
| KENTUCKY PSC | C,I | C,I | C,I | C,I | C,I | | | C,I | C,I |
| LOUISIANA PSC | C,I | C,I | C,I | | | | | | C,I |
| MAINE PUC | C,I | | | C,I | | | | C,I | I |
| MARYLAND PSC | C,I | C,I | | C,I | C,I | | | C,I | C,I |
| MASSACHUSETTS DPU | | C,I | | C,I | C,I | | C,I | C,I | C,I |
| MICHIGAN PSC | C,I | C,I | C,I | C,I | C,I | | | C,I | C,I |
| MINNESOTA PUC | C,I | C,I 2/ | I 2/ | C,I | C,I | | | C,I | C,I |
| MISSISSIPPI PSC | C,I | C,I | C,I | C,I | | | | | C,I |
| MISSOURI PSC | C,I | C,I | C,I | C,I | C,I | | | C,I | C,I |
| MONTANA PSC | I | C | | C,I | C,I | | C,I | C,I | C,I |
| NEBRASKA PSC | | | | | | | | | |
| NEVADA PSC | | | | C,I | C,I | | | C,I | C,I |
| NEW HAMPSHIRE PUC | C,I | C,I | C,I | C,I | C,I | | | C,I | C,I |
| NEW JERSEY BPU | C,I | C,I | C,I | C,I | | | C | C,I | |
| NEW MEXICO PUC | C,I | C,I | | C,I | C,I | | C,I | C,I | C,I |
| NEW YORK PSC | C,I | C,I | C,I | C,I | C,I | | | C,I | C,I |
| NORTH CAROLINA UC | C,I | C,I | C,I | C,I | C,I | | | C,I | I |
| NORTH DAKOTA PSC | C,I | C,I | | C,I | C,I | | | C,I | C,I |
| OHIO PUC | C,I | C,I | C,I | C,I | C,I | C,I | C,I | C,I | C,I |
| OKLAHOMA CC | C,I | C,I | | C,I | | C,I | | C | |
| OREGON PUC | C,I | C | | C,I | C,I | | C | C,I | C,I |
| PENNSYLVANIA PUC | C,I | C,I | I | | C,I | | | C,I | C,I |
| RHODE ISLAND PUC | | | | | | | | | |
| SOUTH CAROLINA PSC | C,I | C,I | C,I | C,I | C,I | C,I | | C,I | C,I |
| SOUTH DAKOTA PUC | C,I | C,I | C,I | | | | | C,I | C,I |
| TENNESSEE PSC | C,I | C | | I | C,I | | | | C,I |
| TEXAS PUC | | | | | | | | | |
| UTAH PSC | C,I | C,I | | C,I | C,I | | C,I | | C,I |
| VERMONT PSB | | | | | | | | | |
| VIRGINIA SCC | C,I | C,I | C,I | C,I | C,I | | | C,I | C,I |
| WASHINGTON UTC | C,I | | | C,I | C,I | | | C,I | |
| WEST VIRGINIA PSC | C,I | C,I | | C,I | C,I | | | | C,I |
| WISCONSIN PSC | C,I | | | C,I | C,I | | | | I |
| WYOMING PSC | C,I | C,I | C,I | C,I | C,I | | | C,I | C,I |
| ALBERTA PUB | C,I | C,I | I | | C | | | I 4/ | I |
| BRITISH COL. UC | I | C | | I | I | | C | C | C,I |
| NOVA SCOTIA UARB | C,I | C,I | | | | | | | C,I |

1/   There are no industrial rates offered.

2/   Phasing out declining-block rates.

3/   Energy rates decline as hours of use increase.

4/   As well as certain other large use customers.

### Table 7  Costing Methodology for Electric Utilities

| AGENCY (SEE KEYS BELOW) | Which Principles are Used Most Often in Establishing Rate Designs in General Rate Cases (SEE KEY BELOW) | Agency Uses or Has Approved a System Expansion Model to Calculate Marginal Costs? Which One; # of Years | To Allocate Costs Among Customer Classes, Agency Uses: (SEE KEY BELOW) | To Allocate Costs to Establish Rates Within Customer Classes, Agency Uses: | If Marginal Cost Principle is Used, Which Used to Reconcile w/Revenue Requirement |
|---|---|---|---|---|---|
| ALABAMA PSC | Approaching R | No | E | E | |
| ALASKA PUC | A | No | E | E | |
| ARIZONA CC | Varies | UPLAN, 10 years | E | Combination | |
| ARKANSAS PSC | R | No | E | E | |
| CALIFORNIA PUC | R | No | L | L | Equal %age Adj. |
| COLORADO PUC | R | Pending IRP rules | E | E | |
| CONNECTICUT DPUC | R | Done by Utilities | E | E | |
| DELAWARE PUC | R | No | E | E | |
| DC PSC | M | PROMOD/Zinder, 20 yrs | L | | Inverse Elastic. |
| FLORIDA PSC | R | Utility model reviewed | E | E | |
| GEORGIA PSC | A | No | E | E | |
| HAWAII PUC | R | No | E | E | |
| IDAHO PUC | R | No | E | E | |
| ILLINOIS CC | CC seeks class parity in marginal cost recovery. | NERA methodology - 10 years | S | Other | Equal %age Adjustment |
| INDIANA URC | R | Yes | E | E | |
| IOWA UB | R | No | E | E--w/some allowance | |
| KANSAS SCC | R | No | E | E | |
| KENTUCKY PSC | R | No | E | E | |
| LOUISIANA PSC | A | No | E | E | |
| MAINE PUC | M (Some still use R) | UPLAN (energy), 5 yrs | L (Some use E) | L | Equal %age Adj. |
| MARYLAND PSC | R | Company-specific, 30 Y | E | Combination | Customer/Demand |
| MASSACHUSETTS DPU | R | No | E | S-energy; L-demand | Fully Distrib. |
| MICHIGAN PSC | R | No | E | E | |
| MINNESOTA PUC | R | No | E | E,L Combined | |
| MISSISSIPPI PSC | Approaching R | No | E | E | |
| MISSOURI PSC | R | Production costing | E | Combination | |
| MONTANA PSC | M | No | L,S Combined | L,S Combined | Equal %age adj. |
| NEBRASKA PSC | | | | | |
| NEVADA PSC | M | No | L | L | Equal %age Adj. |
| NEW HAMPSHIRE PUC | M | No | Moving to L,S | L,S Combined | Equal %age Adj. |
| NEW JERSEY BPU | Full embedded cost | Differential Rev. Req. | E | E | |
| NEW MEXICO PUC | R | No | E | E | |
| NEW YORK PSC | R | No | E,L,S Combined | S | Equal %age Adj. |
| NORTH CAROLINA UC | R | No | E | E | |
| NORTH DAKOTA PSC | A,E | No | E | E | |
| OHIO PUC | R | No | E | E | |
| OKLAHOMA CC | R | No | E | E | |
| OREGON PUC | M | No | L | L,S Combined | Equal %age adj. |
| PENNSYLVANIA PUC | R | No | E | E | |
| RHODE ISLAND PUC | | | | | |
| SOUTH CAROLINA PSC | R | No | E | E | |
| SOUTH DAKOTA PUC | R | No | Various | Variety of methods | |
| TENNESSEE PSC | NONE | No | E | E | |
| TEXAS PUC | | | | | |
| UTAH PSC | R | No | E | E | |
| VERMONT PSB | | | | | |
| VIRGINIA SCC | R | No | E | E | |
| WASHINGTON UTC | M,R | No | E | E | |
| WEST VIRGINIA PSC | R | No | E | E | |
| WISCONSIN PSC | R | No | E | L,S | |
| WYOMING PSC | R | No | E | E | |
| ALBERTA PUB | R | Proxy Plant, 35 yrs | E | L | Equal %age adj. |
| BRITISH COL. UC | A | No | E | L | Equal %age adj. |
| NOVA SCOTIA UARB | R | No | E | E | |

**KEYS**

M=Rates approach Marginal/Incremental Costs
R=Rate of Return for Each Customer Class Approaches Allowed Rate of Return for Co.
A=All Customer Classes Are Given Equal Percentage Increases/Decreases

E=Embedded Cost;
L=Long-Run Marginal Cost;
S=Short-Run Marginal Cost

**Table 8**  Seasonal Peaking Electric Utilities, Demand Cost Allocation Methods Used

| AGENCY | Electric Utilities Display Seasonal Peaking | Which Cost Allocation Method Does Agency Use to Allocate Demand Cost Among Customer Classes:<br><br>A=COINCIDENT PEAK METHOD<br>B=AVERAGE AND EXCESS DEMAND | If Coincident Peak Method Please Describe |
|---|---|---|---|
| ALABAMA PSC | Summer only | Coincident Peak Demands | 12-month average. |
| ALASKA PUC | Summer/Winter | A | 3-day coincident peak |
| ARIZONA CC | Summer/Winter | No firm policy; reviews results of several alternatives, including peak credit | |
| ARKANSAS PSC | Summer only | No firm policy; has recently used Coincident Peak & Average & Peak methods | |
| CALIFORNIA PUC | Summer only | A | 4-month coincident peak |
| COLORADO PUC | Summer/Winter | B | |
| CONNECTICUT DPUC | Summer only | A (Distribution); B (Transmission & Generation) | 12-month average |
| DELAWARE PSC | Summer only | A and B; Other methods as needed | Four-month |
| DC PSC | Summer only | B | |
| FLORIDA PSC | Summer/Winter | A + 1/13th weighted average demand | 12-month average + 1/13th weighted average energy |
| GEORGIA PSC | Summer only | A | Transmission - 4-month; Production - 12-month average |
| HAWAII PUC | Summer/Winter | B | |
| IDAHO PUC | Summer/Winter | A, Weighted Coincident Peak, Other | 12-month average |
| ILLINOIS CC | Summer only | A, B | One-month highest |
| INDIANA URC | Summer/Winter | A (for IOUs); B (for REMCs). Can vary. | 12-month average, but depends on demand characteristics of system |
| IOWA UB | Summer/Winter | A, B | 12-month average |
| KANSAS SCC | Summer only | A, B | 12-month average |
| KENTUCKY PSC | Summer/Winter | No specified method; case by case | |
| LOUISIANA PSC | Summer/Winter | A, B | 4-month |
| MAINE PUC | Winter only | A | Combination of one-month (highest) and 4-month |
| MARYLAND PSC | Summer/Winter | A, B | 4-month |
| MASSACHUSETTS DPU | Summer/Winter | Probability of dispatch | |
| MICHIGAN PSC | Summer/Winter | A--75% coincident peak; 25% energy | 12-month average |
| MINNESOTA PUC | Summer/Winter | A, B & stratification method | One-month highest |
| MISSISSIPPI PSC | Summer only | A | 12-month average |
| MISSOURI PSC | Summer/Winter | Time of Use (hourly cost allocation) | |
| MONTANA PSC | Summer/Winter | A (depends on cost function) | Highest winter and summer |
| NEBRASKA PSC | | | |
| NEVADA PSC | Summer | Contribution to loss of load prob. | |
| NEW HAMPSHIRE PUC | Winter only | A | One-month (highest) |
| NEW JERSEY BPU | Summer only | System Planning and HCAM | |
| NEW MEXICO PUC | Summer/Winter | A, B | 12-month average |
| NEW YORK PSC | Summer/Winter | A, Energy demand % relationship, Probability of negative margin | Peak 20 hours |
| NORTH CAROLINA UC | Summer/Winter | A, Peak and Average | One-month highest |
| NORTH DAKOTA PSC | Summer/Winter | A, B | 12-month average |
| OHIO PUC | Summer/Winter | A, B, Non-Coincident Peak | Depends on company characteristics 12-mo CP most common |
| OKLAHOMA CC | Summer only | A, B | Four-month CP method |
| OREGON PUC | Summer/Winter | A | One-Month highest |
| PENNSYLVANIA PUC | Summer/Winter | B, Multiple Coincident Peaks | |
| RHODE ISLAND PUC | Summer/Winter | A (no firm policy) | 12-month average |
| SOUTH CAROLINA PSC | Summer only | A | One-month highest |
| SOUTH DAKOTA PUC | Summer/Winter | A, B | 12-month average |
| TENNESSEE PSC | Winter only | A | 12-month average |
| TEXAS PUC | | | |
| UTAH PSC | Winter only | A | |
| VERMONT PSB | | | |
| VIRGINIA SCC | Summer/Winter | A, B | 12-month average |
| WASHINGTON UTC | Winter only | A | One-month highest |
| WEST VIRGINIA PSC | Winter only | A | 12-month average |
| WISCONSIN PSC | Summer only | A | 12-month average |
| WYOMING PSC | Summer/Winter | A, B | 12-month average |
| ALBERTA PUB | Summer/Winter | A | 12-month aver., weighted |
| BRITISH COLUMBIA UC | Winter only | 1st-ever rate design for BC Hydro scheduled for 1991 | |
| NOVA SCOTIA UARB | Winter only | B | |

**Table 9**   Choice of Electricity Suppliers, Including Retail Wheeling

| AGENCY | Are Large Commercial/Industrial Customers Allowed to Choose Retail Electricity Provider From More Than One Utility? |
|---|---|
| FERC | |
| ALABAMA PSC | No |
| ALASKA PUC | No |
| ARIZONA CC | No |
| ARKANSAS PSC | No |
| CALIFORNIA PUC | 4/20/94 PUC proposed plan to restructure electric industry. Beginning in 1996, large electricity consumers can choose retail supplier; by 2002, all consumers can do so. |
| COLORADO PUC | No |
| CONNECTICUT DPUC | No |
| DELAWARE PSC | No |
| DC PSC | N/A. There is only one retail electricity supplier in the jurisdiction. |
| FLORIDA PSC | No |
| GEORGIA PSC | Yes, those with a minimum 900 kW load |
| HAWAII PUC | N/A. There is only one retail electricity supplier in the jurisdiction. |
| IDAHO PUC | No |
| ILLINOIS CC | No |
| INDIANA URC | In July 1994, PSI Energy announced it would seek approval from the URC to offer wheeling to its largest industrial customers. |
| IOWA UB | No |
| KANSAS SCC | No |
| KENTUCKY PSC | No |
| LOUISIANA PSC | No |
| MAINE PUC | Not addressed |
| MARYLAND PSC | No |
| MASSACHUSETTS DPU | No |
| MICHIGAN PSC | Yes, if within 300 feet of more than one utility's distribution lines. 4/11/94, PSC approved a 5-year experimental retail wheeling program for end-use customers in service territories of Consumers Power and Detroit Edison. |
| MINNESOTA PUC | Not generally |
| MISSISSIPPI PSC | No |
| MISSOURI PSC | No |
| MONTANA PSC | Not usually |
| NEBRASKA PSC | N/A. Any jurisdiction lies with the Power Review Board, not the PSC. |
| NEVADA PSC | No |
| NEW HAMPSHIRE PUC | No |
| NEW JERSEY BPU | No |
| NEW MEXICO PUC | No |
| NEW YORK PSC | No |
| NORTH CAROLINA UC | No |
| NORTH DAKOTA PSC | Yes, in cities where more than one electric utility has a franchise. |
| OHIO PUC | Yes, if the alternate supplier is a municipal utility (no authority over munis). |
| OKLAHOMA CC | Yes, new load. |
| OREGON PUC | No |
| PENNSYLVANIA PUC | No |
| RHODE ISLAND PUC | No |
| SOUTH CAROLINA PSC | Not generally |
| SOUTH DAKOTA PUC | Yes, those with a minimum 2,000 kW load |
| TENNESSEE PSC | No |
| TEXAS PUC | |
| UTAH PSC | Yes, on service territory borders. |
| VERMONT PSB | |
| VIRGINIA SCC | No |
| WASHINGTON UTC | No |
| WEST VIRGINIA PSC | No |
| WISCONSIN PSC | No |
| WYOMING PSC | No |
| NATL ENERGY BOARD | |
| ALBERTA PUB | No |
| BRITISH COLUMBIA UC | No |
| NEWFOUNDLAND BCPU | |
| NOVA SCOTIA UARB | No |
| ONTARIO EB | |

**Table 10**  Special Promotional Tariffs Offered to Customers of Electric Utilities

| AGENCY | Any Promotional Tariffs? | Space Heating | Water Heating | Air Conditioning | All-Electric Service | Thermal Energy Storage | Electric Vehicles | Other Tariffs |
|---|---|---|---|---|---|---|---|---|
| ALABAMA PSC | YES | R,C,I | | | | X | | |
| ALASKA PUC | NO | | | | | X | | |
| ARIZONA CC | YES | | R | | | X | | |
| ARKANSAS PSC | YES | R,C | R | R | R,C | | | |
| CALIFORNIA PUC | NO | | | | | | | |
| COLORADO PUC | NO | | | | | | | |
| CONNECTICUT DPUC | NO | | | | | | | |
| DELAWARE PSC | YES | R,C | R,C  1/ | R,C,I | R  1/ | X | | |
| DC PSC | YES | C  1/ | | | | | | |
| FLORIDA PSC | YES | | | | | | | |
| GEORGIA PSC | NO | | | | | | | |
| HAWAII PUC | NO | | | | | | | |
| IDAHO PUC | NO | | | | | | | |
| ILLINOIS CC | YES | R,C,I | R | | R,C | X | | YES |
| INDIANA URC | YES | R,C,I | R,C,I | C,I | R,C | | | |
| IOWA UB | NO | | | | | | | |
| KANSAS SCC | YES | R,C,I | R,C,I | | R,C | X | | |
| KENTUCKY PSC | YES | R,C | R,C | | R,C | X | | |
| LOUISIANA PSC | YES | | R | R | | | | YES |
| MAINE PUC | YES | R | R | | I | X | | |
| MARYLAND PSC | YES | R,C  1/ | | | | | | |
| MASSACHUSETTS DPU | YES | R,C,I  1/ | R | | C  1/ | | | |
| MICHIGAN PSC | NO | | | | | | | |
| MINNESOTA PUC | YES | R | 1/ | R,C,I | R,C | X | | |
| MISSISSIPPI PSC | YES | C,I | R,C,I | | R,C | X | | YES |
| MISSOURI PSC | YES | R,C,I | R,C | R | R,C | X | | |
| MONTANA PSC | NO | | | | | | | |
| NEBRASKA PSC  2/ | | | | | | | | |
| NEVADA PUC | NO | | | | | | | |
| NEW HAMPSHIRE PUC | YES | R,C  1/ | R,C  1/ | | R,C  1/ | X | | |
| NEW JERSEY BPU | YES | R | R | R  1/ | R | | | |
| NEW MEXICO PUC | YES | R,C | R,C | | | X | | |
| NEW YORK PSC | NO | | | | | | | |
| NORTH CAROLINA UC | NO | | | | | | | |
| NORTH DAKOTA PSC | NO | | | | | | | |
| OHIO PUC | YES | R,C,I | R,C,I | | R,C,I | X | | YES |
| OKLAHOMA CC | YES | R,C | | R,C,I | | | | |
| OREGON PUC | NO | | | | | | | |
| PENNSYLVANIA PUC | YES | R,C,I | R | R,C | R | X | | |
| RHODE ISLAND PUC | NO | | | | | | | |
| SOUTH CAROLINA PSC | NO | | | | | X | | |
| SOUTH DAKOTA PUC | YES | R | | | | X | | |
| TENNESSEE PSC | YES | | | | | | | |
| TEXAS PUC | | | | | | | | |
| UTAH PSC | NO | | | | | | | |
| VERMONT PSB | | | | | | | | |
| VIRGINIA SCC | YES | R,C  1/ | R,C  1/ | | | X | 3/ | |
| WASHINGTON UTC | NO | | | | | | | |
| WEST VIRGINIA PSC | NO | | | | | | | |
| WISCONSIN PSC | no | | | | | | | |
| WYOMING PSC | YES | R,C | C  1/ | | R | X | | |
| ALBERTA PUB | NO | | | | | | | |
| BRITISH COL. UC | NO | | | | | | | |
| NOVA SCOTIA UARB | NO | | | | | | | |

1/   But no new customers are being accepted under the tariff.

2/   The Nebraska PSC has no jurisdiction over energy utilities; authority lies with the Power Review Board.

3/   Proposal pending before the Commission.

**Table 11**　Special Discount Rates Offered to Customers of Electric Utilities

| AGENCY | Special Discount Rates Have Been Approved for Commercial/Industrial Customers C=Commercial Customers    I=Industrial Customers | | | |
| | Economic Development Rates | Market Retention Rates | Cogeneration Deferral Rates | Other Discount Rates |
|---|---|---|---|---|
| ALABAMA PSC | | | | |
| ALASKA PUC | | C, I | C, I | |
| ARIZONA CC | C, I | C, I | | |
| ARKANSAS PSC | I | | I | |
| CALIFORNIA PUC | I | I | I | I |
| COLORADO PUC | | | | |
| CONNECTICUT DPUC | C, I | C, I | C, I | C, I |
| DELAWARE PSC | I | I | | |
| DC PSC | | | | |
| FLORIDA PSC | | I | I | I |
| GEORGIA PSC | | | | |
| HAWAII PUC | | | | |
| IDAHO PUC | | | | |
| ILLINOIS CC | C, I | I | I | |
| INDIANA URC | C, I | I | I | |
| IOWA UB | C, I | C, I | I | |
| KANSAS SCC | C, I | C, I | I | |
| KENTUCKY PSC | I | C, I | I | |
| LOUISIANA PSC | C, I | C, I | | |
| MAINE PUC | | I | I | C, I |
| MARYLAND PSC | C, I | | | |
| MASSACHUSETTS DPU | C, I | | | |
| MICHIGAN PSC | C, I | | | C, I |
| MINNESOTA PUC | I | I | | |
| MISSISSIPPI PSC | | I | I | |
| MISSOURI PSC | C, I | I | | C, I |
| MONTANA PSC | | I | | YES |
| NEBRASKA PSC | | | | |
| NEVADA PSC | | | | |
| NEW HAMPSHIRE PUC | I | | | |
| NEW JERSEY BPU | C, I | | | |
| NEW MEXICO PUC | C, I | | C, I | |
| NEW YORK PSC | C, I | C, I | I | |
| NORTH CAROLINA UC | | I | | |
| NORTH DAKOTA PSC | I | | | |
| OHIO PUC | C, I | C, I | C, I | C, I |
| OKLAHOMA CC | C, I | C, I | I | |
| OREGON PUC | I | | I | |
| PENNSYLVANIA PUC | C, I | I | I | |
| RHODE ISLAND PUC | I | | | |
| SOUTH CAROLINA PSC | | | | |
| SOUTH DAKOTA PUC | C, I | C, I | | |
| TENNESSEE PSC | | | | |
| TEXAS PUC | | | | |
| UTAH PSC | I | | | |
| VERMONT PSB | | | | |
| VIRGINIA SCC | | | | |
| WASHINGTON UTC | | | I | |
| WEST VIRGINIA PSC | | | | |
| WISCONSIN PSC | | | | |
| WYOMING PSC | C, I | C, I | | |
| GUAM PUC | | | | |
| PUERTO RICO PSC | | | | |
| VIRGIN ISLANDS PSC | | | | |
| NATL ENERGY BOARD | | | | |
| ALBERTA PUB | | | | |
| BRITISH COLUMBIA UC | I | | | |
| NEWFOUNDLAND BCPU | | | | |
| NOVA SCOTIA UARB | | | | |
| ONTARIO EB | | | | |

**Table 12**  Interruptible Sales and Special Contract Service by Electric Utilities

| AGENCY | Are Any Customers Served Under Interruptible Rates? | | Do Interruptible Service Tariffs or Contracts Contain a Maximum Number of Interruptions or Hours of Interruption? If so, Please Specify | Were Any Interruptible Customers Interrupted During the Most Recent Power Year? | Are any Commercial or Industrial Customers Served Under Special Contracts Where Exempted From General Rate Increases Are: | | Has Agency Studied Impact of Specific Rate Design on Consumption in the Past 5 Yrs. |
|---|---|---|---|---|---|---|---|
| | Commercial Customers | Industrial Customers | | | Demand Charges | Energy Charges | |
| ALABAMA PSC | NO | YES | YES-600 HOURS/YEAR | NO | NO | NO | NO |
| ALASKA PUC | NO | YES | ONE TARIFF DOES-12 HOURS | YES | NO | NO | NO |
| ARIZONA CC | YES | YES | YES-SOME DO | YES | NO | NO | YES-TOU |
| ARKANSAS PSC | NO | YES | YES-INDIVIDUAL CONTRACTS | YES | YES | NO | NO |
| CALIFORNIA PUC | YES | YES | YES | NO | YES | YES | NO |
| COLORADO PUC | YES | YES | NO | YES | NO | NO | NO |
| CONNECTICUT DPUC | YES | YES | YES-VARIES BY COMPANY | YES | NO | NO | NO |
| DELAWARE PSC | YES | YES | YES-445 HRS/YEAR | YES | NO | NO | YES |
| DC PSC | YES | NO | YES | YES | NO | NO | NO |
| FLORIDA PSC | YES | YES | YES-VARIES BY COMPANY | YES | NO | NO | NO |
| GEORGIA PSC | YES | YES | YES-240 HRS/YEAR        1/ | NO | NO | NO | NO |
| HAWAII PUC | YES | YES | YES-VARIES | NO | NO | NO | NO |
| IDAHO PUC | NO | YES | YES-VARIES BY CONTRACT | YES | NO | NO | NO |
| ILLINOIS CC | YES | YES | YES-VARIES BY UTILITY | YES | YES | YES | NO |
| INDIANA URC | NO | YES | YES-VARIES BY COMPANY | YES | NO | NO | NO |
| IOWA UB | YES | YES | YES | YES | YES | YES | NO |
| KANSAS SCC | YES | YES | YES-VARIES BY COMPANY 2/ | YES | NO | NO | NO |
| KENTUCKY PSC | NO | YES | YES-VARIES BY COMPANY | YES | NO | NO | NO |
| LOUISIANA PSC | NO | YES | NO | NO | NO | NO | NO |
| MAINE PUC | YES | YES | YES-VARIES, MAX 200HR/YR | UNKNOWN | NO | NO | NO |
| MARYLAND PSC | NO | YES | | YES | NO | NO | NO |
| MASSACHUSETTS DPU | YES | YES | YES-VARIES BY COMPANY | N/A | NO | NO | NO |
| MICHIGAN PSC | YES | YES | YES-VARIES BY UTIL/RATE | YES | NO | NO | NO |
| MINNESOTA PUC | YES | YES | NSP-150 HRS/MAX OF 80 | UNKNOWN | NO | NO | NO |
| MISSISSIPPI PSC | NO | YES | | NO | NO | NO | NO |
| MISSOURI PSC | YES | YES | YES-INDIVIDUAL CONTRACTS | YES | NO | NO | NO |
| MONTANA PSC | YES | YES | YES-800 HOURS/YEAR | YES | YES | YES | NO |
| NEBRASKA PSC | | | | | | | |
| NEVADA PSC | YES | YES | YES | YES | NO | NO | NO |
| NEW HAMPSHIRE PUC | YES | YES | YES-45 HOURS/MONTH | YES | NO | NO | NO |
| NEW JERSEY BPU | YES | YES | YES-15 TO 25 EVENTS/YEAR | YES | NO | NO | NO |
| NEW MEXICO PUC | YES | YES | YES-VARIES BY CONTRACT | YES | YES | YES | NO |
| NEW YORK PSC | YES | YES | YES-VARIES, 45-200 HRS | YES | NO | NO | NO |
| NORTH CAROLINA UC | YES | YES | YES-4 TO 8 HRS/24 HOURS | YES | NO | NO | NO |
| NORTH DAKOTA PSC | YES | YES | NO | YES | NO | NO | NO |
| OHIO PUC | YES | YES | YES-VARIES BY COMPANY | YES | YES | YES | NO |
| OKLAHOMA CC | YES | YES | YES-VARIES BY COMPANY | NO | YES | NO | NO |
| OREGON PUC | NO | YES | YES-INDIVIDUAL CONTRACTS | YES | YES | YES | NO |
| PENNSYLVANIA PUC | YES | YES | YES-20 TO 25, 200 HRS | YES | NO | NO | NO |
| RHODE ISLAND PUC | YES | YES | YES-VARIES BY CONTRACT | UNKNOWN | | | NO |
| SOUTH CAROLINA PSC | YES | YES | YES-VARIES BY COMPANY | YES | NO | NO | NO |
| SOUTH DAKOTA PUC | YES | YES | YES-VARIES BY COMPANY | NO | NO | NO | NO |
| TENNESSEE PSC | NO | NO | | | NO | NO | NO |
| TEXAS PUC | | | | | | | |
| UTAH PSC | NO | YES | YES | YES | YES | YES | NO |
| VERMONT PSB | | | | | | | |
| VIRGINIA SCC | YES | YES | YES-VARIES BY SEASON/CO. | YES | NO | NO | NO |
| WASHINGTON UTC | YES | YES | NO | NO | YES | YES | NO |
| WEST VIRGINIA PSC | NO | YES | YES-VARIES BY COMPANY | NO | NO | NO | NO |
| WISCONSIN PSC | YES | YES | YES-VARIES BY COMPANY | YES | NO | NO | NO |
| WYOMING PSC | YES | YES | YES | NO | YES | YES | NO |
| ALBERTA PUB | NO | YES | YES-800 HRS/YEAR | YES | NO | NO | NO |
| BRITISH COL. UC | NO | NO | | | NO | NO | NO |
| NOVA SCOTIA UARB | NO | YES | NO | NO | NO | NO | NO |

1/  The Interruptible Service (IS) schedule, approved 5/91, calls for interruptions to last no more than 10 hours/day and no more than 240 hours/year. The Supplemental Energy Rider (curtailable) has no maximum.

2/  KCPL tariff limits interruptions to 25 occurrences per year, 8 hours per day and 120 hours per year. KPL tariff limits interruptions to 150 hours per month and 400 hours per year.

**Table 13** Energy Conservation Incentive Programs for Customers of Electric Utilities

| AGENCY | ENERGY CONSERVATION CUSTOMER INCENTIVE PROGRAMS CURRENTLY IN EXISTENCE FOR: Residential Electricity Customer SEE KEY BELOW | | | | Commercial and Industrial Customers SEE KEY BELOW | | | |
|---|---|---|---|---|---|---|---|---|
| | Rebates | Loans | Shared savings | Grants or giveaways | Rebates | Loans | Shared savings | Grants or giveaways |
| ALABAMA PSC | S,A,W,I 6/ | S,A,W,I | | | | | | |
| ALASKA PUC | | A,W,L 1/ | | | H,W,L,M,X1/ | | | H,L |
| ARIZONA CC | A,W,I,L 7/ | | | W 1/ | L,M 2/ | | | W,L 1/ |
| ARKANSAS PSC | A | S,A | | | | | | |
| CALIFORNIA PUC | S,A,W,I,L | | X | I,L | H,W,L,C,P,M | | | |
| COLORADO PUC | W,L,X,Z | | | | H,W,L,C,P,M | | | |
| CONNECTICUT DPUC | A | S,W,I,L,Z | | S,W,I,L,Z | H,W,L,C,P,M,Z,E | | | |
| DELAWARE PSC | | | | | H,L | | | |
| DC PSC | S,A,W,I,L,X,Z,E | | | L | H,W,L,C,X,E | | | |
| FLORIDA PSC | S,A,W,I | S,A,W,I | | | H,W,L,M,Z | | | |
| GEORGIA PSC | A,W,I,L,X,Z,E 7/ | S,A,W,I | | W,L | L,E | L | | |
| HAWAII PUC | L 1/ | W 1/ | | | L 1/ | | | E 1/ |
| IDAHO PUC | | I,Z | | S,W,I,Z | H,L,P,M | | | |
| ILLINOIS CC | S,A,W,L 1/ | | | | L,M 1/ | | | |
| INDIANA URC | S,A,W,I,L 2/ | | | | H,L,P,M 2/ | | | |
| IOWA UB | S,A,W,I,L | S,A,W,I | | W,I,L | H,W,L,C,P,M | | | |
| KANSAS SCC | S,A,W,X | S,A,W,X | | | | | | |
| KENTUCKY PSC 8/ | | | | | | | | |
| LOUISIANA PSC | A,W | | | | | | | |
| MAINE PUC | | S,W,I,L | | W,I,L | H,W,L,C,P,M | H,W,L,C,P,M | H,W,L,C,P,M | W |
| MARYLAND PSC | S,A,W,I,L,X,Z,E | S,A,W,X | | L,Z,E | H,W,L,C,P,M,E | | | |
| MASSACHUSETTS DPU | S,WOI,L,X 7/ | | | W,L,E | H,W,L,C,P,M | | | |
| MICHIGAN PSC | A,W,L,X,P | I | | W,I,L,E,Z 3/ | L,M | | | |
| MINNESOTA PUC | A,W,L | A,L | | L | H,L,P,M | | H,W,L,P,M | |
| MISSISSIPPI PSC | | S,A,W,I | | | H | | | |
| MISSOURI PSC 5/ | | | | | | | | |
| MONTANA PSC | | S,A,W,I | | L,Z 3/ | L,P,M | | | |
| NEBRASKA PSC | | | | | | | | H,W,L |
| NEVADA PSC | A,L | S,I | | S,A,W,I | H,L,P,M | | | |
| NEW HAMPSHIRE PUC | S,W,I,L | S,I,Z 3/ | | W,I,L | H,W,L,C,P,M | H,W,L,C,P,M | | L |
| NEW JERSEY BPU | S,A,W,I,L | S,A,W,I | | S,A,W,I | H,W,L,P,M | | | |
| NEW MEXICO PUC 5/ | | | | | | | | |
| NEW YORK PSC | S,A,W,L,X,E | S,W,I,Z / S,A,W,I | | S,W,I,L | H,W,L,I,M,X | | L,P,M,E | |
| NORTH CAROLINA UC | | S,A,W,I | | | | | | |
| NORTH DAKOTA PSC | S,A,W,X | A,I | | E | H,L,C,P,M | H,L,C,P,M | | E |
| OHIO PUC | A,W,I,L,X,Z | | | W,I,L | H,W,L,M | L,M | | |
| OKLAHOMA CC | S,A,I | | | S,A,W,I,L | H | | | |
| OREGON PUC | W,L,X,Z | Z | | W,E | H,W,L,P,M | H,W,L,P,M | H,W,L,P,M | |
| PENNSYLVANIA PUC | S,A,W,I,L | | | | | | | |
| RHODE ISLAND PUC | I,L | | S,A,W,I,L | S,W,I,L | H,W,L,P,M | | H,W,L,P,M | L,M |
| SOUTH CAROLINA PSC | S,A,X | S,A,I | | I,L 1/ 4/ | H,P,M | | | |
| SOUTH DAKOTA PUC | A,W,X | S,W,I | | L | H,W,L,M | H,W,L,M | | L |
| TENNESSEE PSC 5/ | | | | | | | | |
| TEXAS PUC | | | | | | | | |
| UTAH PSC | | | | I,X,Z 3/ 4/ | H,L,P,M,X,Z | | | E |
| VERMONT PSB | | | | | | | | |
| VIRGINIA SCC | | S,A,I,X,Z | W | | | | | |
| WASHINGTON UTC | | S,A,W,I,L | | S,A,W,I,L | | | | |
| WEST VIRGINIA PSC | L | | | W | H,W,L,C,P,M | | | H,W,L,C,P,M |
| WISCONSIN PSC | S,A,W,I,L,X,Z | W,I,L | | I,L,Z 3/ | H,W,L,C,P,M,X,E | H,W,L,C,P,M | H,W,L,C,P,M | L,E |
| WYOMING PSC 5/ | | | | | | | | |
| ALBERTA PUB | | | | | M | | | |
| BRITISH COL. UC | W,L | I | | W 4/ | W,L,P,M,X | P | | |
| NOVA SCOTIA UARB | | | | | M | | | |

KEY - RESIDENTIAL CUSTOMERS: S=Space Heating; A=Air Conditioning; W=Water Heating; I=Insulation; L=Lighting; X=Energy-Efficient Appliances; Z=Weatherization; E=Energy Audits; P=Appliance Pickup/Turn-In

KEY - COMMERCIAL AND INDUSTRIAL CUSTOMERS: H=HVAC; W=Water Heating; L=Lighting; C=Cooking; P=Industrial Process; M=Motors; X=Energy-Efficient Appliances; Z=Weatherization; E=Energy Audits

1/ Pilot program.

2/ Under investigation.

3/ For low-income customers.

4/ Water heater insulation.

5/ No incentive programs.

6/ Offered mostly through dealers, contractors.

7/ Replacement windows.

8/ Incentives for LG&E only.

## Table 14   Demand-Side Management Programs for Customers of Electric Utilities

| AGENCY | DEMAND-SIDE MANAGEMENT PROGRAMS CURRENTLY IN EXISTENCE FOR - | | | | | |
|---|---|---|---|---|---|---|
| | Residential Electric Customer SEE KEYS BELOW | | | Commercial and Industrial Customers SEE KEYS BELOW | | |
| | Load Manage-ment | Fuel Switch-ing | Other Programs | Load Manage-ment | Fuel Switch-ing | Other Programs |
| ALABAMA PSC | | | | T | | |
| ALASKA PUC | W,O | H | | W | H | |
| ARIZONA CC | W,O | | | | | |
| ARKANSAS PSC | W,A,U | | Thermal storage-heating | W,A,R, T,U | | Thermal storage-cooling |
| CALIFORNIA PUC | A | H,A,W,C | TES | A,E,T | A,C,P | Off-peak cooling |
| COLORADO PUC | | A,W,D | Rebates to switch to gas | W,A,P | | Rebates to switch to gas |
| CONNECTICUT DPUC | W,A | | | W,A,T | | Cool storage |
| DELAWARE PSC | W,A,X | | | A,L,T | | Cool storage |
| DC PSC | W,A,X,U | | Off-peak rates, 2nd fridge removal, eff. heat pumps, eff. A/C, shop doctor | W,A,L, E,T,X,N | | Lighting rebates, thermal storage, hi-efficiency A/C, shop doctor |
| FLORIDA PSC | W,A | C | Swimming pool pump DLC | W,A,T | | |
| GEORGIA PSC | A,X,N | | Energy-efficient mortgages Pilot program | T,X,U | | |
| HAWAII PUC | | | | T,U | | Tariffed rates |
| IDAHO PUC | U | H,W | Builder incentives-new construction | T | | Pilot programs to help offset cost of energy-efficiency improvements |
| ILLINOIS CC | A | | Pilot programs | T | | Group load control cooperative |
| INDIANA URC | W,A,X, U,N | | Promote geothermal | T,X,U,N | | |
| IOWA UB | W,A,O,U | | Tree planting | W,A,T, U,X | | Low-cost technical assistance, tree planting, cool storage |
| KANSAS SCC | W,A | | | A,R,T | | |
| KENTUCKY PSC | W | | | T,U | | |
| LOUISIANA PSC | A | W | | | | |
| MAINE PUC | W,O,U | | | W,T | | |
| MARYLAND PSC | W,A,X, U,N | | 2nd refrigerator, geothermal | A,T,X, U,N | A | curtailable rates, cool storage shop doctor, custom rebates |
| MASSACHUSETTS DPU | W,A,N | N | Public housing, neighborhood blitz, pool pump DLC | A,T,N | N | Cool storage, customer-owned generation assistance |
| MICHIGAN PSC | W,A,O,U | | Conservation rates, builder incentives, new construction | T,U | | Cool storage |
| MINNESOTA PUC | W,A,O,U | | Residential demand control | T,X,U,R | | Cool storage |
| MISSISSIPPI PSC | A,O | W | Promote weatherization | R,T | | |
| MISSOURI PSC | A,X,U,N | | Temp-activated A/C cycling | T,X,U,N | | |
| MONTANA PSC | W,X,N | | Space heating | W,T,X,N | | Space heating |
| NEBRASKA PSC | | | | | | |
| NEVADA PSC | A | | Swimming pool pump trippers | T | | Low-pressure irrigation |
| NEW HAMPSHIRE PUC | W,A,O | | | W,T | | Design assistance |
| NEW JERSEY BPU | W,A,O | | | A,T | A | |
| NEW MEXICO PUC | O | | | T | | |
| NEW YORK PSC | W,A,O, X,N | | | W,A,T, L,X,N | W,A | generation assistance |
| NORTH CAROLINA UC | W,A,X, U,N | | TOU Comparative billing, conservation rates, low-income weatherization | W,A,T, X,U | | TOU Comparative billing, Thermal storage |
| NORTH DAKOTA PSC | W,A,O, X,U | | Residential demand controller | W,A,T | | Encourage standby generators |

KEY - LOAD MANAGEMENT:
W=Water Heating Direct Load Control (DLC);
A=Air Conditioning DLC;
O=Off-Peak Heat;
X=Energy Audits;
U=Time of Use Rates;
N=Energy-Efficient New Construction/Design

KEY - FUEL SWITCHING (ELECTRIC TO GAS):
H=Heating; A=Air Conditioning;
W=Water Heating; C=Cooking;
D=Clothes Drying

KEY - LOAD MANAGEMENT:
W=Water Heating DLC; A=Air Conditioning DLC;
R=Irrigation DLC; L=Lighting DLC;
E=EMS DLC;  T=Interruptible Rates
X=Energy Audits; U=Time of Use Rates;
N=Energy-Efficient New Construction/Design

KEY - FUEL SWITCHING (ELECTRIC TO GAS):
W=Water Heating; A=Air Conditioning;
C=Cooking; P=Industrial Process;
G=Gas Engines

**Table 14**  Demand-Side Management Programs for Customers of Electric Utilities (Continued)

| AGENCY | DEMAND-SIDE MANAGEMENT PROGRAMS CURRENTLY IN EXISTENCE FOR - | | | | | |
|---|---|---|---|---|---|---|
| | Residential Electricity Customers SEE KEYS BELOW | | | Commercial and Industrial Customers SEE KEYS BELOW | | |
| | Load Management | Fuel Switching | Other Programs | Load Management | Fuel Switching | Other Programs |
| OHIO PUC | W,A,O | | | T | | Cool storage |
| OKLAHOMA CC | A,X,U,N | | | T,X,U,N | | |
| OREGON PUC | W,A,U | | | T,U | | Buy back savings from individual customers |
| PENNSYLVANIA PUC | A,O | | | A,T | | |
| RHODE ISLAND PUC | W,N | N | Promote energy efficient home construction, appliance rating | W,N | N | Design 2000 promotes design of energy-efficient buildings |
| SOUTH CAROLINA PSC | W,A,U | | Off-peak water heating | W,A,T | | |
| SOUTH DAKOTA PUC | W,A,O,X | | Dual fuel heating, blower door testing | W,T,X,U | | Dual fuel heating, blower door testing |
| TENNESSEE PSC | U | | TOD rates | U | | TOD rates |
| TEXAS PUC | | | | | | |
| UTAH PSC | U | | | T,U,N | | |
| VERMONT PSB | | | | | | |
| VIRGINIA SCC | W,A,X,U | | Promote energy efficient homes | T | | |
| WASHINGTON UTC | | | WWP just starting | T | | WWP just starting |
| WEST VIRGINIA PSC | | | | | | |
| WISCONSIN PSC | W,A,O,U,N | H,W,C,D | Appliance turn-in | W,A,R,T | W,A,C,P,G | Statewide motor standards |
| WYOMING PSC | W,A | | Service extenders | W,A,R | | |
| ALBERTA PUB | | | Promote energy literacy | T,X,U | | |
| BRITISH COL. UC | | W | Numerous programs | | W | Numerous programs |
| NOVA SCOTIA UARB | | | | | | |

| KEY - LOAD MANAGEMENT: W=Water Heating Direct Load Control (DLC); A=Air Conditioning DLC; O=Off-Peak Heat; X=Energy Audits; U=Time of Use Rates; N=Energy-Efficient New Construction/Design | KEY - LOAD MANAGEMENT: W=Water Heating DLC; A=Air Conditioning DLC; R=Irrigation DLC; L=Lighting DLC; E=EMS DLC; T=Interruptible Rates X=Energy Audits; U=Time of Use Rates; N=Energy-Efficient New Construction/Design |
|---|---|
| KEY - FUEL SWITCHING (ELECTRIC TO GAS): H=Heating; A=Air Conditioning; W=Water Heating; C=Cooking; D=Clothes Drying | KEY - FUEL SWITCHING (ELECTRIC TO GAS): W=Water Heating; A=Air Conditioning; C=Cooking; P=Industrial Process; G=Gas Engines |

**Table 15**  Cost Recovery and Financial Incentive Mechanisms for Demand-Side Activities of Electric Utilities

| AGENCY | COST RECOVERY METHODS CURRENTLY IN USE — Recovered as Operation & Maintenance Expenses | Allowed to Earn Current Return in Rate Base, Capital | True-Up, Balancing Acct, Escrow Acctg to Insure Accurate Cost Recov | Sales Adjustment to Insure Full Recovery of Lost Revenues | FINANCIAL INCENTIVES CURRENTLY IN EFFECT — No Incentives | Incentives Are Based On: Activity With Customers | Engineering Calculation of Saving | Demand and/or Energy Saving | Net System Benefits 7/ | Incentives are Calculated: Net of Free-Riders | On Actual Performance Measure | Designed To Allow Recovery of Lost Revenue |
|---|---|---|---|---|---|---|---|---|---|---|---|---|
| ALABAMA PSC | X | | | | X | | | | | | | |
| ALASKA PUC | X | X | | | | X 13/ | | | | | | |
| ARIZONA CC | X | | 1/ | 1/ | X | | | | | | | 1/ |
| ARKANSAS PSC | X | X | | | X | | | | | | | |
| CALIFORNIA PUC | X | | X | X | | X | X | X | X | X | 20/ | |
| COLORADO PUC | X 2/ | X 2/ | X | | | | X 2/ | X 2/ | X | | X | X |
| CONNECTICUT DPUC | X | X | X | | | X | X | X | | | X | X |
| DELAWARE PSC | X | | | | X | | | | | | | |
| DC PSC | X | | X | | | | | X | | X | X | X |
| FLORIDA PSC | X | X 3/ | X | | X 4/ | | | | | | | |
| GEORGIA PSC | | X | | | | X | | | X 6/ | X | X | |
| HAWAII PUC | X 14/ | | X 15/ | | X | | | | | | | |
| IDAHO PUC | | X | X | | | | | | | | | X 18/ |
| ILLINOIS CC | X 2/ | | X | | X 11/ | | | | | | | |
| INDIANA URC | X 1/ | | | X | X 4/ | | | | | | | |
| IOWA UB | | X | X | | | | X | X | X | X | X | |
| KANSAS SCC | X | X | | | 5/ | | | | | | | |
| KENTUCKY PSC | X | X | X 19/ | X 19/ | | | | | X 19/ | | | |
| LOUISIANA PSC | X | | | | X | | | | | | | |
| MAINE PUC | X | X | X | X | | | X | X | X | X | X 6/ | X 10/ |
| MARYLAND PSC | X | X 16/ | X | X | | X | X | X | X | X | X 6/ | X |
| MASSACHUSETTS DPU | X | | X | | | X | X | X | X | | X | X 17/ |
| MICHIGAN PSC | X | X | X | X | | X | X | X | | | X | X |
| MINNESOTA PUC | X | X | X | X | | | | X | | | X | |
| MISSISSIPPI PSC | X | X | | | X | | | | | | | |
| MISSOURI PSC | | | | | X | | | | | | | 1/ |
| MONTANA PSC | X | X | | | | 9/ | | | | | | |
| NEBRASKA PSC | | | | | | | | | | | | |
| NEVADA PSC | X | X | | | X | | | | | | | |
| NEW HAMPSHIRE PUC | X 1/ | | X | X 11/ | | X | X | X | X | X | | |
| NEW JERSEY BPU | | X | | | X 4/ | | | | | | | |
| NEW MEXICO PUC | X | X | | | X | | | | | | | |
| NEW YORK PSC | X | X | X | X | | X | X | X | X | X | | X |
| NORTH CAROLINA UC | X | X | X | | | | | | | | | X 4/ |
| NORTH DAKOTA PSC | X | X | | | X | | | | | | | |
| OHIO PUC | X | X | X | | | X | X | X | X | X | X | |
| OKLAHOMA CC | X | | X | | X | | | | | | | |
| OREGON PUC | X | X | X | X | | | X | X | 1/ | X | X | |
| PENNSYLVANIA PUC | X | X | | | | X | X | X | X | X | X | |
| RHODE ISLAND PUC | | | | | | | X | X | X | X | 6/ | |
| SOUTH CAROLINA PSC | X | X | X | | X | | | | | | | |
| SOUTH DAKOTA PUC | X | X | X | | X | | | | | | | |
| TENNESSEE PSC | | X | | | X | | | | | | | |
| TEXAS PUC | | | | | | | | | | | | |
| UTAH PSC | | X | | 11/ | X 4/ | | | | | | | |
| VERMONT PSB | | | | | | | | | | | | |
| VIRGINIA SCC | X | X | | | X | | X 1/ | X 1/ | X 1/ | | | X 8/ |
| WASHINGTON UTC | X | X | | X | X | | | | | | | |
| WEST VIRGINIA PSC | | | X | | | | | | | | | |
| WISCONSIN PSC | X | X | X | | X | | | | | | | |
| WYOMING PSC | X | X | | | X | | | | | | | |
| ALBERTA PUB | X | | | | X | | | | | | | |
| BRITISH COL. UC | | X | | | X | | | | | | | |
| NOVA SCOTIA UARB | X | | | | | | | | | | | |

**Table 16**   Cost Allocation and Economic Evaluation of Demand-Side Activities of Electric Utilities

| AGENCY | COST ALLOCATION METHOD USED TO DISTRIBUTE THE COSTS OF ELECTRIC UTILITY DEMAND-SIDE ACTIVITIES TO VARIOUS CUSTOMER CLASSES (See Key Below) | ECONOMIC TESTS USED TO EVALUATE DEMAND-SIDE MANAGEMENT ACTIVITIES OF ELECTRIC UTILITIES (See Key Below) | |
|---|---|---|---|
| | | Primary Economic Test(s) | Other Economic Test(s) |
| ALABAMA PSC | | 6 | 4, 5 |
| ALASKA PUC | | | |
| ARIZONA CC | | 3 (considers future costs, not sunk costs) | |
| ARKANSAS PSC | A, C, D | 1, 4, 5, 6 | |
| CALIFORNIA PUC | A | 1,4(TRC excludes externalities) | 3, 5, 6 |
| COLORADO PUC | D, E | 1, 3, 4, 5, 6 | |
| CONNECTICUT DPUC | A, D, E (One company allocates as a peaking plant would be-demand) | 4 | |
| DELAWARE PSC | Indirectly assigned via cost of service study in rate case. | Pending before Commission | |
| DC PSC | Treated like other costs. | 1 | |
| FLORIDA PSC | D, E | 6 | 6 |
| GEORGIA PSC | A; F proposed for pilot program 1991 | 3, 4 | 1, 5, 6 |
| HAWAII PUC | E proposed for pilot programs | 1 | 4, 5, 6 |
| IDAHO PUC | A, D, E | None specified; use 1, 5 | 4 |
| ILLINOIS CC | D, then E | 1, 3, 4 | 4 |
| INDIANA URC | A, D, E | None ruled out; use 1, 4 | 5, 6 |
| IOWA UB | Based on benefits/costs or rate design | 3 | |
| KANSAS SCC | A, B | 1, 3, 5 (pending) | 4, 5, 6 |
| KENTUCKY PSC | A | 1, 6 | |
| LOUISIANA PSC | | | |
| MAINE PUC | F | 1 | 3, DSM programs with rate impact >1% must meet higher standards |
| MARYLAND PSC | A, E | 1, 3, 4, 5, 6 | 2 - initial screening |
| MASSACHUSETTS DPU | A, F | 3 | |
| MICHIGAN PSC | A, E, Rate Base | 1 | 3, 4, 5, 6 |
| MINNESOTA PUC | F | 1, 3 | |
| MISSISSIPPI PSC | B (on a limited basis) | 6 | 1 |
| MISSOURI PSC | | 1 | 4 |
| MONTANA PSC | Treated like other costs | Analysis based on avoided costs | 3 |
| NEBRASKA PSC | | | |
| NEVADA PSC | NONE | 1 | 3, 4, 5, 6 |
| NEW HAMPSHIRE PUC | A, E | 1 | 4, 6 |
| NEW JERSEY BPU | D, E | 1, 3, 5, 6 (No formal IRP/LCUP Process) | |
| NEW MEXICO PUC | A, B, C, D, E | 4 | |
| NEW YORK PSC | A, E | 3, 4, 6 | |
| NORTH CAROLINA UC | A, B | 4, 5, 6 | 4, 5, 6 |
| NORTH DAKOTA PSC | A | 4 | |
| OHIO PUC | Still under consideration; A likely | 1, 6 for relative equity considerations | |
| OKLAHOMA CC | A | 4 | |
| OREGON PUC | D, E | 1, 3 | |
| PENNSYLVANIA PUC | Still under consideration | 1, 4, 5, 6 | |
| RHODE ISLAND PUC | F | 1 | |
| SOUTH CAROLINA PSC | A | 1, 6 | 2, 3, 4, 5 |
| SOUTH DAKOTA PUC | A, D, E | 4, 5, Positive Net Benefit | |
| TENNESSEE PSC | A | NONE | |
| TEXAS PUC | | | |
| UTAH PSC | Still under consideration | None specified, use 1 | 3, 4, 5, 6 |
| VERMONT PSB | | | |
| VIRGINIA SCC | D, E | 1, 6 | 4, 5 |
| WASHINGTON UTC | E, F | 4 | 1, 6 |
| WEST VIRGINIA PSC | A | 1 | |
| WISCONSIN PSC | A | 2 | 1, 3, 4, 5 |
| WYOMING PSC | A | | |
| ALBERTA PUB | A | 6 | |
| BRITISH COL. UC | E | 1, 3 | 4, 6 |
| NOVA SCOTIA UARB | | 1, 4, 5 | |

KEY - COST ALLOCATION
A=Direct Assignment/Class;
B=Direct Assignment/Participants;
C=Customer Count;
D=Demand;
E=Energy;
F=Demand/Energy Saved

KEY - ECONOMIC EVALUATION METHODS
1=Total Resource Costs;  2=Total Technical Costs;
3=Total Societal Costs;  4=Utility Perspective;
5=Participants Test;  6=Non-Participants Test

(See Introduction for Definitions)

**Table 17**  State Policies Regarding Integrated Resource Planning for Electric Utilities

| AGENCY | IRP Is Required | Citation and Description of State Policies Governing IRP | Some Policies A Direct Result of the EPAct | IRP Has Been Required Since | Utilities Have Changed Resource Acquisition Decisions as Result of IRP | How Often Utilities File IRPs |
|---|---|---|---|---|---|---|
| ALABAMA PSC | | | | | | |
| ALASKA PUC | | | | | | |
| ARIZONA CC | X | Order 56313, Docket No. U-0000-88-093 | | 1989 | X | 3 years |
| ARKANSAS PSC | X | 92-160-U, 92-162-U, 92-165-U, 92-229-U | | 1992 | | 3 years |
| CALIFORNIA PUC | 1/ | | | | X | |
| COLORADO PUC | X | Dec. C92-1646, Dkt. 91R-642E | | 1993 | | 3 years |
| CONNECTICUT DPUC | X | Util. submit plans & forecasts to DPUC | | 1989 | Unknown | 2 years |
| DELAWARE PSC | X | Dkt. 29, Order 3446 has IRP guidelines | | 9/1992 | X | 2 years |
| DC PSC | X | Order 9417, Formal Case 834, Phase II | | 1988 | X | 2 years |
| FLORIDA PSC | X | Order 24989 defines contents of IRPs | | 1981 2/ | X | Annually |
| GEORGIA PSC | X | O.C.G.A. §46-3A, PSC Rule 515-3-4 | | 1992 | X | 3 yrs 3/ |
| HAWAII PUC | X | Order 11523, 3/12/92; Order 11630,5/22/92 | | 1992 | X | 3 years |
| IDAHO PUC | X | Order 22299, Case U-1500-165, 1/89 | 4/ | 1989 | | 2 years |
| ILLINOIS CC | X | Docket 87-0261, 1/88 and 12/88 | | 1985 | X | 3 years |
| INDIANA URC | X | Certificate of need law req. IRP     5/ | | | | 2 years |
| IOWA UB | X | Iowa Code Ch. 476A, 476.6(19) & (20); IA Admin. Code 199-35 | | 1990 | X | 2 years |
| KANSAS SCC | X | Dkt. 180,056-U; proposed rules currently before the Commission | | | | 3 years |
| KENTUCKY PSC | X | 807 KAR 5:058 | | 1991 | X | 2 years |
| LOUISIANA PSC | | | | | | |
| MAINE PUC | X | PUC Rules Ch. 36,380; Dkts. 88-174, 88-175, 88-176; MRS Ch. 35-A §3191 | | 1985 | X | Annually |
| MARYLAND PSC | X | PSC Law §28(g) and 59A | | 1986 | X | Annually |
| MASSACHUSETTS DPU | X | DPU 86-36-C, 86-36-D, 86-36-F, 86-36-G; Dkts. 89-239, 91-131, 93-138, 93-157-A. MA Stats §1, Ch. 164 §691 | | 1988 | X | 2 years |
| MICHIGAN PSC | X | U-10292, U-9172 | | 1990 | X | 2 years |
| MINNESOTA PUC | X | Dkt. E-999/R-89-201, MN Laws 1993 Ch. 356 | | 9/90 | X | 2 years |
| MISSISSIPPI PSC | | | | | | |
| MISSOURI PSC | X | Dkt. EX-92-299, Dkt. OX-92-300 | 6/ | 1993 | Unknown | 3 years |
| MONTANA PSC | X | Admin. Rules 38.5.2001-2012 | | 1993 | Unknown | 2 years |
| NEBRASKA PSC | | | | | | |
| NEVADA PSC | X | SB 161, 1983, Dkt. 89-752 | | 1984 | X | 3 years |
| NEW HAMPSHIRE PUC | X | Order 19052, 19141; RSA 378:37-39[supp.] | | 1989 | X | 2 years |
| NEW JERSEY BPU | | | | | | |
| NEW MEXICO PUC | | NMPUC Case No. 2383; proposed rules currently before the Commission | | | | |
| NEW YORK PSC | X | Opinion 88-20, Case 29409 | | 1989 | X | 7/ |
| NORTH CAROLINA UC | X | Dkt.E-100,Sub58&64;N.C.Gen.Stat.§62-2(3a) | | 1989 | X | 3 years |
| NORTH DAKOTA PSC | X | Case 10,799                          8/ | | 1987 | | 2 years |
| OHIO PUC | X | Order 88-816-EL-OR | | 1990 | X | 2 years |
| OKLAHOMA CC | | | | | | |
| OREGON PUC | X | Order 89-507, Dkt.UM 180, Order 93-695 | | 1989 | X | 2 years |
| PENNSYLVANIA PUC | X | HB1639,Act 114,1986; Dkt.L-860026,I-90005 | | 1988 | | Annually |
| RHODE ISLAND PUC | X | Dkt. 2059, 3/11/93 | | 1988 | X | 2 years |
| SOUTH CAROLINA PSC | X | Order 91-885, 10/21/91 | | 1991 | | 3 years |
| SOUTH DAKOTA PUC | | | | | | |
| TENNESSEE PSC | 9/ | | | | | |
| TEXAS PUC | 10/ | Tex.Rev.Civ.Stat.Ann.art. 1446c | | 1984 | X | 2 years |
| UTAH PSC | X | Dkt. 90-2035-01, 6/18/92 | | 1992 | X | 2 years |
| VERMONT PSB | X | Dkt. 5270, 4/16/90; 30 VSA § 218c(1991) | | 9/90 | X | 3 years |
| VIRGINIA SCC | 11/ | | | 1987 | | 2 years |
| WASHINGTON UTC | X | WAC 480-100-251, Dkt. UE-900385, 5/5/90 | | 1988 | X | 2 years |
| WEST VIRGINIA PSC | | | | | | |
| WISCONSIN PSC | X | Dkt.05-EP-4, 8/86, Dkt.05-EP-6, 9/15/92 | | 1986 | X | 2 years |
| WYOMING PSC | X 12/ | Dkt. 90000-XO-93-68 (GO 68) | X | 13/ | X | Varies |

**Table 17**   State Policies Regarding Integrated Resource Planning for Electric Utilities
(Continued)

### FOOTNOTES – TABLE 17

1/   All future resource planning exercises have been suspended. The Commission believes that resource planning will change in response to industry restructuring and increasing competition. One part of this change will likely be a considerably smaller role for the Commission in the planning process.

2/   Depends on how IRP is defined; hearings will be held on whether to adopt the definition contained in EPAct.

3/   Also when applying for a Certificate of Public Convenience and Necessity.

4/   Order 25260, case GNR-E-93-3 considered the IRP requirements of the EPAct. It did not change existing IRP regulations.

5/   Three utilities have been ordered to file IRPs on a regular basis. Generic IRP rulemaking is in progress.

6/   Case EO-93-222 determined that the adopted IRP rules comply with Sec. 111(a) of the EPAct.

7/   IRP filing required in 1992. New filing date has not yet been set.

8/   One utility is required to submit an IRP. There are not formal IRP rules or legislation.

9/   The Tennessee Commission regulates only one small non-generating electric utility.

10/   State law permits, but does not require, comprehensive IRP regulation. These responses are based on the requirements for biennial forecast and resource plans, energy efficiency plans, and standard avoided cost filings (viewed by some in Texas as the functional equivalent of IRP).

11/   Title 56, Code of Virginia requires electric utilities to file plans. It does not specifically mention IRP.

12/   Some utilities are required to file an IRP; it is decided on a case-by-case basis.

13/   IRP has been required for some utilities for three years. The case-by-case policy has been in effect for two months.

**Table 18**   Required Elements of Electric Utilities' Integrated Resource Plans

| AGENCY | Statement of Plan's Objectives | Length of Energy & Demand Forecasts | Existing Capacity | Potential Supply-Side | Potential Demand-Side | Alternative IRP Plans | Relative Sensitivity | Impact on Demand | Costs and Benefits | Short-Term Action Plan's Length | Externalities | Other |
|---|---|---|---|---|---|---|---|---|---|---|---|---|
| ALABAMA PSC | | | | | | | | | | | | |
| ALASKA PUC | | | | | | | | | | | | |
| ARIZONA CC | | 10-20 yrs | X | X | X | | X | X | X | 3 yrs | X | |
| ARKANSAS PSC | X | 20 yrs | X | X | X | | X | X | X | 3 yrs | X | |
| CALIFORNIA PUC | | | | | | | | | | | | |
| COLORADO PUC | X | 20 yrs | X | X | X | X | X | X | X | 3 yrs | | |
| CONNECTICUT DPUC | X | 20 yrs | X | X | X | | | X | X | | | |
| DELAWARE PSC | | 15 yrs | X | X | X | | X | X | X | 4 yrs | X | |
| DC PSC | X | 15 yrs | X | X | X | X | X | X | X | 4 yrs | X | 1/ |
| FLORIDA PSC | X | 10 yrs | X | X | X | | X | X | | | | |
| GEORGIA PSC | X | 20 yrs | X | X | X | X | X | X | X | 4 yrs | X | 2/ |
| HAWAII PUC | X | 20 yrs | X | X | X | X | X | X | X | 5 yrs | X | |
| IDAHO PUC | | 20 yrs | | X | X | X | X | | | x | | |
| ILLINOIS CC | X | 20 yrs | X | X | X | X | X | | X | 3 yrs | | |
| INDIANA URC | | 20 yrs | X | X | X | X | X | X | X | 2 yrs | | |
| IOWA UB | | 20 yrs | X | X | X | | X | X | X | 5 yrs | X | |
| KANSAS SCC | | 20 yrs | X | X | X | | X | X | X | 4 yrs | | |
| KENTUCKY PSC | X | 15 yrs | X | X | X | | X | | | | | |
| LOUISIANA PSC | | | | | | | | | | | | |
| MAINE PUC | | 30 yrs | X | X | X | X | X | X | X | | | |
| MARYLAND PSC | X | 15 yrs | X | X | X | X | X | X | | 2 yrs | | 3/ |
| MASSACHUSETTS DPU | X | 20 yrs | X | X | X | X | X | X | X | 4 yrs | X | 4/ |
| MICHIGAN PSC | X | 15 yrs | X | X | X | X | X | X | X | | X | |
| MINNESOTA PUC | X | 15 yrs | X | X | X | | X | X | X | 5 yrs | X | 5/ |
| MISSISSIPPI PSC | | | | | | | | | | | | |
| MISSOURI PSC | X | 20 yrs | X | X | X | | X | X | X | 3 yrs | | 6/ |
| MONTANA PSC | | x | X | X | X | X | X | X | X | x | X | 7/ |
| NEBRASKA PSC | | | | | | | | | | | | |
| NEVADA PSC | | 20 yrs | X | X | X | | X | X | X | 3 yrs | X | |
| NEW HAMPSHIRE PUC | X | 15 yrs | X | X | X | | X | | X | x | | T&D plan |
| NEW JERSEY BPU | | | | | | | | | | | | |
| NEW MEXICO PUC | | | | | | | | | | | | |
| NEW YORK PSC | X | 20 yrs | X | X | X | X | X | X | X | x | X | |
| NORTH CAROLINA UC | X | 15 yrs | X | X | X | X | X | X | X | 3 yrs | | T&D plan |
| NORTH DAKOTA PSC | | 10-20 yrs | | X | X | X | | | | 2 yrs | | |
| OHIO PUC | | 20 yrs | X | X | X | | X | | X | 4 yrs | | T&D plan |
| OKLAHOMA CC | | | | | | | | | | | | |
| OREGON PUC | X | 20 yrs | X | X | X | X | X | X | X | 2 yrs | X | |
| PENNSYLVANIA PUC | X | 20 yrs | X | X | X | X | X | X | | 2 yrs | | |
| RHODE ISLAND PUC | X | 10 yrs | X | X | X | | | X | X | | | |
| SOUTH CAROLINA PSC | X | 15 yrs | X | X | X | | X | X | X | 1 yr | | 8/ |
| SOUTH DAKOTA PUC | | | | | | | | | | | | |
| TENNESSEE PSC | | | | | | | | | | | | |
| TEXAS PUC | | 15 yrs | | X | X | | | | X | | | 9/ |
| UTAH PSC | | 20 yrs | X | X | X | X | X | X | X | 4 yrs | X | |
| VERMONT PSB | | 20 yrs | X | X | X | X | X | X | X | | X | |
| VIRGINIA SCC | X | 20 yrs | X | X | X | | X | | | | | |
| WASHINGTON UTC | | 20 yrs | | X | X | | | | | 2 yrs | | |
| WEST VIRGINIA PSC | | | | | | | | | | | | |
| WISCONSIN PSC | | 20 yrs | X | X | X | X | X | X | X | 5-10yr | X | |
| WYOMING PSC | | Varies | X | X | Some | Some | Some | X | Some | Varies | Some | |

1/   Pilot and full-scale DSM programs, process and evaluation programs.

2/   CAA compliance, T&D facilities, purchase and sales options, QF transactions.

3/   Probable environmental costs considered in development of avoided costs used to value benefits of DSM.

4/   RFPs (separate supply- and demand-side or combined) for any capacity need identified within the next 10 years.

5/   Scenarios containing an analysis of renewable resources: the first must contain 50% conservation and renewables, the second must contain 75%.

6/   Environmental factors are considered as "probable environmental costs", i.e., the utilities costs to comply with future regulations that may be imposed, not as external costs.

7/   The only requirements is to file a plan. The contents of the plan is left to the utility's discretion. The commission rules contain guidance for what should be in a plan, these are marked above.

8/   Environmental impacts.

9/   Externalities are considered in power plant licensing proceedings.

**Table 19**   Public Participation in and Agency Authority Over Integrated Resource Planning for Electric Utilities

| AGENCY | Agency Holds Public Hearings on IRP Plans | Other Ways Public Participates and Comments on Utility IRP Plans | Agency Authority Over IRP Plans | Agency Response in Practice to IRP Plans | How Often Utilities Are Required to File Progress Reports |
|---|---|---|---|---|---|
| ALABAMA PSC | | | | | |
| ALASKA PUC | | | | | |
| ARIZONA CC | X | Workshops, collaboratives | R,M | R,M,O  1/ | |
| ARKANSAS PSC | X | Regional focus groups | P,M,Q | 2/ | Every 6 mths |
| CALIFORNIA PUC | | | | | |
| COLORADO PUC | X | Prior to plan's submission to PUC | P,J | 2/ | Annually |
| CONNECTICUT DPUC | X | Written comments | A,R,P,M,Q | A,R,P,M,Q | |
| DELAWARE PSC | X | | R,Q,K | R,Q,K | |
| DC PSC | X | Community hearings, filings w/PSC | A,R,P,M,Q,O | A,R,P,Q,O 3/ | |
| FLORIDA PSC | if nec. | Workshops, conservation goals hearings | R,P,M  4/ | R,P,M | |
| GEORGIA PSC | X | Comment on accompanying res. cert. app | A,R,P,M,J | R,M | Quarterly |
| HAWAII PUC | | Advisory groups, hearings by utilities | A,R,P,M,Q | R  2/ | Annually |
| IDAHO PUC | X | Policy advisory group | A,R | A,R | |
| ILLINOIS CC | X | Circulate notice to interested parties | A,R,P,M,Q | A,R,P,M,Q | |
| INDIANA URC | | Comments made in context of Dkt Case. | A,R,P,Q | R | |
| IOWA UB | X | Collaboration prior to filing of IRP | A,R,P,M,J | A,R,P,M | 3-6 months |
| KANSAS SCC | X | Collaborative proceedings | A | A | |
| KENTUCKY PSC | | Written comments, informal conferences | 5/ | 5/ | |
| LOUISIANA PSC | | | | | |
| MAINE PUC | X | | A,R,Q | A,R,Q | Quarterly |
| MARYLAND PSC | X | Collaboratives, written comments | A,R,P,Q | A,R,Q  6/ | Annually |
| MASSACHUSETTS DPU | X | Settlement negotiations | R,P,M,Q | R,P,M,Q | 7/ |
| MICHIGAN PSC | | Public presentations, written comments | A,R | A,R | |
| MINNESOTA PUC | | Written comments, intervene in proc. | A,R,P,M,Q,J | A,R,M,O 6/ | 6-9 months |
| MISSISSIPPI PSC | X | Workshops | A,R,P,M,Q | | |
| MISSOURI PSC | X | Written comments | R | 2/ | |
| MONTANA PSC | X | Written comments | A,R,Q | R,Q | |
| NEBRASKA PSC | | | | | |
| NEVADA PSC | X | | R,P,Q | R,P,M,Q | w/in 20 mths |
| NEW HAMPSHIRE PUC | X | | R,P,Q | R,P,Q | |
| NEW JERSEY BPU | | | | | |
| NEW MEXICO PUC | | | | | |
| NEW YORK PSC | | Comment period, utility outreach | A,R,P,M,Q | R  8/ | |
| NORTH CAROLINA UC | X | Customer focus/public involv. groups | A,R,P,M,Q | A,R | Annually |
| NORTH DAKOTA PSC | | IRP to be reviewed in another hearing | R | R | |
| OHIO PUC | X | | A,R,P,M | A,R,P,M | Every 6 mths |
| OKLAHOMA CC | | | | | |
| OREGON PUC | X | Advisory Groups, written comments | R,M,Q,K | R,M,O  9/ | Annually 10/ |
| PENNSYLVANIA PUC | | | R | R | |
| RHODE ISLAND PUC | X | Written comments | A,R,P  11/ | Q | |
| SOUTH CAROLINA PSC | X | Comment as programs are instituted | A,R,M,Q,O | A,R,O | Annually |
| SOUTH DAKOTA PUC | | | | | |
| TENNESSEE PSC | | | | | |
| TEXAS PUC | | Written comments, intervene in proceed | A,R | A,R,O  12/ | |
| UTAH PSC | if nec. | Public meetings | Q,K | Q,K | 6-12 months |
| VERMONT PSB | 13/ | Direct intervention, public advocate | R,P,Q,J | A,R,P,Q | Varies |
| VIRGINIA SCC | | Public can comment on IRPs | A,R,P,M,Q | Staff reviews | |
| WASHINGTON UTC | X | Tech. advisory comm., written comments | A,R,Q,J | A | |
| WEST VIRGINIA PSC | | | | | |
| WISCONSIN PSC | X | Public meetings, mailing to ratepayers | A,R,P,M,Q | R,P,M,Q | Varies |
| WYOMING PSC | X | Public participation & comment meeting | A,R,P,M,Q | A,R,M,Q | Varies |

**SEE KEY BELOW**

A=Accept it     R=Review it
P=Approve it    M=Modify it
J=Reject        O=Other
K=Acknowledge it
Q=Require utility to modify and resubmit it

1/   Commission has conducted further studies on key issues.
2/   Currently considering the first plans.
3/   Collaborative working group disbanded, periodic briefing by util.
4/   Comment on plan to other state agencies.
5/   Staff reviews IRP plans and compiles a report with recommendations for the utility's next IRP. Commission does not act on the plan.
6/   Require modifications in the next resource plan.
7/   120 days after issuance of RFP.
8/   Accept planning process
9/   Acknowledge with modifications
10/   Required for DSM activities only.
11/   Under a recent Memorandum of Understanding, the three investor-owned utilities that are owned by interstate holding companies must modify their IRPs until they obtain a consensus of all states in which they operate.
12/   Modify forecasts and plans as part of the Statewide Electrical Energy Plan.
13/   Evidentiary hearings are held which are open to public attendance.

**Table 20**   Open Dockets Regarding Integrated Resource Planning for Electric Utilities

| AGENCY | Agency Has Open Dockets That Affect IRP Process | Citation and Description | Direct Result of the EPAct | Agency Considering a Docket | Some Util. Voluntarily File Plans | Agency Has Decided Not to Require IRP | Citation and Reason |
|---|---|---|---|---|---|---|---|
| ALABAMA PSC | X | Considering IRP | X | | 1/ | | |
| ALASKA PUC | | | | X | | | |
| ARIZONA CC | | | | X | | | |
| ARKANSAS PSC | | | | | | | |
| CALIFORNIA PUC | X | Industry Restructuring | | | | | |
| COLORADO PUC | | | | | | | |
| CONNECTICUT DPUC | | | | | | | |
| DELAWARE PSC | | | | | | | |
| DC PSC | | | | | | | |
| FLORIDA PSC | X | Dkts. 930548 through 930551 | X | | | | |
| GEORGIA PSC | | | | | | | |
| HAWAII PUC | | | | | | | |
| IDAHO PUC | | | | | | | |
| ILLINOIS CC | X. | Docket 92-0274 | | | | | |
| INDIANA URC | 2/ | Generic IRP Rulemaking | | | | | |
| IOWA UB | X | NOI-93-2 | X | | | | |
| KANSAS SCC | X | Proposed rules | | | | | |
| KENTUCKY PSC | | | | | | | |
| LOUISIANA PSC | X | Considering IRP | | | | | |
| MAINE PUC | X | Dkt. 93-244 | X | | | | |
| MARYLAND PSC | X | Case 8630 | X | | | | |
| MASSACHUSETTS DPU | | | | | | | |
| MICHIGAN PSC | X | U-10574 | | | | | |
| MINNESOTA PUC | | | | | | | |
| MISSISSIPPI PSC | | | | X | | | |
| MISSOURI PSC | | | | | | | |
| MONTANA PSC | | | | | | | |
| NEBRASKA PSC | | | | | | | |
| NEVADA PSC | | | | | | | |
| NEW HAMPSHIRE PUC | | | | | | | |
| NEW JERSEY BPU | X | Drafting proposed IRP rules | | X 3/ | X | | |
| NEW MEXICO PUC | X | Considering IRP | | | | | |
| NEW YORK PSC | X | C. 92-E-0886 | | | | | |
| NORTH CAROLINA UC | X | Dkt. E-100, sub. 69 | X | | | | |
| NORTH DAKOTA PSC | | Considering IRP | | X | X | | |
| OHIO PUC | | | | | | | |
| OKLAHOMA CC | X | Considering IRP | | | | | |
| OREGON PUC | X | UM 573 | | | | | |
| PENNSYLVANIA PUC | X | Dkt. L-930079 | | | | | |
| RHODE ISLAND PUC | | | | | | | |
| SOUTH CAROLINA PSC | X | IRP Dockets are on-going | | | | | |
| SOUTH DAKOTA PUC | | | | X | | | |
| TENNESSEE PSC | | | | | | | |
| TEXAS PUC | X | Project 11365, Consid. IRP | | | | | |
| UTAH PSC | X | Dkt. 90-2035-01 | | | | | |
| VERMONT PSB | X | Dkt. 5718 | X | | | | |
| VIRGINIA SCC | | | | | | | |
| WASHINGTON UTC | | | | X | | | |
| WEST VIRGINIA PSC | X | Considering IRP | | X | X | | |
| WISCONSIN PSC | | | | X | | | |
| WYOMING PSC | | | | X | | | |

1/   Some utilities prepare IRP plans but do not file them.

2/   An IRP rulemaking is underway. Technically, this is not an open docket.

3/   Board is in the process of drafting proposed IRP rules.

**Table 21**   Status of State Policies Regarding Recovery of Electric Utility Investments in Conservation and Demand-Side Management

| AGENCY | State Policy on Investment Recovery Currently In Effect | Citation and Description | Agency Currently Has Open Docket | Citation and Description | Direct Result of the EPAct | Agency Considering a Opening a Docket |
|---|---|---|---|---|---|---|
| ALABAMA PSC | | | X | Docket #22943 | X | |
| ALASKA PUC | | | | | | X |
| ARIZONA CC | X | Decided case-by-case basis | | | | |
| ARKANSAS PSC | X | A.C.A. §23-2-401 - 405(a)(3) | X | Generic docket opened 1/94 | X | |
| CALIFORNIA PUC | X | Expensed, recovered in rates | X | Generic DSM rulemaking | | |
| COLORADO PUC | X | Decision No. C93-38 | X | 931-199E | | |
| CONNECTICUT DPUC | X | Dockets 92-07-02, 92-04-01 | | | | |
| DELAWARE PSC | | | | | | |
| DC PSC | X | Order 9868, Formal Case 905 | | | | |
| FLORIDA PSC | X | 1/ | X | Dkts.93-0444-EI,93-0424-EI | | |
| GEORGIA PSC | X | O.C.G.A. §46-3A-9 | X | Dkt. 4229-U lost revenues | X | |
| HAWAII PUC | X | Order 11523, 3/12/92 | X | D.7574,7689,7690,7691,7692 | | |
| IDAHO PUC | X | Order 22299, Case U-1500-165 | | | | |
| ILLINOIS CC | X | Dkt. 91-0021, 91-0057  2/ | | | | X |
| INDIANA URC | X | Cause 39201, 38986, 39672 | X | Cause 39401, 39857 | | |
| IOWA UB | X | Iowa Admin. Code 199-35 | X | NOI-93-2 | X | |
| KANSAS SCC | X | KSA 66.117(d), 1980 | X | 180,056-U | | |
| KENTUCKY PSC | | | X | Case 341 cost recovery | | |
| LOUISIANA PSC | | | X | Docket U-20178 | | |
| MAINE PUC | X | 65-407 CMR 380 | | | | |
| MARYLAND PSC | X | PSC Law §28(g) | X | Case 8630 | X | |
| MASSACHUSETTS DPU | X | DSM costs are expensed-DPU 89-179, 89-175, 89-260, 90-335 and 91-80 | X | DPU 91-234-A | | |
| MICHIGAN PSC | X | Base rate surcharges | | | | |
| MINNESOTA PUC | X | MN Laws 1993, Chp. 49; Dkt. E-002/M-90-1159 | X | annual adjustment for conservation | | |
| MISSISSIPPI PSC | | | | | | |
| MISSOURI PSC | X | Recover same as O&M expenses | | | | X |
| MONTANA PSC | X | MCA §69-3-702, -1204, -1206; Order 5360d, Dkt. 88.6.15 | X | Dkt. 93.6.24 | | |
| NEBRASKA PSC | | | | | | |
| NEVADA PSC | X | Dkt. 88-111, 89-651 | | | | |
| NEW HAMPSHIRE PUC | X | Order 19689, 19773 | | | | |
| NEW JERSEY BPU | X | Recover costs &lost revenues | | | | |
| NEW MEXICO PUC | | | X | Cases 2383, 2449, 2450 | | |
| NEW YORK PSC | X | Case 29409, Opinion 88-20 | | | | |
| NORTH CAROLINA UC | X | Dkt. E-100, Sub. 64 | | | | |
| NORTH DAKOTA PSC | X | PU-400-92-399 | | | | X |
| OHIO PUC | X | Case 90-723-El-COI mod.10/92 | | | | |
| OKLAHOMA CC | X | Order 240281, 327685 | X | Cause No. PUD 001342 | | |
| OREGON PUC | X | 3/ | | | | |
| PENNSYLVANIA PUC | X | Dkt. I-900005, 11/93 | | | | |
| RHODE ISLAND PUC | X | Dkt. 1939 | | | | 4/ |
| SOUTH CAROLINA PSC | X | Ord.93-465, Dkt.92-619-E; SB 1273 §58-37-20 | X | Dkt. 87-223-E | | |
| SOUTH DAKOTA PUC | X | Recover same as O&M expenses | | | | X |
| TENNESSEE PSC | X | | | | | |
| TEXAS PUC | X | Subst. Rule 23.22(d), 1984 | X | Project 11365 | | |
| UTAH PSC | X | Dkt. 92-2035-04 | X | Dkt. 92-2035-04 | | |
| VERMONT PSB | X | Dkt. 5270, 4/16/90 | X | Dkt. 5270-CUC-2 | | |
| VIRGINIA SCC | X | Dkt. PUE90070, 3/27/92 | | | | |
| WASHINGTON UTC | X | Rev. Code Wash. 80.28.260 | | | | |
| WEST VIRGINIA PSC | X | Recover same as O&M expenses | | | | X |
| WISCONSIN PSC | X | 6680-GR-3, 10/10/77 and  5/ | | | | |
| WYOMING PSC | | | | | | |

1/     Load management programs are capitalized and amortized; all others are expensed.

2/     Commission authorization in Docket 91-0057 was reversed by State Appellate Court on June 8, 1993. There were also orders issued Feb. 1992, Sept. 1992, Feb. 1993.

3/     Order 89-1700 and DSM cost recovery/incentive mechanisms approved for some utilities.

4/     As a result of the EPAct, the utilities that do not currently receive compensation for lost revenues will request it in their conservation filings next fall.

5/     Wis. Stats. 196.374(3) 1983a27. 6630-UR-100, 12/30/86.

**Table 22**  Agency Authority Over Rate of Return – Electric Utilities

| AGENCY | Agency determines rate of return under its general authority | Capital structure is adjusted to exclude non-utility financing when it is traceable | Method Agency favors in determining rate of return | | | | | | | | Duration of call protection provision influences judgment in determining rate of return |
| --- | --- | --- | --- | --- | --- | --- | --- | --- | --- | --- | --- |
| | | | No ONE method ALL are considered | Dis-counted cash flow | Comp-arable earn-ings test | Earn-ings/ price ratio | Mid-point app-roach | Capital asset pricing model | Risk prem-ium | Other | |
| FERC | X | X | X | X | | | | | | | | |
| ALABAMA PSC | X | X | | X | | | | | | | | |
| ALASKA PUC | X | X | | | X | | | | | | | Possible. |
| ARIZONA CC | X | X | X 2/ | | | | | | | | | |
| ARKANSAS PSC | X | | X | X 11/ | | | | | | | | |
| CALIFORNIA PUC | X | X 1/ | X 2/ | X | X | | | X | X | X | Possible. |
| COLORADO PUC | X | X | | X 9/ | X | | | | | | | |
| CONNECTICUT DPUC | X | X | | X | | | | | | | | |
| DELAWARE PSC | X | | X 2/ | X | X | | | | X | | |
| D.C. PSC | X | X | | X | | | | | | | | |
| FLORIDA PSC | X | X 1/ | X 2/ | | | | | | | | | |
| GEORGIA PSC | X | X | X 2/ | X | | | | | X | X 8/ | |
| HAWAII PUC | X | X | X 2/ | | X | | | | X | | |
| IDAHO PUC | X | X | | X 9/ | X | X | | X | | | |
| ILLINOIS CC | X | X | X 2/ | | | | X | | X | | |
| INDIANA URC | X | | X | | | | | | | | | |
| IOWA UB | X | X 1/ | X | X | | | | | X | X 6/ | |
| KANSAS SCC | X | X | | X | | | | | | | | |
| KENTUCKY PSC | X | X | X 2/ | X | X | X | | | X | | |
| LOUISIANA PSC | X | | | X | | | | | | | | |
| MAINE PUC | X | 10/ | X 9/ | X | | | | | | | |
| MARYLAND PSC | X | X | | X | | | | | | X 6/ | |
| MASSACHUSETTS DPU | X | X | | X 5/ | | | | | | X 5/ | |
| MICHIGAN PSC | X | X | | 2/ | X | X | | X | X | X | |
| MINNESOTA PUC | X | X | | X | | | | | | | | |
| MISSISSIPPI PSC | X | X | | X | X | | | | | | |
| MISSOURI PSC | X | X | | X | | | | | | | | |
| MONTANA PSC | X | X | | X | X | | | | | | |
| NEBRASKA PSC 4/ | X | X | | X | X | | | | | | |
| NEVADA PSC | X | X | | X | X | X | | | | | |
| NEW HAMPSHIRE PUC | X | X | | X | | | | | | | Yes |
| NEW JERSEY BPU 12/ | X | X | X | | X | | | X | X | X | |
| NEW MEXICO PUC | X | X | X 2/ | X | | | | | | X | |
| NEW YORK PSC | X | X | X | X 7/ | | | | | | X | |
| NORTH CAROLINA UC | X | X | X 2/ | X | X | | | X | X | X | |
| NORTH DAKOTA PSC | X | | X | | | | | | | | | |
| OHIO PUC | X | X | X | X 7/ | | | | | | X 7/ | No decision. |
| OKLAHOMA CC | X | X | | X | X | | | X | X | | |
| OREGON PUC | X | X 1/ | | X | | | | X | | | |
| PENNSYLVANIA PUC | X | X | X 2/ | X | X | X | | X | | X | Maybe, if soon |
| RHODE ISLAND PUC | X | X | X | X | X | | | | | X 3/ | |
| SOUTH CAROLINA PSC | X | X | X | X | | | | X | X | | |
| SOUTH DAKOTA PUC | X | X | | X | | | | | | | | |
| TENNESSEE PSC | X | X | X 2/ | X | X | X | | X | X | | |
| TEXAS PUC | X | X | X 2/ | X | X | | | | X | X | |
| UTAH PSC | X | X | | X | | | | | | | | |
| VERMONT PSB 12/ | X | X | | X | X | | | | | X | |
| VIRGINIA SCC | X | X | X 2/ | | | | | | | | |
| WASHINGTON UTC | X | X | | X | | | | | | | | |
| WEST VIRGINIA PSC | X | X | X 2/ | X | X | | | X | X | X | |
| WISCONSIN PSC | X | X | X 2/ | X | | | | X | X | X | |
| WYOMING PSC | X | | X 2/ | X | X | | | X | X | X | |
| PUERTO RICO PSC 12/ | | | | | | | | | | | |
| VIRGIN ISLANDS PSC | X | 10/ | X 2/ | X | X | | | | | X | |
| ALBERTA PUB | X | X | X 2/ | X | X | | | | | X | |
| NOVA SCOTIA UARB | X | X | X 2/ | X | X | | | | X | X | |
| ONTARIO EB 12/ | X | X | X 2/ | | X | | | | | X | |

**Table 22**   Agency Authority Over Rate of Return – Electric Utilities (Continued)

## FOOTNOTES – TABLE 22

1/   Non-utility investment dollars are always excluded from rate base. Where non-utility investment is comparatively small, capital ratios are not adjusted. When on-utility investment is large, we usually remove non-utility investment from equity.

2/   Commission favors no single method, but rather that which produces the most reasonable results.

3/   It may use any method it desires especially in the case of a small company.

4/   No Commission regulation of electric or gas utilities.

5/   DCF is preferred, but Department approves other methods which check DCF result; risk spread analysis preferred by a slight margin. Financial condition of utility also given serous consideration.

6/   DCF is preferred; all methods are considered including econometric modeling approach.

7/   No single method, however, discounted cash flow is frequently used.

8/   Discounted cash flow most often used, but risk premium method used also. Determined case by case.

9/   DCF has been the preferred method, but its results should be checked with other methods.

10/   Never an issue before this agency.

11/   Agency favors DCF, but any method presented is considered.

12/   Commission did not respond to request for update information; this data may not be current.

**Table 23**  Rate of Return on Common Equity – Electric Utility Most Recently Approved Rate and Rate Actually Earned by the Same Company

| AGENCY / Company Name | Approved Date | % Granted | Earned Date | % Earned | Comment |
|---|---|---|---|---|---|
| FERC / Virginia Power | 06/22/92 | 09.78 | | | |
| ALABAMA PSC / Alabama Power | 03/05/90 | 13.00-14.50 | 1993 | 13.14 | Under Rate RSE |
| ALASKA PUC / AK Electric L&P | 11/01/90 | 15.25 | 1993 | 15.30 | |
| ARIZONA CC / Tucson Electric Power | 01/13/94 | 11.00 | | | |
| ARKANSAS PSC / Empire Dist. Electric | 06/26/91 | 12.25 | | | |
| CALIFORNIA PUC / SoCal Edison Co. | 12/03/93 | 11.00 | | | |
| COLORADO PUC / Public Service Colo. | 10/14/93 | 11.00 | 1993 | 08.56 | |
| CONNECTICUT DPUC / Conn. Light & Power | 06/16/93 | 11.50 | 04/94 | 09.62 | |
| DELAWARE PSC / Delmarva Power/Light | 10/05/93 | 11.50 | 1993 | 13.20 | |
| DC PSC / PEPCO | 03/04/94 | 11.00 | 1993 | 12.35 | |
| FLORIDA PSC / Tampa Electric | 12/92 | 12.00 | 1992 | 12.55 | |
| GEORGIA PSC / Georgia Power | 10/01/91 | 12.25 | | | |
| HAWAII PUC / Citizens Util.-Kauai | 11/02/93 | 11.68 | 12/31/93 | 04.15 | |
| IDAHO PUC / Idaho Power Co. | 1986 | 12.25 | | | |
| ILLINOIS CC / Iowa-Illinois G&E | 07/21/93 | 11.38 | | | |
| INDIANA URC / IN-MI Power Co. | 11/12/93 | 12.00 | | | |
| IOWA UB / Iowa-Illinois G&E | 02/25/94 | 11.25 | | | |
| KANSAS SCC / Empire Dist. Electric | 10/23/91 | 11.00 | 1992 | 16.67 | |
| KENTUCKY PSC / Union Light, Heat | 05/05/92 | 11.50 | | | |
| LOUISIANA PSC / Gulf States Utilities | 10/26/90 | 12.75 | | | |
| MAINE PUC / Bangor Hydro Electric | 03/16/94 | 10.60 | | | |
| MARYLAND PSC / Potomac Electric | 10/13/93 | | | | Settlement-ROE not specified |
| MASSACHUSETTS DPU / Cambridge Electric | 05/28/93 | 11.00 | | | |
| MICHIGAN PSC / Detroit Edison Co. | 01/21/94 | 11.00 | | | |
| MINNESOTA PUC / Northern States Power | 09/01/93 | 11.00 | | | |
| MISSISSIPPI PSC / MS Power Co. | 03/03/93 | 11.94 | | | |
| MISSOURI PSC / Show-Me Power Corp. | 02/13/92 | 12.22 | | | |
| MONTANA PSC / Montana Power Co. | 04/28/94 | 11.00 | | | |
| NEBRASKA PSC / Does not regulate | | | | | |
| NEVADA PSC / Nevada Power Co. | 07/24/92 | 12.50 | | | |
| NEW HAMPSHIRE PUC / Granite State Elec. | 02/26/93 | 10.50 | 1992 | 09.86 | |
| NEW JERSEY BPU / Jersey Central P&L | 06/15/93 | 12.20 | | | |
| NEW MEXICO PUC / Public Service NM | 04/12/90 | 12.52 | | | |
| NEW YORK PSC / Central Hudson G&E | 12/16/93 | 10.60 | | | |
| NORTH CAROLINA UC / NC Power (VEPCO) | 02/26/93 | 11.80 | 12/31/93 | 10.63 | |
| NORTH DAKOTA PSC / Northern States Power | 04/07/93 | 11.50 | 12/92 | 06.71 | |
| OHIO PUC / Monongahela Power | 07/15/92 | 11.99 | | | |
| OKLAHOMA CC / OK Gas & Electric Co. | 02/25/94 | 12.00 | | | |
| OREGON PUC / Portland Gen. Elec. | 02/05/91 | 12.50 | | | |
| PENNSYLVANIA PUC / West Penn Power | 05/14/93 | 11.50 | | | |
| RHODE ISLAND PUC / Newport Electric | 09/28/92 | 11.40 | | | |
| SOUTH CAROLINA PSC / SCE&G Co. | 06/07/93 | 11.50 | | | |
| SOUTH DAKOTA PSC / Northern States Power | 01/01/91 | 12.00 | | | |
| TENNESSEE PSC / Kingsport Power Co. | 11/1992 | 12.00 | 12/93 | 13.86 | |
| TEXAS PUC / Texas Utilities Co. | 01/28/94 | 11.35 | | | |
| UTAH PSC / Utah Power & Light | 02/09/90 | 12.10 | | | |
| VERMONT PSB / Citizens Utilities | 01/26/94 | 09.89 | | | |
| VIRGINIA SCC / Virginia Power | 02/03/94 | 10.50-11.50 | | | 11.40% used to set rates |
| WASHINGTON UTC / Puget Sound P&L | 10/29/93 | 10.50 | | | |
| WEST VIRGINIA PSC / WV Power | 02/10/93 | 10.60 | | | |
| WISCONSIN PSC / Wisconsin Electric | 08/01/93 | 11.80 | 12/31/93 | 12.91 | Based on settlement agreement |
| WYOMING PSC / Montana-Dakota Utils. | 12/01/93 | | | | Stipulated case, not stated |
| PUERTO RICO PSC | | | | | |
| VIRGIN ISLANDS PSC | | | | | |
| ALBERTA PUB / TransAlta Utilities | 12/10/93 | 11.88 | | | |
| NOVA SCOTIA UARB / Nova Scotia Power Inc | 03/24/93 | 11.50-12.00 | 12/31/93 | 12.00 | 1st ROE hearing since privati-zation. |
| ONTARIO EB | | | | | |
| QUEBEC NGB / Does not regulate electric utilities. | | | | | |

# Appendix D

# Listing of Retail Wheeling Information Publications

Listed in this section are (7) publications that address and discuss retail wheeling from varying viewpoints. Any of these publications may be of interest to a retail electricity customer since each publication addresses the subject of retail wheeling from a different prospective.

1. **Publisher –**    Edison Electric Institute
701 Pennsylvania Avenue, NW
Washington, DC 20004
(202) 508-5533

   **Publication –**    "Retail Wheeling Report"

   **Cost –**    $210 per year (4 issues per year)

   **Publication Description –** This publication, as its name indicates, addresses and analyzes retail wheeling of electricity. On a quarterly basis, an update on retail wheeling on a state-by-state basis is provided. For someone who wants to remain current on the status of retail wheeling, this publication will be of benefit.

2. **Publisher –**        The National Regulatory Research Institute
                          Ohio State University
                          1080 Carmack Road
                          Columbus, OH 43210
                          (614) 292-9404

   **Publication –**      "Overview of Issues Relating to the Retail
                          Wheeling of Electricity"

   **Cost –**             $30

**Publication Description** – This publication provides a good objective analysis of the items that affect retail wheeling of electricity. A good discussion by supporters as well as opponents to retail wheeling is outlined; and, included in this are the legal, technical and economic considerations. For someone that wants a good, broad overview of retail electricity wheeling, this publication could be of value.

3. **Publisher –**        The EOP Foundation
                          1727 DeSalles, NW
                          Washington, DC 20004
                          (202) 833-3940

   **Publication –**      A report to the U.S. Department of Energy on
                          the "Role of Integrated Resource Plans (IRP) in a
                          Rapidly Changing Industry." (Grant No. DEFG
                          4493R410608)

   **Cost –**             Free

**Publication Description** – Although the title of this publication does not even have "retail wheeling" of electricity in its title, the subject is addressed in the text. One whole chapter (IV) discusses competition in the electric utility industry. Many aspects of retail wheeling are examined and discussed in this chapter. This publication provides a good overview of many things that are happening in the electric utility industry that will ultimately impact every electricity user.

4. **Publisher –**        Edison Electric Institute
                       701 Pennsylvania Avenue, NW
                       Washington, DC 20004
                       (202) 508-5533

    **Publication –**    "Issues and Trends – Moving Forward – 18 Key Trends Affecting the Electric Utility Industry." (Report #70)

    **Cost –**          $20

    **Publication Description –** This publication details 18 different things that are currently taking place that will ultimately affect all electricity users. While retail wheeling of electricity is not directly discussed, many other cost reduction strategies are explored. This publication gives an interesting overview of the many changes that are taking place in the electric utility industry.

5. **Publisher –**        Edison Electric Institute
                       701 Pennsylvania Avenue, NW
                       Washington, DC 20004
                       (202) 508-5533

    **Publication –**    Special Report – "Innovative Rates" Volume I and II.

    **Cost –**          $25 (both volumes)

    **Publication Description –** These two volumes provide an insight to (170) different innovative rate structures that have been established by various electric utilities to fight competition. While each of the rates are specific to a particular customer, they do provide a good insight to the types of rates that are being developed to fight competition in the electricity industry.

6. **Publisher –**          Edison Electric Institute
                            701 Pennsylvania Avenue, NW
                            Washington, DC 20004
                            (202) 508-5533

   **Publication –**        "The British Model: An Assessment – Power
                            Supply Monograph, Issue #2."

   **Cost –**               $13

**Publication Description –** This publication describes the breakup of
the British government-owned electric utility industry. The investigation of how this privatization occurred, and what has transpired as
a result of it, is detailed in this monograph. This information may
be of value to anyone interested in how retail wheeling of electricity
may evolve in the United States as well as what may happen to the
utilities involved.

7. **Publisher –**          Electricity Consumers
                            Resource Council (ELCON)
                            1333 H Street, NW
                            Washington, DC 20005
                            (202) 682-1390

   **Publication –**        "Retail Competition in the United States
                            Electricity Industry."

   **Cost –**               Free

**Publication Description –** This publication lists (8) principles for
achieving competitive, efficient and equitable retail electricity markets. Even though this organization is supported by electricity users,
these (8) principles are objectively presented and merit investigation
by anyone interested in how retail wheeling of electricity should be
evaluated by both users as well as producers.

# Appendix E

# Listing of General Electricity Information Publications

There are many publications concerning electricity that can be of value to any electricity user. Following is a listing of 20 current publications that, at least in the opinion of this writer, may be of value to anyone who is seriously trying to understand or reduce electricity.

1. **Publisher** –     United States Government
                       Printing Office
                       McPherson Square Bookstore
                       1510 H Street, NW
                       Washington, DC 20005
                       (202) 376-5055

   **Publication** –   "Electric Power Monthly"
                       (DOE/EIA – 0226, Distribution Category UC-
                       950)

   **Cost** –          $210 per year (4 issues per year)

   **Publication Description** – This publication provides in-depth data on electric utilities operating in the United States on a monthly basis. This publication typically contains at least 250 pages and addresses electric utility as follows:

1. United States electric power at a glance.
2. United States electric utility net generation.
3. United States electric utility consumption of fossil fuels.
4. United States electric utilities sales, revenues and average revenue per kilowatthour.
5. Miscellaneous utility generation, fuel consumption, fuel cost and operational data statistics.

This publication is very comprehensive in its electric utility coverage and can be of value to anyone that is interested in base utility operational characteristics and costs.

2. **Publisher** –        Cogen Publications
                          747 Leight Mill Road
                          Great Falls, VA 22066
                          (703) 759-5060

   **Publication** –      "Cogen"

   **Cost** –             $55 per year (monthly)

   **Publication Description** – This publication discusses electric cogeneration topics and provides good insight into the costs and operational characteristics of cogeneration installations. It generally contains 25-35 pages and as such, can be read and understood rather quickly. This publication could be of benefit to cogeneration operators or to those that are investigating the potential for cogeneration.

3. **Publisher** –        Flanagan Group, Inc.
                          84-54 118th Street
                          Kew Gardens, NY 11415
                          (218) 723-9477

   **Publication** –      "World Cogeneration"

   **Cost** –             $35 per year (4 issues per year)

   **Publication Description** – This publication gives a good overview of worldwide cogeneration. It is a relatively small 20-25 page publication and is easily read. It could be of benefit to anyone considering a cogeneration installation.

4.  **Publisher –**      American Public Power Association
                         2301 M Street, NW
                         Washington, DC 20037-1484

    **Publication –**    "Public Power"

    **Cost –**           $50 per year (monthly)

    **Publication Description –** This publication addresses public power, primarily municipal utilities. It is of value to anyone that purchases their electricity from a municipal utility. It covers all aspects of public utilities including the impact of retail wheeling on these entities.

5.  **Publisher –**      Public Utilities Reports, Inc.
                         2111 Wilson Boulevard
                         Arlington, VA 22201-3008
                         (703) 243-7000

    **Publication –**    "Public Utilities Fortnightly"

    **Cost –**           $99 per year (22 issues)

    **Publication Description –** This publication covers all electric utilities especially for-profit entities. This publication has probably the most continuing information on retail electric wheeling across the United States.

6.  **Publisher –**      Energy Resources
                         P.O. Box 8467
                         Gaithersburg, MD 29898-8476
                         (301) 601-4365

    **Publication –**    "DSM Quarterly"

    **Cost –**           $50 per year (4 issues)

    **Publication Description –** This publication addresses demand-side management processes. It gives a good overview of many energy service companies that are in the business of assisting electricity users in the implementation of demand-side management programs.

7. **Publisher –**          The Electricity Journal
                            1932 First Avenue, Suite 809
                            Seattle, WA 98101-1040
                            (206) 448-4078

   **Publication –**        "The Electricity Journal"

   **Cost –**               $395 per year (10 issues per year)

   **Publication Description –** This publication provides varying analysis and commentary on the full range of issues facing the electric utility industry. Areas covered include retail competition, integrated resource planning, transmission policy, industry structure and environmental policy. Generally, both sides of an issue are presented so that the reader can have enough information to draw their own conclusions.

8. **Publisher –**          Edison Electric Institute
                            701 Pennsylvania Avenue, NW
                            Washington, DC 20004
                            (202) 508-5533

   **Publication –**        "Retail Wheeling Report"

   **Cost –**               $210 per year (4 issues per year)

   **Publication Description –** This publication sets forth the Federal Government policies and guidelines relating to energy in the United States. This publication should be of interest to any energy user, electricity or natural gas, since many Federal directives are described in this publication. As Federal publications go, this one is easily understood and in this writer's opinion is a must for any energy user.

9. **Publisher** –          McGraw Hill, Inc.
                            1221 Avenue of the Americas
                            New York, NY 10124-0027
                            (800) 223-6180

**Publication** –    "Industrial Energy Bulletin"

**Cost** –           $635 per year (biweekly)

**Publication Description** – This publication covers FERC (Federal Energy Regulatory Commission) actions on a weekly basis. Since FERC regulates on an interstate basis both electricity and natural gas, their actions are of importance to all electricity and natural gas users. With retail wheeling of electricity becoming a very real possibility, knowing the FERC's regulatory actions concerning this matter is very important. Anyone that wants to remain informed on interstate regulation of both electricity and natural gas might be interested in this publication.

10. **Publisher** –         National Association of
                            Regulatory Utility Commissioners
                            1102 Interstate Commerce
                            Commission Building
                            P.O. Box 684
                            Washington, DC 20044-0684
                            (202) 898-2200

**Publication** –    "NARUC Bulletin"

**Cost** –           $110 per year (monthly)

**Publication Description** – This bulletin is distributed by the National Association of Regulatory Utility Commissioners and covers all areas regulated by these Commissioners. Included are electricity, natural gas, energy in general, oil products, railroads, and water and sewer. Since this bulletin is a recap of regulatory actions across the United States, it gives a good overview of what is happening in utility regulation on a national intrastate basis. Since this publication is put out by the various intrastate regulatory commissioners, it tends to be factual and not overly editorialized. Its cost makes it somewhat more affordable than some other publications that are put out by for-profit entities.

11. **Publisher** –      King Publishing Group
                      627 National Press Building
                      529 14th Street, NW
                      Washington, DC 20077-1289
                      (202) 638-4260

**Publication** –     "The Energy Daily"

**Cost** –     $1,260 per year (daily, 250 issues per year)

**Publication Description** – As its name implies, it is published every working day of the year. It addresses both electricity as well as natural gas and provides very current information since it is published daily. As with any daily information, if the time to read the material is not taken, the value of the information is diminished. The publication contains about 4 pages and as such can be read in a minimal amount of time. If a need for immediate information concerning both electricity and natural gas is needed, this publication may be of value to you.

12. **Publisher** –      Inside Washington Publishers
                      P.O. Box 7167
                      Ben Franklin Station
                      Washington, DC 20044
                      (703) 892-8500

**Publication** –     "Electric Power Alert"

**Cost** –     $445 per year (26 issues per year)

**Publication Description** – This publication covers electricity generation, transmission and pricing. It also covered the rules, court cases and Congressional actions that affect the electric power industry. Coverage is on a state-by-state basis where applicable. This publication provides a broad range of electricity topics that could be of general interest to any commercial or industrial electricity user.

13. **Publisher** –          United States Government
                             Printing Office
                             McPherson Square Bookstore
                             1510 H Street, NW
                             Washington, DC 20005
                             (202) 376-5055

**Publication** –          "Electric Sales and Revenue"

**Cost** –          $13 per year (1 issue per year)

**Publication Description** – The "Electric Sales and Revenue" is prepared by the Survey Management Division, Office of Coal, Nuclear, Electric and Alternate Fuels; Energy Information Administration (EIA); U.S. Department of Energy. This publication provides information about sales of electricity, its associated revenue, and the average revenue per kilowatthour sold to residential, commercial, industrial and other consumers throughout the United States.

The sales, revenue and average revenue per kilowatthour provided in the "Electric Sales and Revenue" are based on annual data reported by electric utilities on a calendar year basis. The electric revenue reported by each electric utility includes the applicable revenue from kilowatthours sold; revenue from income; unemployment and other State and local taxes; energy, demand and consumer service charges; environmental surcharges; franchise fees; fuel adjustments; and miscellaneous charges. The revenue does not include taxes such as sales and excise taxes that are assessed on the consumer and collected through the utility. Average revenue per kilowatthour is defined as the cost per unit of electricity sold and is calculated by dividing retail sales into the associated electric revenue. The sales of electricity, associated revenue, and average revenue per kilowatthour provided in this report are presented at the national, state and electric utility levels.

The data presented in this publication would be of use to any analyst, researcher or statistician engaged in regulatory policy and program areas for electricity customers, or for the electric utilities themselves.

14. **Publisher** –        National Association of
                            Regulatory Utility Commissioners
                            1102 Interstate Commerce
                            Commission Building
                            P.O. Box 684
                            Washington, DC 20044-0684
                            (202) 898-2200

    **Publication** –       "Utility Regulatory Policy in the United States
                            and Canada"

    **Cost** –              $70 per year (1 issue per year)

**Publication Description** – This publication is of great value to anyone that wants/needs data on electric and natural gas utility regulation. The book is organized into nine major parts:

1. **Part A** contains names and addresses of regulatory agencies,
   names and terms of office of commissioners.

2. **Part B** displays the general jurisdiction of the agencies: electric, gas, telephone, water and sewer, carriers, as well as other
   functions performed by the agencies and other types of businesses under the agency's jurisdiction.

3. **Part C** contains national tables on utility regulation, covering
   electric, gas and telephone utilities.

4. **Part D** covers regulation of communications companies.

5. **Part E** contains information about regulation of energy (electric
   and gas) utilities.

6. **Part F** contains information about regulation of electric utilities.

7. **Part G** covers gas utilities.

8. **Part H** is about water and sewer utilities.

9. **Part I** reports on utility rate cases considered by each agency.

15. **Publisher** –          Public Utilities Reports, Inc.
                             Suite 200
                             2111 Wilson Boulevard
                             Arlington, VA 22201
                             (800) 368-5001

**Publication** –          "PUR Utility Weekly"

**Cost** –                 $459 per year (weekly)

**Publication Description** – This weekly publication covers State Commission rulings and Federal Regulatory issues. It may be of value to electricity users as a means of keeping informed on regulatory actions concerning retail wheeling of electricity in a particular state.

16. **Publisher** –          PennWell Publishing Company
                             1421 South Sheridan Road
                             Tulsa, OK 74112
                             (708) 382-2450

**Publication** –          "Electric Light and Power"

**Cost** –                 $45 per year (12 issues per year)
                           Note: Sometimes this publication is available
                           free to qualified individuals.

**Publication Description** – This publication gives a good general overview of the electric utility industry including power generation. It provides a good quick overview of many electric utility related items including retail wheeling when appropriate.

17. **Publisher –**          McGraw Hill
                             11 West 19th Street
                             New York, NY 10011
                             (609) 426-5667

    **Publication –**     "Power"

    **Cost –**            $55 per year (monthly)
                             Note: Sometimes this publication is available
                             free to qualified individuals.

**Publication Description** – This publication covers power generation technology for electric utilities and independent power and cogeneration plants including boilers and combustion systems, environmental management, hydro, solar and wind instrumentation, controls, computers and software. Natural gas, oil, coal and renewable fuels, nuclear power, pumps, compressors, valves, piping, turbines, engines, generators, and water treatment. This publication provides a good overview of the above topics.

18. **Publisher –**          Intertec Publishing Corp.
                             9800 Metcalf Avenue
                             Overland Park, KS 66212-2215
                             (913) 341-1300

    **Publication –**     "Transmission and Distribution"

    **Cost –**            $35 per year (monthly)
                             Note: Sometimes this publication is available
                             free to qualified individuals.

**Publication Description** – This publication covers the electric power delivery industry. It contains information that could be beneficial to electricity users interested in transmission by and for electric utilities. Retail wheeling problems/potentials are discussed when appropriate.

19. **Publisher –**      McGraw Hill
                         11 West 19th Street
                         New York, NY 10011
                         (609) 426-5667

   **Publication –**     "Electrical World".

   **Cost –**            $55 per year (monthly)
                         Note: Sometimes this publication is available
                         free to qualified individuals.

**Publication Description –** This publication provides a general overall analysis of the electric power industry. It could be of value to anyone wanting to remain current with electric utilities in general. It covers the areas of power marketing, transmission and distribution, and power generation.

20. **Publisher –**      National Regulatory Research Institute
                         1080 Carmack Road
                         Columbus, OH 43210
                         (614) 292-9404

   **Publication –**     "The National Regulatory Research Institute
                         Quarterly Bulletin"

   **Cost –**            $120 per year (4 issues per year)
                         Note: Sometimes this publication is available
                         free to qualified individuals.

**Publication Description –** This publication on a quarterly basis provides updates on regulatory activities in electricity, natural gas, telecommunications, and water/sewer. It provides a good source of information on regulatory activities all over the United States. Retail wheeling regulatory activities are addressed as they occur.

## SYNOPSIS OF PUBLICATIONS

Twenty (20) different publications have been presented here and each is of value to the right person. Obviously not all of these publications will apply to all persons but they all have merit. There are many other magazines, periodicals and specialized reports that address various aspects of electricity but space does not allow the inclusion of them in this publication. When trying to decide which, if any, of the listed publications would be of benefit, always request a free sample copy from the publisher. Generally, publishers are willing to do this and this will assist you in making an intelligent decision on the worth of a particular publication to a specific need. The 20 publications listed are not necessarily endorsed or recommended by this writer but rather are presented to provide examples of the types of materials that are available.

# Appendix F

# Glossaries of Electricity Terms

The following director of electricity related terms or glossary is excerpted from information provided by the National Association of Regulatory Utility Commissioners and the Energy Information Administration Agency of the United States Department of Energy. For a complete listing of electricity related terms, the following publications are recommended:

A. **"Utility Regulatory Policy in the United States and Canada."** Compilation 1993-1994. (See Item #15 in Appendix E in this publication.)

B. **"Energy Information Administration Electric Power Monthly."** (See Item #1 in Appendix E in this publication.)

C. **"Energy Information Administration Electric Power Monthly."** (See Item #14 in Appendix E in this publication.)

# GLOSSARY
## –A–

*Excerpted From –*

## "UTILITY REGULATORY POLICY IN THE UNITED STATES AND CANADA"

*National Association*

*of*

*Regulatory Utility Commissioners*

# GLOSSARY OF TERMS

**AAV (Alternative Access Vendor)** – See CAP.

**AFUDC (Allowance for Funds Used During Construction)** – A percentage amount added to Construction Work in Progress (CWIP) account to compensate the utility for funds used to finance new plant under construction prior to its inclusion in rate base.

**ALJ** – See Administrative Law Judge.

**AM/FM** – (Automated Mapping/Facilities Management).

**ANSI** – American National Standards Institute.

**APPA (American Public Power Association)** – Represents the interests of publicly owned electric power utilities.

**ASCII (American Standard code of Information Interchange)** – Computer machine language recognized by many different software packages.

**Abandonment** – Abandonment of facilities – Retirement of utility plant on the books without its physical removal from its installed location. Abandonment of service – ceasing to provide service.

**Above-the-Line** – Expenses incurred in operating a utility that are charged to the ratepayer (utility customer), by being allowed in a utility's rate base. The term originated because they are written above a line drawn on the income statement separating them from costs paid by investors (shareholders). See also Below-the-Line.

**Accelerated Depreciation** – Accounting method allowing company to write off asset more quickly in early years, with progressively smaller increments in later years.

**Accrued Depreciation** – Monetary difference between the original cost of an article and its remaining value.

**Accumulated Deferred Income Taxes** – Income taxes collected by utilities through their rates in advance of the time they are actually owed to the government.

**Accumulated Deferred Investment Tax Credit** – The next unamortized balance of investment tax credits spread over the average useful life of the related property, or some other shorter period. This balance sheet account is built up by charges against income in the years in which such credits are realized and is reduced subsequently through credits to income.

**Acquisition Adjustment** – The difference between the price paid to acquire an operating unit or system of a utility and the rate base of the acquired property. (See also Plant Acquisition Adjustment).

**Administrative Law Judge (ALJ)** – A Commission staff member who serves as a hearing officer at formal PUC proceedings. He or she may conduct public hearings, issue subpoenas, question witnesses, and prepare draft decisions and orders for the Commission's consideration. See also Hearing Examiner.

**Advice Letter** – A filing by letter made by a utility to change rate or services. An advice letter filing usually does not require public hearings.

**Allocation of Costs** – See Cost Allocation.

**Allowance for Funds Used During Construction** – See AFUDC.

**Alternative Regulatory Scheme (or Framework)** – A means of regulating a utility other than by the traditional rate base, rate of return, method.

**American Public Power Association** – See APPA.

**Amortization** – Similar to depreciation. A method by which costs for non-tangible assets, such as a patent, are charged to ratepayers over a number of years until the costs have been recovered by the utility.

**Amp (Ampere)** – Unit of measurement of electric current; proportional to the quantity of electrons flowing through a conductor past a given point in one second.

**Appellate Authority** – The authority to hear and decide an appeal to a decision. See also Original Authority.

**Automated Mapping/Facilities Management (AM/FM)** – Digitized geographic maps on which is shown the infrastructure of interest (such as location and type of utility poles, transmission lines, substations, generating plant, etc.) See also Geographic Information Systems.

**Automatic Adjustment Clause** – Allows a utility to increase or decrease its rates to cover costs of specific items without a formal hearing before a Commission. Utility can automatically raise its rates only when the price it pays for those specified items goes up. Changing fuel costs are the primary example of such clauses.

**Average Demand** – The demand on, or power output of, an electric system over any interval of time, as determined by dividing the total number of kilowatthours by the number of units of time in the interval.

**Average Rate Base** – Rate base determined on average investment during the test year.

**Average Service Life** – Used in determining depreciation, the average expected life of all the units in a group of assets.

**Avoided Cost** – The cost an electric utility would otherwise incur to generate power if it did not purchase electricity from another source. Also the basis of the rate required to be paid to QFs for purchased power under PURPA. See also Negawatt.

**BPA (Bonneville Power Administration)** – One of five Department of Energy power marketing administrations. It operates federal hydroelectric generating facilities in the Pacific Northwest, wholesaling the power to electric distribution companies.

**BTU** – See British Thermal Unit.

**Back-up Power** – Electric energy supplied by a utility to replace power and energy lost during an unscheduled equipment outage.

**Base Load** – The minimum quantity of electric power or gas delivered over a given period of time; minimum demand on the system. Excludes peak usage.

**Base Load Capacity** – Generating capacity which serves the base load, usually the utility's largest, most efficient facilities with the lowest operating cost.

**Base Load Station** – A generating station which operates to take all or most of the base load of a system and therefore operates at a nearly constant output. See also Peak Load Station.

**Base Rate** – component of utility rates – a fixed amount charged each month for any of the classes of utility service provided to a customer. This rate excludes all special rate components, such as FAC and PGA.

**Below-the-Line** – Expenses incurred in operation of utility that are charged to the investor, not the ratepayer. These expenses are not allowed in rate base. See also Above-the- Line.

**Blanket Certificate** – Broad approval by the FERC of a particular type of energy transaction, allowing qualifying transactions to take place without case-by-case litigation and approval. Certain contract carriage natural gas arrangements currently hold blanket certificates.

**Book Value** – The accounting value of an asset. The book value of a capital asset equals its original cost minus accumulated depreciation. The book value of a share of common stock equals the net worth of the company divided by the number of shares of stock outstanding.

**British Thermal Unit (BTU)** – The standard unit for measuring quantity of heat energy. The amount of heat energy needed to raise the temperature of one pound of water one degree Fahrenheit.

**Bundled Rate** – Several services combined into one tariff offering for single charge. See also Unbundled Rate and Vertical Service.

**Buyback Rates** – Rates paid to an electric utility's customer who produces his own electricity in excess of his needs.

**Bypass** – Use of transmission facilities which avoid local utility company network.

**CIAC (Contributions In Aid of Construction)** – Non-refundable donations or contributions in cash or properties from individuals to pay for construction of facilities.

**CPCN (Certificate of Public Convenience and Necessity, also known as CCN)** – License or permit granted to a utility proving that a proposed new facility or service is in the public interest; often required before a utility can start construction or begin doing business.

**CWIP (Construction Work in Progress)** – A subaccount in the utility plant section of the balance sheet representing the costs of utility plant under construction but not yet place in service.

**Capacity Costs** – Fixed costs of facilities required for the utility to provide service.

**Capital Asset Pricing Model** – Method of estimating cost of equity in determining rate of return.

**Capital Structure** – The permanent long-term financing of a firm represented by relative proportions of long-term debt, preferred stock and net worth.

**Capitalized Costs** – Costs are capitalized when they are expected to provide benefits over a period longer than one year. Capitalized costs are considered investments and are included in rate base to be recovered from customers over a number of years.

**Certificate of Public Convenience and Necessity** – See CPCN.

**Classification of Service** – A group of customers with similar characteristics (i.e., residential, commercial, etc.) which are identified for the purpose of setting a rate for utility service.

**Cogeneration** – Production of electricity from steam, heat, or other forms of energy produced as a by-product of another process.

**Cogeneration Deferral Rates** – Special discount rates offered to large users who may have the potential capacity to generate their own power via cogeneration.

**Coincident Peak** – Any demand for electricity that occurs simultaneously with any other demand for electricity on the same system. See also Non-Coincident Peak.

**Collocation of Facilities** – Generally the requirement that an embedded utility allows access to its network by others on a non-discriminatory basis.

**Combined Cycle** – The increased thermal efficiency produced by a steam electric generating system when otherwise waste heat is converted into electricity rather than discharged into the atmosphere. One of the technologies of cogeneration in which electricity is sequentially produced from two or more generating technologies. An electricity generating technology in which hot gases turn a turbine and then heat a boiler, which makes team to turn another turbine.

**Common Costs** – Costs incurred jointly for two or more types of operations that must be allocated among the operations. (See also Cost Allocation).

**Construction Work in Progress** – See CWIP.

**Contributions in Aid of Construction** – See CIAC.

**Cooperative (Co-op)** – A group of persons organized in a joint venture to supply services to a specified area.

**Cost Allocations** – Method of separating and assigning different costs to interstate or intrastate operations. Generally used for costs not readily assignable or for common costs. See also Separations.

**Cost of Service Pricing** – Method of pricing service strictly in accordance with the costs (expenses and allowable profit) that are attributable to it. Customers of services priced below cost are generally subsidized by customers paying above cost for their services. See also Value of Service Pricing.

**Cross-subsidization** – Practice of using revenues generated from one (often unregulated) product or service to support another (often regulated) one.

**Customer Advances for Construction** – A deferred credit account representing cast advances paid to the utility by customers requiring the construction of facilities in their behalf. These advances are refundable – the time or extent of refund depends on revenues from the facilities. This is not the same as Contributions in Aid of Construction (CIAC).

**Customer Charge** – A component of electric rates designed to cover those costs (such as metering and billing costs) that are related to the existence of the customer rather than to either the size and extent of the facilities needed to serve him or the quantity of electricity the customer uses.

**DSM** – See Demand-Side Management.

**Declining Block Rates** – As more energy is consumed the unit price goes down. For example, the first 500 kilowatthours cost 8 cents each; the next block of 500 kWh is priced at 6 cents each; etc.

**Decommissioning** – The process of removing a nuclear facility from operation.

**Deferred Fuel Costs** – Those fuel costs spent in one accounting period which are not reflected in billings to customers until a later billing period.

**Deferred Tax Treatment** – Actual taxes plus deferred taxes are included in the income statement.

**Demand** – The maximum rate at which energy is delivered to a specific point at a given moment. Demand is created by a customer's power consuming equipment and differs from load in that load is a measurement of the amount of energy delivered.

**Demand/Capacity Cost** – The expenses incurred by a utility on behalf of an individual customer in providing sufficient capacity to meet that customer's maximum demand on an as- needed basis.

**Demand Change Credit** – A credit applied against the buyer's demand charges when the delivery terms of the contract cannot be met by the seller.

**Demand Factor** – The ration of the maximum demand over a specified time period to the total connected load on any defined system.

**Demand Rate** – A method of pricing under which prices vary according to differences in usage or costs.

**Demand-Side Management (DSM)** – Generally refers to reducing a consumer's demand for energy through many means, including conservation, more efficient appliances, weatherization, etc. Demand and Supply Side Management are combined in Least Cost Utility Planning (LCUP).

**Depreciation** – Accounting procedure used to set aside the difference between the first cost of an item of plant (capital) and its estimated net salvage at the end of its expected life. This "amount to be depreciated" is treated as an expense to offset revenues for tax purposes over the years of expected life.

**Differential Revenue Requirement** – A method of calculating a utility's avoided cost. One calculates the utility's revenue requirement both with and without the costs that would be incurred if the utility were to obtain the power in question from some other source, then one calculates the difference.

**Direct Load Control (DLC)** – When the utility has the ability to directly control a customer's devices and can turn them on or off as necessary to control load.

**Discounted Cash Flow** – Method of determining the cost of common equity capital where the cost of common equity is equal to the dividends per share divided by the market price per share plus an assumed growth rate.

**Distribution Line** – For electricity, the line which carries electricity from a substation to the ultimate consumer. See all Transmission Line.

**Docket** – Formal regulatory proceeding; may also be referred to as a case.

**Dual-Fuel Plant** – Any plant which can operate on either of two different fuels, such as coal or natural gas.

**EEI (Edison Electric Institute)** – Represents the interests of the investor owned electric utilities.

**EIS (Environmental Impact Statement)** – Required by the National Environmental Policy Act, as EIS must analyze the environmental effects of major actions or projects.

**EMF** – Electro-Magnetic Field or Electric and Magnetic Field. A common form of radiation generated by appliances, equipment, machinery, transmission lines, distribution lines.

**EPAct (Energy Policy Act of 1992)**

**Earnings/Price Ration** – The annual earnings per share of common stock divided by the market price per share of common stock.

**Economic Development Rates** – Special discount rates offered to attract new businesses to the area.

**Electro-Magnetic Field (EMF) Effect** – Effect on health resulting from proximity to energized electric facilities. Whether there are such effects and how significant they may be is still being argued by the experts. Also referred to as Electric and Magnetic Field Effect.

**Embedded Costs** – Money already spent for investment in plant and in operating expenses.

**Emissions Trading** – A company that reduces emissions beyond what is required by law at one pollution source can use the excess reduction to permit higher emissions at other sources.

**Energy Charge** – A component of rates which covers the cost of the energy actually used. See also Commodity Charge and Customer Charge.

**Energy Cost Adjustment Clause** – The utility may adjust its rates to offset changes in the cost of fuel used to produce electricity. In some states, these adjustments may be made automatically by the utility, subject to Commission review; other States require an Adjustment Clause hearing first. See also Automatic Adjustment Clause.

**Equal Life Group Method of Depreciation** – Utility plant items with the same life expectancy are depreciated under a common formula.

**Equity** – The utility investment supplied by the sale of common stock. There is no fixed interest on these common stocks.

**Excess Capacity** – The amount of energy available over and above the amount of energy needed, plus reasonable reserves, at any given period.

**Excess Deferred Taxes** – When a utility collects from its ratepayers some portion of the income taxes it will owe in the future, the difference between the amount collected (including future tax obligation) and the amount of its current tax liability. See also Normalization and Flow-Through Tax Treatment.

**Externality** – Benefit or cost, generated as a by-product of an economic activity, that does not accrue to the parties involved in the activity. Must be considered to determine the true cost or benefit to society.

**FAC (Fuel Adjustment Clause)** – See Automatic Adjustment Clause and Energy Cost Adjustment Clause.

**FERC (Federal Energy Regulatory Commission)** – Federal agency established in 1977, concurrently with the creation of the Department of Energy, charged with regulating sale, transportation and price of natural gas and of wholesale electric power moved in interstate commerce. Successor to the Federal Power Commission (FPC), which was established in 1930.

**FPC (Federal Power Commission)** – Federal agency with authority over interstate energy utilities. It was replaced in 1977 with FERC.

**Facilities Charge** – Component of rates which reimburses the utility for investment in facilities which benefit the ratepayer.

**Fall Rate of Return** – The rate of return a utility is entitled to have the opportunity to earn on either its rate base or its common equity. Fair implies balancing keeping rates low for ratepayers, financial integrity of the utility, and investment return for shareholders.

**Fair Value Method of Valuation** – The value which would be ascertained by a prudent purchaser making thorough inquiry relating to all circumstances affecting value.

**Federal Energy Regulatory Commission** – See FERC.

**Firm Power** – Delivery of utility service on a non- interruptible, always-available basis. A utility must supply its firm power customers whenever they demand it, despite conditions. See also Interruptible Rates.

**Firm Wheeling** – Transmission of electricity for another party that is not subject to interruption except for circumstances beyond the transmitting utility's control.

**Fixed Costs** – Business costs that remain unchanged regardless of quantity of output or traffic. See also Non-Traffic-Sensitive Plant, Customer Charge, Facilities Charge.

**Flat Rate** – A rate structure in which everyone within a customer class pays the same price per unit for all energy consumed; method of pricing local telephone service so that customers pay a fixed charge each month for unlimited number of calls. See also Metered Service and Local Measured Service.

**Flow-Through Tax Treatment** – Only actual taxes to be paid for the period are included in the income statement and collected from ratepayers. See also Excess Deferred Taxes and Normalization.

**Forecast Test Year** – Use of future 12-month period projected utility financial data to evaluate a proposed tariff revision. See also Test Year.

**Fossil Fuel** – Any fuel, such as coal, oil and natural gas, derived from the remains of ancient plants or animals.

**Franchise** – A privilege to do business which may be limited to a specified period of time or geographical area and may or may not be exclusive.

**Freedom of Information (Sunshine) Statutes** – Any laws designed to guarantee public access to governmental actions.

**Fuel Adjustment Clause** – See Automatic Adjustment Clause.

**Fuel Factor** – A component of rates designed to recover changes in the cost of fuel; differs from automatic adjustment in that it requires prior Commission approval.

**Fully Distributed Costs (FDC)** – Regulatory accounting procedure that directly assigns, or arbitrarily allocates, to specific service categories the total costs of providing that service.

**G & T** – Generation and Transmission. Identifies a utility which both generates and transmits electricity as distinguished from an entity which provides transmission only.

**Generating Plant** – A facility where electricity is generated.

**Geothermal Energy** – The natural heat available in the rocks, hot water and steam of the earth's subsurface. Geothermal energy can be used to generate electric power.

**Heat Rate** – A measure of the efficiency of generating facilities. The number of BTUs used to produce a kilowatthour of electricity; a low heat rate indicates high efficiency.

**Historic Test Year** – Use of a past 12-month period (usually the immediately preceding period) utility financial data to evaluate a proposed tariff revision. See also Test Year.

**Historical Cost** – Original cost minus any expenditures deemed by a Commission to be fraudulent, unwise or extravagant.

**Hydroelectric** – An electric generating station driven by water power.

**IPP (Independent Power Producer)** – As defined by FERC under PURPA, a generating entity, other than a qualifying facility (QF) and not a utility, that is – (1) unaffiliated with the utility purchaser and (2) lacks significant market power. The facility must not be in the utility's rate base. See also QF.

**IRP** – See Integrated Resource Planning.

**Incremental Costs** – The additional amount of money it takes to generate or transmit energy above a previously determined base amount.

**Incremental Pricing** – A method of charging customers for energy consumption based on the incremental costs involved in energy production.

**Independent Power Producer** – See IPP.

**Informal Complaint** – Informal request for assistance from a Commission where resolution is attempted without public hearing or Commission order.

**Integrated Resource Planning** – Effort to identify all possible options of satisfying end-use energy needs at the lowest possible cost to all ratepayers while minimizing external costs to society. Also called Least-Cost Utility Planning (LCUP).

**Interim Rates** – Rates that are allowed to go into effect, usually subject to refund and sometimes under bond, until the Commission issues its final order.

**Interim Relief Request** – An application to a Commission showing that the applicant will suffer irreparable injury, immediate special hardship or inequity if relief from a regulation is denied.

**Interruptible Rates** – Special rates for energy consumers who are willing to have their energy delivery service interrupted by the utility when necessary. This is a low-priority service with generally lower unit rates. See also Firm Power.

**Interstate** – From one state to another, or across state lines. Interstate activities generally fall under the jurisdiction of the Federal government. See also Intrastate.

**Intervenor** – A third party who receives permission from a Commission to participate in a rate case.

**Intrastate** – Completely within the borders of a single state. Intrastate activities generally fall under the jurisdiction of the State government. See also Interstate.

**Inverted Rate Structure** – A rate design in which the unit price increases with usage.

**Investor-Owned Utility (IOU)** – A utility owned by and responsible to its shareholders (investors). See also Municipal Utility and Public Power.

**Jurisdictional** – Within the jurisdiction, or authority, of a particular agency. See also Non-Jurisdictional.

**Kilovolt (kV)** – One thousand volts; measure of electromotive force.

**Kilowatt (kW)** – One thousand watts; measure of electric capacity or load.

**Kilowatthour (kWh)** – 1,000 watts of consumption for one hour. Electric bills are measured in kilowatthours.

**LCUP (Least-Cost Utility Planning)** – See Least Cost Planning.

**Least Cost Planning** – See Integrated Resource Planning (IRP).

**Life Expectancy** – Time period during which an article is expected to render efficient service.

**"Lifeline" Rates** – Special local telephone rates for low- income customers. As approved by the FCC, customers meeting certain eligibility tests may apply to have an amount equal to the Subscriber Line Charge (SLC) deducted from their monthly bills. Also used generically to designate special rate plans offering very basic utility service at low rates to eligible customers. May also be called "Baseline" rates.

**Load** – The amount of electric power or gas delivered at any specified point or points on a system. Load originates primarily at the power-consuming equipment of customers.

**Load Factor** – The ration of the average load supplied during a designated period to the peak load occurring during that period.

**Load Management** – Techniques designed to reduce the demand for electricity at peak times, such as remote devices to temporarily turn off appliances.

**Long-Term Debt** – Indebtedness (notes, drafts, bonds, etc.) payable over a period of time longer than one year. See also Short-Term Debt and Capital Structure.

**MMBTU** – One Million BTU of energy.

**MW (Megawatt)** – One million watts of electric energy. Used to designate the capacity of an electric generating plant and/or measure demand or load.

**Maintenance Expenses** – Part of operating expenses, including labor, materials, and other expenses, incurred for preserving the operating efficiency and/or physical condition of utility plant.

**Management Audit** – Analysis of the management practices of a company with an eye toward improving efficiency and effectiveness.

**Marginal Cost** – The extra cost of producing one more unit at any production level. Marginal Cost of Capital is the cost of an additional dollar of new funds.

**Market-Based Prices** – Prices fixed in the free market under conditions of pure competition.

**Market Retention Rates** – Special discount rates offered to large users to keep them from leaving the system.

**Market-to-Book Ratio** – Comparison of the market and book value of stock. A one-to-one market-to-book ration means the stock is selling on the market at book value.

**Master Metering** – Installation of one bulk power meter for multiple tenants.

**Megawatt** – See MW.

**Megawatthour (MWh)** – One megawatt of power for one hour.

**Metered Service** – Meters record actual energy use in order to accurately bill a customer. See also Flat Rate.

**Municipal Utility** – Utility (electric, gas, telephone, sewer, water) owned and operated by a city, town or other municipality. Rates charged by a municipal utility within its municipal boundaries are usually exempt from state agency regulatory. See also Public Power.

**NARUC (National Association of Regulatory Utility Commissioners)** – Represents state regulatory agencies in Washington, DC.

**NASUCA (National Association of State Utility Consumer Advocates)** – Members are state officials representing consumer interests in utility matters.

**NERC (North American Electric Reliability Council)** – Established by the industry in the 1970s, it tracks usage and capacity.

**NOI (Notice of Intent, also Notice of Inquiry)**

**NOPR (Notice of Proposed Rulemaking)** – Also know as NPRM.

**NRC (Nuclear Regulatory Commission)** – Established in 1946 to oversee the nuclear industry.

**NRECA (National Rural Electric Cooperative Association)** – Represents the interests of rural electric cooperatives.

**NRRI (National Regulatory Research Institute)** – Established in 1976, the research arm of the NARUC.

**Negawatt** – A watt of electric energy that is created by conservation rather than generation. See also Avoided Cost.

**Net Original Cost** – The original cost of utility property minus any accumulated depreciation.

**Net Worth** – Capital plus capital surplus plus retained earnings.

**Non-Coincident Peak** – When one customer class reaches maximum energy use. This peak may or may not coincide with the peak for the total system. See also Coincident Peak.

**Non-Discrimination** – In general usage, reasonably equal treatment for all. See Equal Access and Divestiture.

**Non-Firm Power** – See Interruptible.

**Non-Interruptible Rates** – See Firm Power.

**Normalization** – An accounting method that allows a utility to recover from its customers income taxes that it must pay evenly over its years of operation. See also Flow-Through Tax Treatment.

**Notice of Inquiry (NOI)** – Public notice soliciting information and comments on a specific subject.

**Notice of Intent (NOI)** – A filing of preliminary data which indicates the applicant's intent to pursue a formal proceeding.

**Notice of Proposed Rulemaking (NOPR)** – Notice to the public that an agency is proposing specific new rules.

**Off-Peak Period** – Period of relatively low system demands.

**On-Peak** – Period of relatively high system demands.

**Operating Costs** – Expenses related to maintaining day-to-day utility functions, including operation and maintenance expenses, taxes and depreciation and amortization costs, but not interest payments or dividends. Operating costs are recovered from customers on a current basis, as opposed to capitalized costs.

**Operating Ratio** – The ratio, generally expressed as a percentage, of operating expenses to operating revenues.

**Operating Revenues** – Amounts billed by the utility for utility services rendered.

**Operating Unit or System** – Complete and self-sustaining facility or group of facilities acquired and operated intact.

**Original Authority (Or Original Jurisdiction)** – The jurisdiction or authority conferred on or inherent in an agency in the first instance. See also Appellate Authority.

**Original Cost Depreciated** – See Net Original Cost.

**Original Cost Method of Valuation** – The cost of the property to the person first devoting it to public service.

**Outage** – The period during which a generating unit, transmission line, or other facility, is out of service.

**Overall Rate of Return** – The monetary allowance for shareholders and bondholders granted by a Commission. It consists of the fixed rate of return in the bondholders' contracts and the Commission's determination of a fair market return to the shareholders' investment.

**Overhead Expenses** – Expenditures connected with the development and operation of any revenue-producing property.

**PUHCA (Public Utilities Holding Company Act)** – Enacted in 1935, its intent was to prevent electric and gas utilities from using complex corporate structure to evade regulatory oversight.

**PURPA (Public Utility Regulatory Policies Act)** – Part of the National Energy Act of 1978, it requires State regulatory agencies to consider a variety of issues affecting electric and gas utility customers. The intent is to establish standards and policies that promote energy conservation, encourage the efficient use of facilities and resources, and provide equitable rates for consumers. Public Law 95-617, 92 Stat. 3117.

**Partial Forecast Test Year** – A 12-month period, usually comprised of the immediately preceding 6 months and the immediately following 6 months, utility financial data used to evaluate a proposed tariff revision. See also Test Year.

**Party-in-Interest** – An individual or group appearing in a formal proceeding.

**Peak Demand** – The maximum level of operating requirements placed on the system by customer usage during a specified period of time.

**Peak Load Pricing** – Pricing which reflects different prices for system peak periods or for hours of the day during which loads are normally high.

**Peak Load Station** – Generating station normally in operation only to provide power during maximum load periods; usually a high operating cost facility or facility which cannot be operated for long periods of time. See also Base Load Station.

**Peak Shaving** – Means by which an electric utility lowers the peak demand on its system.

**Peaking Capacity** – See Peak Load Station.

**Petitioner** – Any party to a proceeding who seeks to appeal a Commission Decision, modify a proposed decision, or intervene during a Commission hearing. See also Intervenor.

**Photovoltaics (PV)** – A technology that produces electricity directly from sunlight.

**Plant Acquisition Adjustment** – The difference between the cost to the utility of acquired plant and the original cost of the plant less the amount credited at the time of acquisition for depreciation and amortization and contributions in aid of construction. See also Acquisition Adjustment.

**Plant in Service** – The land, facilities and equipment used to generate, transmit and/or distribute utility service. See also Utility Plant.

**Pool Capacity** – Capacity provided by a power pool member in order for the member to meet installed or reserve capacity obligations.

**Pool-to-Pool** – An arrangement between power pools to provide electric services to each other.

**Pooling** – Different utilities share their physical plants or resources to increase their efficiency and conserve energy.

**Power Marketing Administration (PMA)** – Energy Department agencies that sell electricity generated by federally owned power generation projects in five regions of the country. Western Area Power Administration (WAPA), Bonneville Power Administration (BPA), Southeastern Power Administration, Southwestern Power Administration, Alaska Power Administration.

**Power Pool** – Two or more interconnected electric systems planned and operated to supply power in the most reliable and economical manner for their combined load requirements and maintenance programs.

**Preferential Tariffs or Rates** – A tariff or rate by which a specified class of customers is given special treatment, for example a "lifeline" rate to provide very basic service to low-income customers.

**Price Caps** – Relatively recently devised means of regulating utility rates as an alternative to rate of return regulation. The prices the utility charges are capped at a certain level, allowing the utility to earn a larger rate of return if it cuts expenses, increases productivity, etc.

**Price/Earnings Ration (P/E)** – The market price per share of common stock divided by the annual earnings per share of common stock.

**Prudent Investment Method of Valuation** – Historical cost less any amounts found to be dishonest or obviously wasteful.

**Prudently Incurred** – Only investments or expenses that were prudent at the time they were made are includable in Rate Base and Cost of Service.

**Public Power** – Electric utility owned by a government entity such as a municipality or utility district. See also Municipal Utility.

**Public Utilities Holding Company act** – See PUHCA.

**Public Utility** – A business or service engaged in regulatory supplying the public with some commodity or service. Also, a utility owned and/or operated by a public authority, such as a municipality or district or public housing authority.

**Public Utility District** – Publicly owned energy producer or distributor. Normally districts incorporate areas larger than a single municipality and operate as special government districts, independent of State regulatory agencies.

**QF (Qualifying Facility)** – Cogenerator who satisfies Section 201 of PURPA (among other things, the owner must not be primarily engaged in generation or sale of electric power, the facility also must meet certain size, fuel use and fuel efficiency requirements).

**REA (Rural Electrification Administration)** – Part of Department of Agriculture established in 1935 and authorized in 1949 to make loans for extending electric and telephone service into rural areas, by making available low cost loans.

**ROE** – Return on Equity. Rate of return allowed on Common Stock Equity. Also called ROCE.

**ROR** – Rate of Return. May refer to overall rate of return or rate of return on rate base.

**RTG** – Regional Transmission Group.

**Rate Base** – Investment in operating plant, less depreciation, upon which regulated utility is entitled to earn profit.

**Rate Base Regulation** – Method of regulation in which utility is limited in operations to revenue level which will recover no more than its expenses plus an allowed rate of return on its rate base.

**Rate Case** – Procedures followed by a regulatory authority so that a utility may present and justify its need for a rate change.

**Rate Case Audit** – Audit performed in the course of a rate case.

**Rate of Return** – Percentage allowed by the Commission as a fair and reasonable profit. May refer to rate of return on rate base or overall rate of return.

**Rate Structure** – The design and organization of billing charges by customer class to distribute the revenue requirement among customer classes and rating periods.

**Regulatory Lag** – The time elapsed between the filing of an application for a rate change and the issuance of a final decision.

**Remaining Life** – The expected future service life of an asset at any given age.

**Removal Costs** – The costs of disposing of plant, whether by demolishing, dismantling, abandoning, sale or other. Removal costs increase the amount to be recovered as depreciation expense.

**Renewables** – Energy sources that in theory are indefinitely sustainable, such as solar energy, geothermal heat, hydropower and wind.

**Reproduction Cost** – Estimated cost to reproduce existing properties in their current form and capability at current cost.

**Reserve Generating Capacity** – A utility's back-up ability to insure sufficient energy supply despite occasional loss of some production capability due to mechanical failures or other problems.

**Retained Earnings** – Corporate earnings that are not paid out in dividends.

**Return on Common Stock Equity** – Shareholders' earnings based on Commission's determination of a fair market return on shareholder's investment.

**Revenue Requirement** – Amount of return (rate base times rate of return) plus operating expenses.

**SEC (Securities and Exchange Commission)** – The federal agency which supervises the operation of securities exchanges and related aspects of the securities business.

**Seasonal Rates** – Rates designed to encourage conservation during time of the year when energy consumption is high.

**Separations** – Process by which a utility's expenses and investment in plant are divided between interstate operations and intrastate operations. See also Cost Allocation.

**Service Area** – Territory in which a utility is required or has the right to supply service to ultimate customers.

**Service Life** – The period of time from the date a unit of property is place in service until it is taken out of service. Average service life is the weighted average of the lives for all units within a plant account or group.

**Service Value** – The difference between original cost and net salvage value of utility plant.

**Small Power Producer** – One that has production capacity of no more than 80 megawatts and uses biomass, waste, or renewable resources (such as wind, water, or solar energy) to produce electric power. Defined under PURPA.

**Standby Service** – A class of service wherein the utility does not serve the customer on a regular basis, but only when called upon to do so by the customer.

**Statutory** – Deriving from or ordered by state or federal legislation which has been enacted, thus is a statute (law).

**Stipulation** – Prior to a rate increase hearing, the different parties may agree on the resolution of one or more issues. The resulting agreement (stipulation) is presented at the hearing.

**Straight Line Method of Depreciation** – The cost of an asset is spread equally over the number of years the asset is estimated to be useful.

**Straight Line Average Service Life** – Principal objective is the determination for each year of the expenses of depreciation attributable to that year's operation.

**Straight Line Remaining Life** – Depreciation reserve is reviewed before applying this method; only the rate is reviewed thereafter.

**Substation** – An assemblage of equipment for the purpose of switching and/or changing or regulating the voltage of electricity. See also Distribution Line and Transmission Line.

**Supply-Side Management** – Generally refers to the utility's management of its generating and transmission facilities for maximum efficiency. Demand and Supply Side Management techniques are combined in Integrated Resource Planning (IRP).

**TVA (Tennessee Valley Authority)** – A Federal Government owned corporation established in 1933 to conduct a unified program of resource development in the seven state Tennessee River Valley. Principal efforts are electric power generation, agricultural development and flood control, water supply and river navigation projects.

**Tail Block** – The last priced block of energy in a stepped rate structure.

**Take and Pay** – Energy sales contract which requires payment only for energy actually delivered.

**Take or Pay (TOP)** – Energy sales contract which requires payment for a given amount of energy whether the customer takes it or not.

**Tariff** – A statement that sets forth the services offered and the rates, terms and conditions for the use of those services. Tariffs must often be submitted to, and approved by, the agency with jurisdiction over the utility or carrier.

**Tax Treatment** – See Flow-Through Tax Treatment and Normalization.

**Testimony** – A declaration, oral or written, given under oath at a public hearing and subject to cross-examination.

**Therm** – Heat measurement equal to 100,000 British Thermal Units (BTUs). Equivalent to about 100 cubic feet of natural gas.

**Time-of-Day (TOD) Rates** – Rate design which prices energy consumption higher during peak usage times of the day. Used to encourage energy conservation. In telecommunications, TOD rates are used to encourage calling during off-peak times.

**Time-of-Use Rates** – Rate design which prices energy consumption higher during peak usage times. Used to encourage energy conservation.

**Total Factor Productivity (TFP)** – A method of measuring an electric utility's overall productivity.

**Transformation** – The process by which electricity voltage is increased or decreased. Generally, voltage is increased before electricity enters the Transmission Line, and decreased before it enters the Distribution Line.

**Transmission** – The movement or transfer of electric energy in bulk. Ordinarily, transmission ends when the energy is transformed for distribution to the ultimate customer.

**Transmission Line** – For electricity, the line which carries electricity at high voltage from points of supply (generating plant or interconnection with other utilities) to a substation where it is reduced in voltage and handed off to Distribution Lines.

**Unbundled Rate** – Individual services are listed and priced separately. See also Bundled Rate. Historically, monopoly utilities provided all, or a number of, services for a single rate. With increasing competition, rates for component parts of services are being disaggregated (or unbundled) and offered separately. See also Vertical Service.

**Used and Useful Test** – Criteria for determining the admissibility of utility plant as a component of rate base. Generally, plant must be in use (not under construction or standing idle awaiting abandonment) and useful (actively helping the utility provide efficient service). See also Imminence Test.

**Utility Plant** – All equipment used for the generation, transmission and/or distribution of utility service, or an account in which record is kept of this equipment. See also Plant in Service.

**Value of Service Pricing** – Method of pricing which puts more weight on the perceived value of the service, rather than the cost of the service. See also Cost of Service Pricing.

**Variable Costs** – Costs which change with the increase or decrease of output or traffic. Also called Traffic-Sensitive Costs.

**Vertical Service** – The utility company performs all major utility services for its customers, including production, transforming, transmittal and distribution. Monopoly utilities in the past frequently provided vertical service; with increasing competition, rates for component parts of service are being disaggregated (or unbundled) and offered separately. See also Bundled Rates and Unbundled Rates.

**Wheeling** – Movement of electricity on the transmission system of one utility for someone other than that utility; transmission for others.

# GLOSSARY
## –B–

*Excerpted From –*

## "ENERGY INFORMATION ADMINISTRATION ELECTRIC POWER MONTHLY"

*Energy Information Administration Agency*
*of the*
*United States Department of Energy*

## GLOSSARY

**Ampere** – The unit of measurement of electrical current produced in a circuit by 1 volt acting through a resistance of 1 ohm.

**Average Revenue per Kilowatthour** – The average revenue per kilowatthour of electricity sold by sector (residential, commercial, industrial, or other) and geographic area (State, Census division, and national), is calculated by dividing the total monthly revenue by the corresponding total monthly sales for each sector and geographic area.

**Baseload** – The minimum amount of electric power delivered or required over a given period of time at a steady rate.

**Baseload Capacity** – The generating equipment normally operated to serve loads on an around-the-clock basis.

**Baseload Plant** – A plant, usually housing high-efficiency steam-electric units, which is normally operated to take all or part of the minimum load of a system, and which consequently produces electricity at an essentially constant rate and runs continuously. These units are operated to maximize system mechanical and thermal efficiency and minimize system operating costs.

**Boiler** – A device for generating steam for power, processing, or heating purposes or for producing hot water supply. Heat from an external combustion source is transmitted to a fluid contained within the tubes in the boiler shell. This fluid is delivered to an end-use at a desired pressure, temperature, and quality.

**Btu (British Thermal Unit)** – A standard unit for measuring the quantity of heat energy equal to the quantity of heat required to raise the temperature of 1 pound of water by 1 degree Fahrenheit.

**Capability** – The maximum load that a generating unit, generating station, or other electrical apparatus can carry under specified conditions for a given period of time without exceeding approved limits of temperature and stress.

**Capacity** – The full-load continuous rating of a generator, prime mover, or other electric equipment under specified conditions as designated by the manufacturer. It is usually indicated on a nameplate attached to the equipment.

**Capacity (Purchased)** – The amount of energy and capacity available for purchase from outside the system.

**Circuit** – A conductor or a system of conductors through which electric current flows.

**Coincidental Demand** – The sum of two or more demands that occur in the same time interval.

**Coincidental Peak Load** – The sum of two or more peak loads that occur in the same time interval.

**Combined Pumped-Storage Plant** – A pumped-storage hydro-electric power plant that uses both pumped water and natural streamflow to produce electricity.

**Commercial Operation** – Commercial operation begins when control of the loading of the generator is turned over to the system dispatcher.

**Compressor** – A pump or other type of machine using a turbine to compress a gas by reducing the volume.

**Consumption (Fuel)** – The amount of fuel used for gross generation, providing standby service, start-up and/or flame stabilization.

**Contract Receipts** – Purchases based on a negotiated agreement that generally covers a period of 1 or more years.

**Costs** – The amount paid to acquire resources, such as plant and equipment, fuel or labor services.

**Current (Electric)** – A flow of electrons in an electrical conductor. The strength or rate of movement of the electricity is measured in amperes.

**Demand (Electric)** – The rate at which electric energy is delivered to or by a system, part of a system, or piece of equipment, at a given instant or averaged over any designated period of time.

**Demand Interval** – The time period during which flow of electricity is measured (usually in 15-,30-,or 60-minute increments.)

**Electric Plant (Physical)** – A facility containing prime movers, electric generators, and auxiliary equipment for converting mechanical, chemical, and/or fission energy into electric energy.

**Electric Utility** – An enterprise that is engaged in the generation, transmission, or distribution of electric energy primarily for use by the public and that is the major power supplier within a designated service area. Electric utilities include investor-owned, publicly owned, cooperatively owned, and government-owned (municipals, Federal agencies, State projects, and public power districts) systems.

**Energy** – The capacity for doing work as measured by the capability of doing work (potential energy) or the conversion of this capability to motion (kinetic energy). Energy has several forms, some of which are easily convertible and can be changed to another form useful for work. Most of the world's convertible energy comes from fossil fuels that are burned to produce heat that is then used as a transfer medium to mechanical or other means in order to accomplish tasks. Electrical energy is usually measured in kilowatthours, while heat energy is usually measured in British thermal units.

**Energy Deliveries** – Energy generated by one electric utility system and delivered to another system through one or more transmission lines.

**Energy Receipts** – Energy generated by one electric utility system and received by another system through one or more transmission lines.

**Energy Source** – The primary source that provides the power that is converted to electricity through chemical, mechanical, or other means. Energy sources include coal, petroleum and petroleum products, gas, water, uranium, wind sunlight, geothermal, and other sources.

**Fahrenheit** – A temperature scale on which the boiling point of water is at 212 degrees about zero on the scale and the freezing point is at 32 degrees above zero at standard atmospheric pressure.

**Generation (Electricity)** – The process of producing electric energy by transforming other forms of energy; also, the amount of electric energy produced, expressed in watthours (Wh).

*Gross Generation* – The total amount of electric energy produced by the generating units at a generating station or stations, measured at the generator terminals.

*Net Generation* – Gross generation less the electric energy consumed at the generating station for station use.

**Generator** – A machine that converts mechanical energy into electrical energy.

**Generator Nameplate Capacity** – The full-load continuous rating of a generator, prime mover, or other electric power production equipment under specific conditions as designated by the manufacturer. Installed generator nameplate rating is usually indicated on a nameplate physically attached to the generator.

**Geothermal Plant** – A plant in which the prime mover is a steam turbine. The turbine is driven either by steam produced from hot water or by natural steam that derives its energy from heat found in rocks or fluids at various depths beneath the surface of the earth. The energy is extracted by drilling and/or pumping.

**Gigawatt (GW)** – One billion watts.

**Gigawatthour (GWh)** – One billion watthours.

**Gross Generation** – The total amount of electric energy produced by a generating facility, as measured at the generator terminals.

**Horsepower** – A unit for measuring the rate of work (or power) equivalent to 33,000 foot-pounds per minute or 746 watts.

**Hydroelectric Plant** – A plant in which the turbine generators are driven by falling water.

**Instantaneous Peak Demand** – The maximum demand at the instant of greatest load.

**Integrated Demand** – The summation of the continuously varying instantaneous demand averaged over a specified interval of time. The information is usually determined by examining a demand meter.

**Internal Combustion Plant** – A plant in which the prime mover is an internal combustion engine. An internal combustion engine has one or more cylinders in which the process of combustion takes place, converting energy released from the rapid burning of a fuel-air mixture into mechanical energy. Diesel or gas-fired engines are the principal types used in electric plants. The plant is usually operated during periods of high demand for electricity.

**Kilowatt (kW)** – One thousand watts.

**Kilowatthour (kWh)** – One thousand watthours.

**Maximum Demand** – The greatest of all demands of the load that has occurred within a specified period of time.

**Megawatt (MW)** – One million watts.

**Megawatthour (MWh)** – One million watthours.

**Net Energy for Load** – Net generation of main generating units that are system-owned or system-operated plus energy receipts minus energy deliveries.

**Net Generation** – Gross generation minus plant use from all electric utility owned plants. The energy required for pumping at a pumped-storage plant is regarded as plant use and must be deducted from the gross generation.

**Net Summer Capability** – The steady hourly output, which generating equipment is expected to supply to system load exclusive of auxiliary power, as demonstrated by tests at the time of summer peak demand.

**Noncoincidental Peak Load** – The sum of two or more peak loads on individual systems that do not occur in the same time interval. Meaningful only when considering loads within a limited period of time, such as a day, week, month, a heating or cooling season, and usually for not more than 1 year.

**North American Electric Reliability Council (NERC)** – A council formed in 1968 by the electric utility industry to promote the reliability and adequacy of bulk power supply in the electric utility systems of North America. NERC consists of nine regional reliability councils and encompasses essentially all the power regional of the contiguous United States, Canada, and Mexico. The NERC Regions are –

| | | |
|---|---|---|
| **ASCC** | – | Alaskan System Coordination Council |
| **ECAR** | – | East Central Area Reliability Coordination Agreement |
| **MAIN** | – | Mid-America Interconnected Network |
| **MAAC** | – | Mid-Atlantic Area Council |
| **MAPP** | – | Mid-Continent Area Power Pool |
| **NPCC** | – | Northeast Power Coordinating Council |
| **SERC** | – | Southeastern Electric Reliability Council |
| **SPP** | – | Southwest Power Pool |
| **WSCC** | – | Western Systems Coordinating Council |

**Nuclear Fuel** – Fissionable materials that have been enriched to such a composition that, when placed in a nuclear reactor, will support a self-sustaining fission chain reaction, producing heat in a controlled manner for process use.

**Nuclear Power Plant** – A facility in which heat produced in a reactor by the fissioning of nuclear fuel is used to drive a steam turbine.

**Ohm** – The unit of measurement of electrical resistance. The resistance of a circuit in which a potential difference of 1 volt produces a current of 1 ampere.

**Operable Nuclear Unit** – A nuclear unit is "operable" after it completes low-power testing and is granted authorization to operate at full power. This occurs when it receives its full power amendment to its operating license from the Nuclear Regulatory Commission.

**Other Generation** – Electricity originating from these sources – biomass, fuel cells, geothermal heat, solar power, waste, wind, and wood.

**Other Unavailable Capability** – Net capability of main generating units that are unavailable for load for reasons other than full-forced outage or scheduled maintenance. Legal restrictions or other causes make these units unavailable.

**Peak Demand** – The maximum load during a specified period of time.

**Peak Load Plant** – A plant usually housing old, low- efficiency steam units; gas turbines, diesels; or pumped- storage hydroelectric equipment normally used during the peak-load periods.

**Peaking Capacity** – Capacity of generating equipment normally reserved for operation during the hours of highest daily, weekly, or seasonal loads. Some generating equipment may be operated at certain times as peaking capacity and at other times to serve loads on an around-the-clock basis.

**Percent Differences** – The relative change in a quantity over a specified time period. It is calculated as follows – the current value has the previous value subtracted from it; this new number is divided by the absolute value of the previous value; then this new number is multiplied by 100.

**Plant** – A facility at which are located prime movers, electric generators, and auxiliary equipment for converting mechanical, chemical, and/or nuclear energy into electric energy. A plant may contain more than one type of prime mover. Electric utility plants exclude facilities that satisfy the definition of a qualifying facility under the Public Utility Regulatory Policies Act of 1978.

**Plant Use** – The electric energy used in the operation of a plant. Included in this definition is the energy required for pumping at pumped-storage plants.

**Plant-Use Electricity** – The electric energy used in the operation of a plant. This energy total is subtracted from the gross energy production of the plant; for reporting purposes the plant energy production is then reported as a net figure. The energy required for pumping at pumped-storage plants is, by definition, subtracted, and the energy production for these plants is then reported as a net figure.

**Power** – The rate at which energy is transferred. Electrical energy is usually measured in watts. Also used for a measurement of capacity.

**Price** – The amount of money or consideration-in-kind for which a service is bought, sold, or offered for sale.

**Prime Mover** – The motive force that drives an electric generator (e.g., steam engine, turbine, or water wheel).

**Production (Electric)** – Act or process of producing electric energy from other forms of energy; also, the amount of electric energy expressed in watthours (Wh).

**Pumped-Storage Hydroelectric Plant** – A plant that usually generates electric energy during peak-load periods by using water previously pumped into an elevated storage reservoir during off-peak periods when excess generating capacity is available to do so. When additional generating capacity is needed, the water can be released form the reservoir through a conduit to turbine generators located in a power plant at a lower level.

**Pure Pumped-Storage Hydroelectric Plant** – A plant that produces power only from water that has previously been pumped to an upper reservoir.

**Qualifying Facility (QF)** – This is a cogenerator or small power producer that meets certain ownership, operating and efficiency criteria established by the Federal Energy Regulatory Commission (FERC) pursuant to the PURPA, and has filed with the FERC for QF status or has self-certified. For additional information, see the Code of Federal Regulation, Title 18, Part 292.

**Reserve Margin (Operating)** – The amount of unused available capability of an electric power system at peak load for a utility system as a percentage of total capability.

**Retail** – Sales covering electrical energy supplied for residential, commercial, and industrial end-use purposes. Other small classes, such as agriculture and street lighting, also are included in this category.

**Running and Quick-Start Capability** – The net capability of generating units that carry load or have quick-start capability. In general, quick-start capability refers to generating units that can be available for load within a 30-minute period.

**Sales** – The amount of kilowatthours sold in a given period of time; usually grouped by classes of service, such as residential, commercial, industrial, and other. Other sales include public street and highway lighting, other sales to public authorities and railways, and interdepartmental sales.

**Scheduled Outage** – The shutdown of a generating unit, transmission line, or other facility, for inspection or maintenance, in accordance with an advance schedule.

**Standby Facility** – A facility that supports a utility system and is generally running under no-load. It is available to replace or supplement a facility normally in service.

**Standby Service** – Support service that is available, as needed, to supplement a consumer, a utility system, or to another utility if a schedule or an agreement authorizes the transaction. The service is not regulatory used.

**Steam-Electric Plant (Conventional)** – A plant in which the prime mover is a steam turbine. The steam used to drive the turbine is produced in a boiler where fossil fuels are burned.

**Substation** – Facility equipment that switches, changes, or regulates electric voltage.

**Switching Station** – Facility equipment used to tie together two or more electric circuits through switches. The switches are selectively arranged to permit a circuit to be disconnected, or to change the electric connection between the circuits.

**System (Electric)** – Physically connected generation, transmission, and distribution facilities operated as an integrated unit under one central management, or operating supervision.

**Transformer** – An electrical device for changing the voltage of alternating current.

**Transmission** – The movement or transfer of electric energy over an interconnected group of lines and associated equipment between points of supply and points at which it is transformed for delivery to consumers, or is delivered to other electric systems. Transmission is considered to end when the energy is transformed for distribution to the consumer.

**Transmission System (Electric)** – An interconnected group of electric transmission lines and associated equipment for moving or transferring electric energy in bulk between points of supply and points at which it is transformed for delivery over the distribution system lines to consumers, or is delivered to other electric systems.

**Turbine** – A machine for generating rotary mechanical power from the energy of a stream of fluid (such as water, steam, or hot gas). Turbines convert the kinetic energy of fluids to mechanical energy through the principles of impulse and reaction, or a mixture of the two.

**Watt** – The electrical unit of power. The rate of energy transfer equivalent to 1 ampere flowing under a pressure of 1 volt at unity power factor.

**Watthour (Wh)** – An electrical energy unit of measure equal to 1 watt of power supplied to, or taken from, an electric circuit steadily for 1 hour.

**Wheeling Service** – The movement of electricity from one system to another over transmission facilities of intervening systems. Wheeling service contracts can be established between two or more systems.

# GLOSSARY
## –C–

*Excerpted From –*

## "ELECTRIC SALES AND REVENUE – 1992"

*Energy Information Administration Agency*
*of the*
*United States Department of Energy*

# GLOSSARY

**Base Bill** – A charge calculated by taking the rate from the appropriate electric rate schedule and applying it to the level of consumption.

**Base Rate** – A fixed per kilowatthour charge for electricity consumed that is independent of other charges and/or adjustments.

**Block Rate Schedule** – An electric rate schedule with a provision for charging a different unit cost for various increasing blocks of demand or energy. Usually a reduced price is charged on succeeding blocks.

**Census Divisions** – The nine geographic divisions of the United States established by the Bureau of the Census, U.S. Department of Commerce for statistical analysis. The boundaries of Census divisions coincide with State boundaries. The Pacific Division is subdivided into the Pacific Contiguous and Pacific Noncontiguous areas.

**Classes of Service** – Consumers grouped by similar characteristics in order to be identified for the purpose of setting a common rate for electric service. Usually classified into groups identified as residential, commercial, industrial and other.

**Class Rate Schedule** – An electric rate schedule applicable to one or more specified classes of service, groups of businesses, or customer uses.

**Commercial Sector** – The commercial sector is generally defined as nonmanufacturing business establishments, including hotels, motels, restaurants, wholesale businesses, retail stores, and health, social, and educational institutions. Electric utilities may classify commercial service that includes all consumers whose demand or annual use exceeds some specified limit. The limit may be set by the utility based on the rate schedule of the utility. Consumers (i.e. farms and irrigation) that the utility has no system for separating into residential, commercial, and industrial classifications, should be classified based on the schedule they most closely resemble. If there is no rate schedule distinction, utilities may define commercial consumers as those having a demand of less than 1,000 kilowatts.

**Consumer Charge** – An amount charged periodically to a consumer for such utility costs as billing and meter reading, without regard to demand or energy consumption.

**Cooperative Electric Utility** – A group organized under the law into a utility company that will generate, transmit, and/or distribute supplies of electric energy to a specified area not being serviced by another utility. Such ventures are generally exempt from the Federal income tax laws. Most electric cooperatives have initially been financed by the Rural Electrification Administration, U.S. Department of Agriculture.

**Cost of Service** – A ratemaking concept used for the design and development of rate schedules to ensure that the filed rate schedules recover only the cost of providing the electric service at issue. These costs include operating and maintenance expenses, depreciation and amortization expenses, and income and other taxes found just and reasonable by the regulatory agency for ratemaking purposes plus, in the case of privately owned electric utilities, an allowance for a return on capital (usually computed by applying a rate of return to the rate base). This concept attempts to equate the cost incurred by the utility to the revenue received for the service provided to each of the consumer classes.

**Demand Charge** – That portion of the consumer's bill for electric service based on the consumer's maximum electric capacity usage and calculated based on the billing demand charges under the applicable rate schedule.

**Energy Information Administration (EIA)** – An independent agency within the U.S. Department of Energy that develops surveys, collects energy data, and does analytical and modeling analysis of energy issues. The Agency must meet the requests of Congress, other elements within the Department of Energy, Federal Energy Regulatory Commission, the Executive Branch, its own independent needs, and assist the general public, or other interest groups, without taking policy position.

**Economy of Scale** – The principle that larger production facilities have lower unit costs than smaller facilities.

**Electric Power Industry** – The privately, publicly, federally and cooperatively owned electric utilities of the United States taken as a whole. This includes all electric systems serving the public – regulated investor-owned electric utility companies, Federal power projects; State, municipal, and other government-owned systems, including electric public utility districts; electric cooperatives, including generation and transmission entities. Excluded from this definition are the special purpose electric facilities or systems that do not offer service to the public.

**Electric Rate** – The price set for a specified amount of electricity in an electric rate schedule or sales contract.

**Electric Rate Schedule** – A statement of the electric rate and the terms and conditions governing its application, including attendant contract terms and conditions that have been accepted by a regulatory body with appropriate oversight authority.

**Federal Energy Regulatory Commission (FERC)** – A quasi-independent regulatory agency within the Department of Energy having jurisdiction over interstate electricity sales, wholesale electric rates, hydroelectric licensing, natural gas pricing, oil pipeline rates, and gas pipeline certification.

**Flat and Meter Rate Schedule** – An electric rate schedule consisting of two components, the first of which is a service charge, and the second a price for the energy consumed.

**Flat Demand Rate Schedule** – An electric rate schedule based on billing demand that provides no charge for energy.

**Industrial Sector** – The industrial sector is generally defined as including manufacturing, construction, mining, agriculture, fishing and forestry establishments under Standard Industrial Classification (SIC) codes 01-39. The utility may classify industrial service using the SIC codes, or based on demand or annual usage exceeding some specified limit. The limit may be set by the utility based on its own rate schedule. Sales for consumers (i.e. farms and irrigation) that the utility has no system for separating into residential, commercial, and industrial classifications, should be classified based on the classification of their rate most closely resembles. If there is no rate schedule distinction, utilities may define industrial consumers as those having a demand equal to or greater than 1,000 kilowatts.

**Investor-Owned Electric Utility** – A class of utility that is investor owned and organized as a tax paying business, usually financed by the sales of securities in the capital market.

**Other Sector** – Electricity supplied to public street and highway lighting, other service to public authorities, service to railroads and railways, and interdepartmental service.

**Power (Electrical)** – An electric measurement unit of power called a voltampere is equal to the product of 1 volt and 1 ampere. This is equivalent to 1 watt for a direct current system and a unit of apparent power is separated into real and reactive power. Real power is the work-producing part of apparent power that measures the rate of supply of energy and is denoted as kilowatts (kW). Reactive power is the portion of apparent power that does no work and is referred to as kilovars; this type of power must be supplied to most types of magnetic equipment, such as motors, and is supplied by generator or by electrostatic equipment. Voltamperes are usually divided by 1,000 and call kilovoltamperes (kVA). Energy is denoted by the product of real power and the length of time utilized; this product is expressed as kilowatthours.

**Public Authorities** – Electricity supplied to municipalities or divisions or agencies of State and Federal governments, usually under special contracts or agreements that are applicable only to public authorities.

**Publicly Owned Electric Utility** – A class of utility that includes those utilities operated by municipalities, political subdivisions, utility or power districts, and State and Federal power agencies.

**Rate Base** – The value of property upon which a utility is permitted to earn a specified rate of return as established by a regulatory authority. The rate base generally represents the value of property used by the utility in providing service and may be calculated by any one or a combination of the following accounting methods – fair value, prudent investment, reproduction cost, or original cost. Depending on which method is used, the rate base includes cash, working capital, materials and supplies, and deductions for accumulated provisions for depreciation, contributions in aid of construction, customer advances for construction, accumulated deferred income taxes, and accumulated deferred investment tax credits.

**Residential Sector** – The residential sector includes private household establishments that consume energy primarily for space heating, water heating, air conditioning, lighting, refrigeration, cooking, and clothes drying. The classification of an individual consumer's account, where the use is both residential and commercial, is based on principal use. Apartment houses are included.

**Retail** – Sales covering electrical energy supplied for residential, commercial, and industrial end-use purposes. Other small classes, such as agriculture and street lighting, also are included in this category.

**Rural Electrification Administration (REA)** – A lending agency of the U.S. Department of Agriculture, the REA makes self-liquidation loans to qualified borrowers to finance electric and telephone service to rural areas. The REA also finances the construction and operation of generating plants, electric transmission and distribution lines, or systems for the furnishing of initial and continued adequate electric services to persons in rural areas not receiving central station service.

**Sales** – The amount of kilowatthours sold in a given period of time; usually grouped by classes of service, such as residential, commercial, industrial, and other. Other sales include public street and highway lighting, other sales to public authorities, sales to railroads and railways, and interdepartmental sales.

**Special Contract Rate Schedule** – An electric rate schedule for an electric service agreement between a utility and another party in addition to, or independent of, any standard rate schedule.

**Special Purpose Rate Schedule** – An electric rate schedule limited in its application to some particular purpose or process within one, or more than one, type of industry or business.

**Tariff** – A published volume of rate schedules and general terms and conditions under which a product or service will be supplied.

**Time-of-Day Rate** – The rate charged by an electric utility for service to various classes of customers. The rate reflects the different costs of providing the service at different times of the day.

# Appendix G

# Miscellaneous Electricity Conversion Factors

| TO CONVERT | INTO | MULTIPLY BY |
|---|---|---|
| **-A-** | | |
| amperes/sq cm | amps/sq in. | 6.452 |
| amperes/sq cm | amps/sq meter | $10^{-4}$ |
| amperes/sq in. | amps/sq cm | 0.1550 |
| amperes/sq in. | amps/sq meter | 1,550.0 |
| amperes/sq meter | amps/sq cm | $10^{-4}$ |
| amperes/sq meter | amps/sq in. | $6.452 \times 10^{-4}$ |
| ampere-hours | coulombs | 3,600.0 |
| ampere-hours | faradays | 0.03731 |
| ampere-turns | gilberts | 1.257 |
| ampere-turns/cm | amp-turns/in. | 2.540 |
| ampere-turns/cm | amp-turns/meter | 100.0 |
| ampere-turns/cm | gilberts/cm | 1.257 |
| ampere-turns/in. | amp-turns/cm | 0.3937 |
| ampere-turns/in. | amp-turns/meter | 39.37 |
| ampere-turns/in. | gilberts/cm | 0.4950 |
| ampere-turns/meter | amp/turns/cm | 0.01 |
| ampere-turns/meter | amp-turns/in. | 0.0254 |
| ampere-turns/meter | gilberts/cm | 0.01257 |

| TO CONVERT | INTO | MULTIPLY BY |
|---|---|---|

### –B–

| | | |
|---|---|---|
| BTU | Liter-Atmosphere | 10.409 |
| Btu | ergs | $1.0550 \times 10^{10}$ |
| Btu | foot-lbs | 778.3 |
| Btu | gram-calories | 252.0 |
| Btu | horsepower-hrs | $3.931 \times 10^{-4}$ |
| Btu | joules | 1,054.8 |
| Btu | kilogram-calories | 0.2520 |
| Btu | kilogram-meters | 107.5 |
| Btu | kilowatt-hrs | $2.928 \times 10^{-4}$ |
| Btu/hr | foot-pounds/sec | 0.2162 |
| Btu/hr | gram-cal/sec | 0.0700 |
| Btu/hr | horsepower-hrs | $3.929 \times 10^{-4}$ |
| Btu/hr | watts | 0.2931 |
| Btu/min | foot-lbs/sec | 12.96 |
| Btu/min | horsepower | 0.02356 |
| Btu/min | kilowatts | 0.01757 |
| Btu/min | watts | 17.57 |
| Btu/sq ft/min | watts/sq in. | 0.1221 |

### –C–

| | | |
|---|---|---|
| calories, gram (mean) | B.T.U. (mean) | $3.9685 \times 10^{-3}$ |
| candle/sq cm | lamberts | 3.142 |
| candle/sq inch | lamberts | .4870 |
| circular mills | sq cms | $5.067 \times 10^{-6}$ |
| circular mils | sq mils | 0.7854 |

### –D–

| | | |
|---|---|---|
| dyne/cm | erg/sq millimeter | .01 |
| dyne/sq cm | atmospheres | $9.869 \times 10^{-7}$ |
| dyne/sq cm | inch of mercury at 0°C | $2.953 \times 10^{-5}$ |
| dyne/sq cm | inch of water at 4°C | $4.015 \times 10^{-4}$ |

| TO CONVERT | INTO | MULTIPLY BY |
|---|---|---|
| **--D--** | | |
| dynes | grams | $1.020 \times 10^{-3}$ |
| dynes | joules/cm | $10^{-7}$ |
| dynes | joules/meter (newtons) | $10^{-5}$ |
| dynes | kilograms | $1.020 \times 10^{-6}$ |
| dynes | poundals | $7.233 \times 10^{-5}$ |
| dynes | pounds | $2.248 \times 10^{-6}$ |
| dynes/sq cm | bars | $10^{-6}$ |
| **--E--** | | |
| em, pica | inch | .167 |
| em, pica | cm | .4233 |
| erg/sec | dyne – cm/sec | 1.000 |
| ergs | Btu | $9.480 \times 10^{-11}$ |
| ergs | dyne-centimeters | 1.0 |
| ergs | foot-pounds | $7.367 \times 10^{-8}$ |
| ergs | gram-calories | $0.2389 \times 10^{-7}$ |
| ergs | gram-cms | $1.020 \times 10^{-3}$ |
| ergs | horsepower-hrs | $3.7250 \times 10^{-14}$ |
| ergs | joules | $10^{-7}$ |
| ergs | kg-calories | $2.3898 \times 10^{-11}$ |
| ergs | kg-meters | $1.020 \times 10^{-8}$ |
| ergs | kilowatt-hrs | $0.2778 \times 10^{-13}$ |
| ergs | watt-hours | $0.2778 \times 10^{-10}$ |
| ergs/sec | Btu/min | $5,688 \times 10^{-9}$ |
| ergs/sec | ft-lbs/min | $4.427 \times 10^{-6}$ |
| ergs/sec | ft-lbs/sec | $7.3756 \times 10^{-8}$ |
| ergs/sec | horsepower | $1.341 \times 10^{-10}$ |
| ergs/sec | kg-calories/min | $1.433 \times 10^{-9}$ |
| ergs/sec | kilowatts | $10^{-10}$ |

| TO CONVERT | INTO | MULTIPLY BY |
|---|---|---|

### –F–

| | | |
|---|---|---|
| farads | microfarads | $10^6$ |
| faraday/sec | ampere (absolute) | $9.6500 \times 10^4$ |
| faradays | ampere-hours | 26.80 |
| faradays | coulombs | $9.649 \times 10^4$ |
| foot-candle | lumen/sq meter | 10.764 |
| foot-pounds | Btu | $1.286 \times 10^{-3}$ |
| foot-pounds | ergs | $1.356 \times 10^7$ |
| foot-pounds | gram-calories | 0.3238 |
| foot-pounds | hp-hrs | $5.050 \times 10^{-7}$ |
| foot-pounds | joules | 1.356 |
| foot-pounds | kg-calories | $3.24 \times 10^{-4}$ |
| foot-pounds | kg-meters | 0.1383 |
| foot-pounds | kilowatt-hrs | $3.766 \times 10^{-7}$ |
| foot-pounds/min | Btu/min | $1.286 \times 10^{-3}$ |
| foot-pounds/min | foot-pounds/sec | 0.01667 |
| foot-pounds/min | horsepower | $3.030 \times 10^{-5}$ |
| foot-pounds/min | kg-calories/min | $3.24 \times 10^{-4}$ |
| foot-pounds/min | kilowatts | $2.260 \times 10^{-5}$ |
| foot-pounds/sec | Btu/hr | 4.6263 |
| foot-pounds/sec | Btu/min | 0.07717 |
| foot-pounds/sec | horsepower | $1.818 \times 10^{-3}$ |
| foot-pounds/sec | kg-calories/min | 0.01945 |
| foot-pounds/sec | kilowatts | $1.356 \times 10^{-3}$ |

### –G–

| | | |
|---|---|---|
| gilberts | ampere-turns | 0.7958 |
| gilberts/cm | amp-turns/cm | 0.7958 |
| gilberts/cm | amp-turns/in | 2.021 |
| gilberts/cm | amp-turns/meter | 79.58 |
| gram-calories | Btu | $3.9683 \times 10^{-3}$ |
| gram-calories | ergs | $4.1868 \times 10^7$ |
| gram-calories | foot-pounds | 8.0880 |

| TO CONVERT | INTO | MULTIPLY BY |
|---|---|---|

## –G–

| TO CONVERT | INTO | MULTIPLY BY |
|---|---|---|
| gram-calories | horsepower-hrs | $1.5596 \times 10^{-6}$ |
| gram-calories | kilowatt-hrs | $1.1630 \times 10^{-6}$ |
| gram-calories | watt-hrs | $1.1630 \times 10^{-3}$ |
| gram-calories/sec | Btu/hr | 14.286 |
| gram-centimeters | Btu | $9.297 \times 10^{-8}$ |
| gram-centimeters | ergs | 980.7 |
| gram-centimeters | joules | $9.807 \times 10^{-5}$ |
| gram-centimeters | kg-cal | $2.343 \times 10^{-8}$ |
| gram-centimeters | kg-meters | $10^{-5}$ |

## –H–

| TO CONVERT | INTO | MULTIPLY BY |
|---|---|---|
| horsepower | Btu/min | 42.44 |
| horsepower | foot-lbs/min | 33,000 |
| horsepower | foot-lbs/sec | 550.0 |
| horsepower (metric) (542.5 ft lb/sec) | horsepower (550 ft lb/sec) | 0.9863 |
| horsepower (550 ft lb/sec | horsepower (metric) (542.5 ft lb/sec) | 1.014 |
| horsepower | kg-calories/min | 10.68 |
| horsepower | kilowatts | 0.7457 |
| horsepower | watts | 745.7 |
| horsepower (boiler) | Btu/hr | 33,479 |
| horsepower (boiler) | kilowatts | 9.803 |
| horsepower-hrs | Btu | 2,547 |
| horsepower-hrs | ergs | $2,6845 \times 10^{13}$ |
| horsepower-hrs | foot-lbs | $1.98 \times 10^{6}$ |
| horsepower-hrs | gram-calories | 641,190 |
| horsepower-hrs | joules | $2.684 \times 10^{6}$ |
| horsepower-hrs | kg-calories | 641.1 |
| horsepower-hrs | kg-meters | $2.737 \times 10^{5}$ |
| horsepower-hrs | kilowatt-hrs | 0.7457 |

| TO CONVERT | INTO | MULTIPLY BY |
|---|---|---|
| **–I–** | | |
| international ampere | ampere (absolute) | .9998 |
| international volt | volts (absolute) | 1.0003 |
| international volt | joules (absolute) | $1.593 \times 10^{-19}$ |
| international volt | joules | $9.654 \times 10^{4}$ |
| **–J–** | | |
| joules | Btu | $9.480 \times 10^{-4}$ |
| joules | ergs | $10^{7}$ |
| joules | foot-pounds | 0.7376 |
| joules | kg-calories | $2.389 \times 10^{-4}$ |
| joules | kg-meters | 0.1020 |
| joules | watt-hrs | $2.778 \times 10^{-4}$ |
| **–K–** | | |
| kilograms-calories | Btu | 3.968 |
| kilograms-calories | foot-pounds | 3,088 |
| kilograms-calories | hp-hrs | $1.560 \times 10^{-3}$ |
| kilograms-calories | joules | 4,186 |
| kilograms-calories | kg-meters | 426.9 |
| kilograms-calories | kilojoules | 4.186 |
| kilograms-calories | kilowatt-hrs | $1.163 \times 10^{-3}$ |
| kilogram meters | Btu | $9.294 \times 10^{-3}$ |
| kilogram meters | ergs | $9.804 \times 10^{7}$ |
| kilogram meters | foot-pounds | 7.233 |
| kilogram meters | joules | 9.804 |
| kilogram meters | kg-calories | $2.342 \times 10^{-3}$ |
| kilogram meters | kilowatt-hrs | $2.723 \times 10^{-6}$ |
| kilowatts | Btu/min | 56.92 |
| kilowatts | foot-pounds/min | $4,426 \times 10^{4}$ |
| kilowatts | Foot-pounds/sec | 737.6 |
| kilowatts | horsepower | 1,341 |
| kilowatts | kg-calories/min | 14.34 |

| TO CONVERT | INTO | MULTIPLY BY |
|---|---|---|

### –K–

| | | |
|---|---|---|
| kilowatts | watts | 1,000.0 |
| kilowatts-hrs | Btu | 3,413 |
| kilowatts-hrs | ergs | $3,600 \times 10^{13}$ |
| kilowatts-hrs | foot-pounds | $2,655 \times 10^{6}$ |
| kilowatts-hrs | gram-calories | 859.850 |
| kilowatts-hrs | horsepower-hrs | 1,341 |
| kilowatts-hrs | joules | $3.6 \times 10^{6}$ |
| kilowatts-hrs | kg-calories | 860.5 |
| kilowatts-hrs | kg-meters | $3,671 \times 10^{5}$ |
| kilowatts-hrs | pounds of water evaporated from and at 212° F. | 3.53 |
| kilowatts-hrs | pounds of water raised from 62° to 212° F. | 22.75 |

### –L–

| | | |
|---|---|---|
| lumens/sq ft | foot-candles | 1.0 |
| lumen | spherical candle power | .07958 |
| lumen | watt | .001496 |
| lumen/sq ft | lumen/sq meter | 10.76 |
| lux | foot-candles | 0.0929 |

### –M–

| | | |
|---|---|---|
| megohms | microhms | $10^{12}$ |
| megohms | ohms | $10^{6}$ |
| microfarad | farads | $10^{-6}$ |
| micrograms | grams | $10^{-6}$ |
| microhms | megohms | $10^{-12}$ |
| microhms | ohms | $10^{-6}$ |
| microliters | liters | $10^{-6}$ |

# Index